Penal Company
on the Falklands

Dedication

To the 'band of brothers' of D Company 2 PARA in 1982, and to their families – *Utrinque Paratus*

Though much is taken, much abides; and though
We are not now that strength which in old days
Moved earth and heaven; that which we are, we are;
One equal temper of heroic hearts,
Made weak by time and fate, but strong in will
To strive, to seek, to find, and not to yield.

(*Ulysses*, by Lord Tennyson)

Penal Company on the Falklands

A Memoir of the Parachute Regiment at War, 1982

Philip Neame

Foreword by
Lieutenant General Sir Cedric Delves

Pen & Sword
MILITARY

AN IMPRINT OF PEN & SWORD BOOKS LTD
YORKSHIRE – PHILADELPHIA

First published in Great Britain in 2022 by
PEN & SWORD MILITARY
an imprint of Pen & Sword Books Ltd
Yorkshire – Philadelphia

Copyright © Philip Neame, 2022

ISBN 978-1-39907-071-3

A CIP catalogue record for this book is available from the British Library.

Typeset by Concept, Huddersfield, West Yorkshire, HD4 5JL.
Printed and bound in England by CPI Group (UK) Ltd, Croydon CR0 4YY.

Pen & Sword Books Ltd incorporates the Imprints of Aviation, Atlas, Family History, Fiction, Maritime, Military, Discovery, Politics, History, Archaeology, Select, Wharncliffe Local History, Wharncliffe True Crime, Military Classics, Wharncliffe Transport, Leo Cooper, The Praetorian Press, Remember When, White Owl, Seaforth Publishing and Frontline Books.

For a complete list of Pen & Sword titles please contact
PEN & SWORD BOOKS LTD
47 Church Street, Barnsley, South Yorkshire, S70 2AS, England
E-mail: enquiries@pen-and-sword.co.uk
Website: www.pen-and-sword.co.uk
or
PEN & SWORD BOOKS
1950 Lawrence Rd, Havertown, PA 19083, USA
E-mail: uspen-and-sword@casematepublishers.com
Website: www.penandswordbooks.com

Contents

List of Plates and Maps vii

Foreword *by Lieutenant General Sir Cedric Delves* ix

Author's Note and Acknowledgements xiii

Glossary xvii

Chronology of Events, 1982 xxv

2 PARA Group Roll of Honour xxvi

Prologue 1

1. MV *Norland*: Midnight, 20 May 1982, Falklands Time 3

2. Penal Company 5

3. An Ocean Cruise 13

4. Welcome to the Falkland Islands 33

5. The Battle for Darwin and Goose Green: the Prelude 43

6. The Battle for Darwin and Goose Green: 'Operation Dinosaur' 55

7. The Battle for Darwin and Goose Green: the Aftermath 83

8. On to Fitzroy and Bluff Cove 93

9. The Battle for Wireless Ridge 105

10. Into Stanley 133

11. Back to the Mother Ship 139

12. Homecoming: the Hard Part 147

Epilogue 159

Appendices

   I: The Surrender Ultimatum to the Argentinian Garrison in
      Goose Green 167

  II: Enemy and Friendly Forces at Goose Green 169

 III: Enemy and Friendly Forces at Wireless Ridge 171

 IV: D Company Honours and Awards 173

List of Plates and Maps

Plates

D Company, 2 PARA on MV *Norland*, South Atlantic, May 1982.

The battalion band playing 'Don't Cry for Me, Argentina' at Portsmouth Docks, 26 April 1982.

MV *Norland* at Ascension Island.

The author compering the prize-giving at the end of the battalion sports day shortly after leaving Ascension Island.

Standing to against enemy air attack on MV *Norland*.

Bomb Alley. San Carlos Water seen from Sussex Mountain.

A peat igloo on Sussex Mountain.

The CO, Colonel H. Jones, on top of Sussex Mountain with his Tac HQ.

Goose Green 'O' Group.

Aerial view of Goose Green.

An Argentinian 0.5in heavy machine-gun position beyond Boca House.

Argentinian Triple A anti-aircraft cannon at Goose Green airfield, depressed for use in the ground role.

Approaching the Boca position after the white flags.

Occupying the Boca position.

The surrender at Boca.

Captain Steve Hughes at work in the regimental aid post.

Preparing for the surrender at Goose Green.

The Goose Green field of surrender covered in downed weapons and equipment.

Local civilians after being liberated from Goose Green community hall.

An Argentinian Skyhawk attack at Goose Green.

Chris Waddington at Goose Green, wearing the smock borrowed from one of our dead in exchange for his soaked clothing the night before.

The site of the Argentinian mass burial undertaken by local civilians.

The burial of 2 PARA men killed at Goose Green and Ajax Bay.

Argentinian POWs at their temporary camp, the sheep-shearing sheds at Goose Green.

Rescuing Welsh Guardsmen from the LSL *Sir Galahad*, Fitzroy, 8 June 1982.

Helicopter move of 2 PARA to Bluff Cove Peak prior to the attack on Wireless Ridge.

Wireless Ridge seen from the Anchor observation post on Mt Longdon, looking toward Hearnden Water.

Wireless Ridge. Looking back from *Dirty Dozen* towards *Blueberry Pie* where D Company were shelled by friendly fire.

Night fire at Wireless Ridge.

Wireless Ridge. A dead Argentinian on *Dirty Dozen*.

'Endex' Wireless Ridge. Helmets off, red berets on!

Corporal Owen's section celebrating their success at Wireless Ridge.

D Company on the road to Stanley.

D Company returning from the battalion thanksgiving service in Stanley Cathedral, tired after a job well done.

The three rifle company commanders on Darwin Hill for the thirtieth anniversary return to the Falklands.

The British cemetery at San Carlos.

The Argentinian cemetery near Goose Green.

Maps

2 PARA Group operations on East Falkland, 21 May–14 June 1982   xxiv

2 PARA manoeuvres at the Battle of Darwin and Goose Green . . .   50

2 PARA manoeuvres at the Battle for Wireless Ridge 113

Foreword

I learnt of 2 PARA's battle for Darwin Goose Green when I was up at Mount Kent, in front of Stanley, commanding an SAS squadron. Danny West told me, my second-in-command. It was a still night, bitterly cold and damp. He had arrived to join me by helicopter, bringing the squadron with him; and very welcome they were too – we had been feeling a touch isolated out there on our own, me and my four-man recce patrol. After deploying the troops Danny and I settled down to catch up on each other's news. He started by saying he had both good and bad news. I opted to hear the good first. 'We have taken Darwin Goose Green,' he said. 'What on earth for?', I responded, less elegantly than is recorded here. I had been expecting to hear of an advance out of San Carlos up towards Stanley, not one down to Darwin.

'And the bad news?'

'Your friend 'H' is dead'.

I knew 'H' well, a fellow Devon and Dorset, Commanding Officer of 2 PARA. I felt stunned, and bloody angry, not with Danny, not with the conduct of the war, but with the war itself. Then, as the initial shock subsided, I realized that we had just won. There would be more things to do, more battles to fight, more losses to endure, and yet I knew, right then and there, with utmost certainty: 2 PARA had set the seal. We were going to win the war.

The British Task Force that fought in the South Atlantic that austral winter of 1982 did so at distinct numerical and physical disadvantage. The enemy were closer to home, prepared and plentifully supplied, more numerous in the air, thicker on the ground, sheltered from the worst of the weather, perhaps more evenly matched at sea. However, war is not all about hardware and related physical issues. It is also about how things get done, and the spirit of those involved. The relationship between the three is both complex and in constant flux; even so, the British operation to retake the Falklands demonstrates how physical limitations can be offset by know-how and self-belief. Of course, all members of the Task Force played their part, the Navy quickly sweeping the sea of enemy, more than matching them in the air, setting the conditions for success on land. Yet notwithstanding the evident interplay, and instances of interdependence, all acknowledge the signal contribution of 2 PARA. And here is their story, told from the inside by Phil Neame, one of the company commanders. It is a strikingly honest and vivid account that tells of how decisions were made and difficulties overcome, shedding light on many details of the battalion's war, and indeed the Parachute Regiment itself. Field Marshal Montgomery, an acute and unsentimental judge of military matters, once posed the question 'What manner of men are these that wear the maroon beret?', before going on to conclude that 'of all the factors, which make for success in battle, the spirit of the warrior is the most decisive', stressing 'that spirit will be found in full measure in the men who wear the maroon beret'. Through Phil's words you get to know what that means: none better to be alongside, none more daunting to be up against.

Phil's military background is unusual: the RAF Regiment, Special Duties in Northern Ireland, an accomplished mountaineer – somehow it brings him to the Parachute Regiment. If any of this registers with his soldiers, his 'Toms' as they are respectfully and affectionately known, it counts for much less than the fact he has passed 'P Company': parachute selection, which 'enables you to join the tribe'. He is posted to 2 PARA, recently returned from a tough two years in Northern Ireland. 'H' Jones, their new CO, is determined to get them reorientated back to 'conventional' warfare. 'H' explains this to Phil, who finds it all 'all very obvious' while noting his commanding officer's restless, nervous energy: 'it was like watching a fizzing firework, waiting for the bang'. Phil is given command of D Company, one of three rifle companies. Coming after A and B, D always seems to be last in all and any sequence, and 'to be the parking lot for other companies' "HR" problems; we were the Battalion's gulag'. In that typical way of British soldiers, the company takes pride in their apparently low hierarchical standing, labelling themselves Penal Company.

When war breaks out somebody somewhere has the good sense to reinforce 3 Commando Brigade with the two available Parachute Regiment battalions: 2 PARA and 3 PARA. And so it is that 2 PARA is carried forward in the MV *Norland*, a North Sea ferry, a ship taken up from trade. A lasting bond forms between crew and unit. As they approach San Carlos, the chosen landing area, the battalion sense that they are not fully in the picture, and still uncertain about exactly when they are to land: 'By lunchtime H was all restless energy and busily chewing his fingernails ... we managed to flash a signal to a nearby frigate, HMS *Broadsword*: "Is there anything we should know about?" "Yes but it's too secret to tell you" came the answer.' Fortunately, HMS *Broadsword* managed to pass on a copy of the landing orders, issued 48 hours previously! Such is the fog of war. And things wouldn't go that smoothly when they did eventually land.

What follows is an operational pause. The troops get ashore only to go to ground, to witness the Navy fight a pitched air battle for which they are not best suited. It lasts for days. Ships are hit. The Task Force is facing failure. Phil records, 'it was on Day 4 that the muttering started; and I took up smoking again'. One of his Toms asks, 'what are we doing here?', another 'when are we going to give some back?', yet another 'is this another Gallipoli?' It is not in the nature of many soldiers to hang around once they have crossed a start line, definitely not Paras, and so we come to the battle of Darwin Goose Green.

The genesis of the battle is likely to remain shrouded, although Phil throws fresh light on how a raid could become an all-out battle for repossession. I can say with certainty that 2 PARA's frustrations were shared. My CO had ordered me forward to Mount Kent as much to spur a more general move out from San Carlos as to get my squadron's relatively limited capacities back into play; we simply had to get on, to take the fight to the enemy. I believe 'H' saw it the same way. I knew 'H'. He was rather impatient, not one for hanging around. Phil attests: 'Later on, the next day, 'H' called me to his HQ again. He had got the go-ahead for a raid on Darwin and Goose Green.' As I departed for Mount Kent, 'H' contacted me, wanting to discuss Darwin. I regret to this day that we never managed to have that meeting. But he did get to speak to my CO, Michael Rose. And I left instructions that should 'H' call by our way, he was to see all that we had on the enemy. Actually, much of the detailed intelligence we held had come to us from or through 'Brigade'. So, yes, we knew what was down there. And if we knew, 2 PARA must surely have known because at that juncture 'Brigade' was their HQ every bit as much if not more than ours. Similarly, it pains me to read 'SAS patrols observing the isthmus ... had also opined that they [the enemy garrison] seemed ill prepared, with poor field discipline and were unlikely to put up much resistance.' This assessment did not come from D Squadron, my squadron, nor G Squadron which conducted the surveillance patrols.

2 PARA go into battle with their original raiding mission adjusted, as Phil says: 'to recapture the settlements with virtually the same resources as the "hit and run" raid, a task of immeasurably different scale, risk and commitment'. They should have failed. Phil's description of the battle is gripping, often heart rending. There is much to absorb. There is his composure under fire. Confronted by confusion, swamped by complexity,

the mind can shut down, go blank. But Phil sees clearly throughout. He maintains an extraordinary detachment, as he methodically and determinedly chips away at what must have seemed near insurmountable tactical difficulties. And out of all the turmoil come seminal, profoundly defining moments, such as when he stops his people looting the enemy dead. It 'was nothing to do with sentiment or respect for the dead. It was about being a professional soldier, in the most professional regiment in the world,' he explains. He sees this as perhaps his most significant 'intervention' for 'it set the tone for Penal Company and the way it would conduct itself for the rest of the war'. Then there is the impact of 'H's death: the management of the battle was loosened. Company commanders and leaders at all levels started to exercise more initiative. And gradually and certainly the enemy yield. As Phil so insightfully observes: 'Here is the irony in 'H'. He was a classic authoritarian, obsessed with being in control. But some have defined great leadership as building a team that can deliver great performance without you. Well, that is what we went on to do ...'

After their triumph at Darwin Goose Green 2 PARA is temporarily subordinated to the recently arrived 5 Brigade, taking a lead in opening up a southern axis to Stanley, before returning to 3 Commando Brigade. They are not sorry to leave the 'hapless' 5 Brigade: as Phil openly admits, back 'with the Commandos and 3 PARA, there seemed every reason to hope that the reserve [2 PARA] might not be needed. After Goose Green, there was undeniably a feeling that we had done our share and more; we had no burning desire to stretch our necks again.' Yet they do; they go on to take Wireless Ridge, on the very last night of the war, the final set-piece battle that has come to be regarded as one of the finest examples of integrated, all-arms fighting.

Phil Neame concludes his enthralling book with reflections on how the war impacted the lives of those involved. He tells of the difficulties of readjusting, how near impossible it is to explain the experience of war to others: 'Where do I start? You've not been there, so you'll never get it,' he records with sorrow. Nevertheless, he gives us an utterly lucid description of war, of a war fought without hate and in a most just cause. His book serves as a fitting tribute not only to his people, but to 2 PARA, and indeed his regiment; it chronicles some of the Parachute Regiment's finest hours. I feel honoured to have been there with them, nearby, in a sense alongside.

Cedric Delves
September 2021

Author's Note and Acknowledgements

The dawning of this book occurred ten years ago. I was in the Falklands to help with a film about 2 PARA's exploits being produced by Jeremy Freeston for the thirtieth anniversary of the war in the Falklands. The film was then called 'Return to the Falklands,' but has since been retitled on YouTube, a little melodramatically, 'Fix Bayonets.' It was Jeremy who, over several evenings and Chilean wine in the Waterfront Hotel at Port Stanley, first suggested, indeed insisted, I should write a book. He saw it as embracing my mountaineering and Falkland stories; thank you Jeremy, although I acknowledge I have so far only tackled half the job.

Despite several attempts, I never got very far until I attended a course provided by Curtis Brown Creative tutored by Cathy Rentzenbrink early in 2021. I was looking for a kick-start, and Cathy and my fellow students provided it, and much more besides. I learnt so much, but their encouragement and inspiration were what got me going. Without Jeremy and Cathy, there was a story, but there would have been no book.

To fill in gaps in my knowledge, and occasionally to verify my own recollections, I referred often to the record put together by my old friend David Benest, the regimental signals officer in the war, on the orders of David Chaundler following our return to the UK. His *The Falklands Campaign 1982 – Operation Corporate* was a monumental piece of work to which many of my company contributed. Sadly, I only saw it twelve months ago, and it was not peer-reviewed at the time. This would have enabled a more accurate collation of people, time and place, which was lacking. As a historical record, it therefore proved flawed, but as a collection of individual experiences it is remarkable. I should like to pay tribute to his research, which sadly haunted him until his premature death in 2020.

Many of the pictures I have used are from 2 PARA's library. These were assigned to the battalion after the war by those who took the photographs. I am unaware of who took them all, but I know many were taken by

Corporal 'Doc' Owen, one of D Company's section commanders. I give him due praise for adding a large single lens reflex camera to his already massive load, and for the coolness to use it when most of us were just thinking it was good to be still alive. Piers Farrar-Hockley produced with much care the map showing 2 PARA Group's operations on East Falkland with great clarity. I would also like to thank Tony Banks for allowing me to use his wonderful introduction to 'Wendy' Gibson, one of the *Norland*'s stewards, in his book *Storming the Falklands*.

I would like to take this opportunity to thank two Falkland families for their hospitality when I was on the Islands: Eric and Shirley Goss, who so generously provided my company HQ with shelter, warmth and friendship after the battle for Goose Green; and Tony and June McMullen who provided similar kindness to me and my family on numerous visits to the settlement when I returned in 1989. You made it all worthwhile.

I am truly grateful, and honoured, that Cedric Delves agreed to write the Foreword to this memoir. He ticks so many boxes – amongst them, as a companion in arms in the Falklands War, where he commanded an SAS squadron; as someone who knew and served with 'H' Jones, 2 PARA's iconic commanding officer who took us to war; and as an astute and uniquely experienced observer at every level of command of people in conflict.

Without my family, again I would not have been able to write this story. From Rachel, Fred and Jen I learnt to see the humanity of the story, to which I hope I have done justice. I thank them for their encouragement. Jen also helped with some of the maps, and I thank Rachel for her constructive editing of my writing. Most of all, however, I thank her for staying by me all these years, particularly in the aftermath of the war when my behaviour I can now see sometimes left a lot to be desired. I hope this memoir makes up for what we should have been talking about then. Perhaps our honeymoon on a mountain in China was useful training.

Then without my 'band of brothers', there would have been no story. I feel I was truly blessed with the people I had around me. At least as much as I led them, they carried me. I owe them a huge amount which I hope this account starts to repay.

Finally, I would like to thank my editors at Pen & Sword for their support and forbearance in bringing my endeavours to publication, and my publishers for kindly donating an extra 1 per cent of royalties from any sales of this book to the Ulysses Trust. I intend to match this. I was ever at least as much a mountaineer as a soldier, and my time spent testing myself with friends 'on the Hill' largely defined who I am. I helped establish the

Trust (www.ulyssestrust.co.uk) thirty years ago on the back of a Territorial Army attempt to make the first British ascent of Mount Everest in winter, which I led. Potential commercial sponsors blanched at the risks involved with the endeavour but offered charitable donations if there was an appropriate charity. We duly set up the charity with the thought that it could go on and help young cadets and others less fortunate than ourselves also to benefit from life-changing adventures in the great outdoors.

This book has largely been written from memory. After forty years I found some details had blurred. The events I personally experienced remain as vivid for me today as they did forty years ago, as I am sure they do for most. Dates, timings, and the experiences recounted by others are less so. I have referred extensively to my notebook that I carried with me to verify as far as possible my orders received and given, and who was doing what, where and when. A diary would have been better, but I must confess to finding the circumstances not conducive to such an exercise.

On our return, I thought that I knew most of what had taken place in so far at least as D Company was concerned. Over the years, from casual conversation with various alumni of D Company '82, from David Benest's work, and finally from the act of writing this memoir, I have come to see the arrogance of that assumption. There is undoubtedly still more for me to learn. The fact is that what one person sees on a battlefield can look very different to someone a hundred yards away, and in the heat of action one can be blissfully unaware of what others just yards away are experiencing. I am conscious, therefore, that I will neither have captured the totality of D Company's, or indeed of 2 PARA's, story; and neither have I been able to do full justice to every individual. One difficulty is that everyone of D Company '82 rose to the occasion beyond measure.

It is also a truism that General Hindsight never lost a battle. Looking back, it is easy to be wise and see the errors of our own or others' ways; equally it can be tempting to endow what went well with a prescience or judgement that at the time was perhaps just good fortune. I have tried to resist that or at least to make it clear where I am opining with wisdom that came after an event.

I take full responsibility and apologise for any errors or omissions. I tell the story as I saw it, but I hope it nevertheless paints a true and honest picture of D Company, its exploits and its people, over the remarkable time that I was privileged to command it.

Glossary

2ic – Second-in-command.

AA – Anti-aircraft.

ABI – Airborne Initiative.

A Echelon – Forward logistics team responsible for replenishment of combat supplies to combat sub-units. This was based at Camilla Creek during the battle for Goose Green.

AEW – Airborne Early Warning [radar].

Airborne snake – A column of [airborne] soldiers on the move.

Assembly Area – An area of ground selected for bringing the component parts for an operation together.

AWOL – Absent without leave.

B Echelon – Main logistics team responsible for obtaining equipment and combat supplies from higher formations and depots. This was still on *Norland* for Goose Green, later moving ashore to collocate with 3 Commando Brigade's FMA at Ajax Bay.

BC – Battery Commander (artillery). Normally part of the CO's Tac HQ.

BCR – Battle Casualty Replacements.

Bergen – Issue rucksack, named after the make of rucksack first issued to British Special Forces.

Blowpipe – Man-portable guided AA missile fired from the shoulder.

Blue-on-Blue – A hostile engagement between or from Friendly Forces. Blue on a map denotes Friendly Forces, red denotes enemy forces.

BV – A tracked vehicle made by Volvo and designed for over-snow transport. Part of the Royal Marine inventory for their NATO role on the northern flank, but equally effective and important for over-peatbog operations in the Falklands.

CAP – Combat Air Patrol providing 'top-cover' from enemy air attack.

Casevac – Casualty Evacuation, used as a noun or a verb – as in 'casevac'd'.

Carl Gustav – Shoulder-fired Medium Anti-tank Weapon (MAW) which launches an 84mm rocket with a shaped explosive charge for penetrating armour. Referred to as the Charlie G or the '84'.

CLF – Commander Land Forces.

CO – Commanding Officer.

COMAW – Commander Amphibious Warfare.

'Crap-hat' – Para term of pity or contempt for any soldier whose headgear is not maroon. On a good day the SAS with their sand-coloured berets might be omitted, or the Royal Marines who, with their green berets, might be referred to as 'cabbage-tops', although the Marines seem happy to be referred to as 'boot-necks' or 'booties'. After the Army decreed that the term was disrespectful and should not be used, a 'crap-hat' is now more commonly referred to simply as a 'hat'.

CSM – Company Sergeant Major.

CVR(T) – Combat Vehicle Reconnaissance (Tracked). In the Falklands these were used as light tanks. There were two models: the Scorpion equipped with a 75mm gun and the Scimitar with a 30mm cannon. Both were also armed with a mounted GPMG and second-generation image intensification passive (non-detectable – as opposed to active infra-red, which is) night viewing sights.

DF – Defensive Fire on to a pre-recorded target – normally registered by artillery to provide a quick response, rather than having to be adjusted; but also applicable for GPMG (SF) firing on targets at night on targets registered by day.

Direct Fire – Aimed, line-of-sight supporting fire brought to bear from weapons such as Milan, MAW, LAW, GPMG (SF) and CVR(T); as opposed to indirect fire which is 'lobbed' by artillery or mortars.

DMS boot – Directly Moulded Sole boot. The standard issue rubber-soled boot – made of cheap reconstituted leather which absorbs water like a sponge.

DS – Directing Staff.

Endex – End-of-Exercise. Time-honoured order to terminate an exercise, greeted with relief by participants eagerly anticipating a return to barracks and a warm bed.

FAC – Forward Air Controller. An officer trained to direct air attacks onto enemy positions by radio.

FAP – Final Assault Position. The point from which troops charge the enemy, or transition from advancing (preferably with support of artillery fire on the enemy) to fire-and-manoeuvre in teams.

Fire-and-Manoeuvre – Coordinated movement when in contact with the enemy, some advancing while others are directly engaging the enemy. Can be at any size of team, but at section level often referred to as 'skirmishing' or 'pepper-potting'.

FMA – Forward Maintenance Area.

FN – Fabrique Nationale. Belgian arms manufacturer which produced both the FN rifles used by the Argentinians and the self-loading rifles (SLR) used by the British Army. Both fired a standard 7.62mm round. The SLR could only fire semi-automatic, self-loading single shots, whereas the FN could also fire in bursts on fully automatic.

FOO – Forward Observation Officer. As the battery commander is normally the CO's right-hand man when in contact with the enemy, so is the FOO to a company commander.

Forward slope – The slope of a hill facing the enemy, and so exposed to observation by and direct fire from the enemy; as opposed to reverse slope, the other side of the hill not directly exposed to the enemy.

FUP – Forming-up point. The point where troops gather before moving in for an assault – ideally on the reverse slope from the position to be assaulted.

Go firm – Establishing a defensive position.

GPMG – General Purpose Machine Gun. Standard issue fully automatic weapon per infantry section using belt-fed or linked 7.62mm ammunition. Often referred to as the 'jimpy'. Usually used supported on a bipod, but can be mounted on a tripod and equipped with target-recording sights for sustained fire, hence GPMG (SF).

Green Maggot – Slang for khaki army-issue sleeping bag. Usually abbreviated to 'maggot': as in 'I'm off to my maggot' meaning 'I'm turning in'.

H Hour – The time at which the Start Line (SL) is crossed. Other timings can be coordinated from that, should the time of H Hour change. For example: the Artillery Fire Plan might start at H -30 minutes; phase 2 might be ordered to start at H +45.

HE – High Explosive. HE shells from mortar or artillery normally explode on impact, but artillery shells can be equipped with proximity fuses that can be set to detonate at a given height above the ground, providing 'air-burst'. Impact detonation is good for destroying physical objects and fortifications, while air-burst is particularly effective against troops in the open.

HLS – Helicopter Landing Site (often abbreviated to LS).

HQ – Headquarters.

KIP – Kit Individual Protection. A strong plastic sheet, cord and tent pegs placed over half a two-man trench for shelter; with the trench's spoil thrown on top, it provides overhead protection from shellfire and air attack.

LAW – Light Anti-tank Weapon. Ours was a throw-away recoilless shoulder-fired rifle launching a 66mm rocket with a shaped charge (see MAW below). As with the MAW, to reduce recoil the blast of the launch is expended through a venturi at the back. Not standing behind the firer and being caught in the back-blast is a Health and Safety instruction for once worth heeding!

LCU – Landing Craft Utility. Large Royal Marine craft to get troops onto the beach. Four of these were carried by the two amphibious assault ships, the LPDs HMS *Fearless* and HMS *Intrepid*.

LO – Liaison Officer.

LPD – Landing Platform Dock.

LSL – Landing Ship Logistic, manned by Royal Fleet Auxiliaries – thus the RFA *Sir Lancelot*.

LMG – Light Machine Gun, known after its manufacturer as the Bren gun, a stalwart of the Second World War.

L2 – HE grenade.

LZ – Landing Zone.

M-79 – A hand-held launcher of a 79mm grenade.

Main HQ – Headquarters coordinating all the operations, support and movement of a unit or formation, sometimes also including A Echelon. To undertake these tasks ideally requires it to be static, so it may also include a Step-up HQ that can move separately and function at a basic level when Main is moving.

MoD – Ministry of Defence.

MFC – Mortar Fire Controller. A soldier from the mortar platoon attached to companies to direct and control mortar fire.

Milan – Missile d'Infanterie Leger Antichar. A wire-guided anti-tank missile system. Ideal also for busting prepared fortifications from up to 2,000 yards.

MO – Medical Officer. Also RMO – Regimental Medical Officer.

MT – Military Transport, hence MTO – Motor Transport Officer.

MV – Motor Vessel, hence MV *Norland*.

NBC – Nuclear, Biological and Chemical, as in NBC Warfare, NBC protective over-boots.

ND – Negligent Discharge. The unintended firing of a weapon, never regarded as an accident by the Army and therefore always subject to disciplinary action.

NAAFI – Navy, Army and Air Force Institute – an organization that provides canteen and shopping facilities for the Services in barracks and on operations.

NCO – Non-commissioned officer. Lance corporals and corporals are Junior or JNCOs. Sergeants, colour sergeants and sergeant majors are Senior or SNCOs.

NGO – Naval Gunfire Observer; or Naval Gunfire Forward Observer (NGFO).

NOK – Next of kin.

OC – Officer Commanding.

'O' Group – The formal gathering together of subordinates for the issue of orders by a commander.

On-stag – On sentry duty or on-watch.

OP – Observation Post.

OR – Other Rank, anyone not a commissioned officer.

Patch – Slang for the married quarters of a garrison. This might further break down to the 'officers' patch' and the 'ORs' patch'.

PRI – President of the Regimental Institute. Normally the 2iC, and used in connection with private funds held by the regiment, the PRI Account which he manages.

PTSD – Post-Traumatic Stress Disorder.

POW – Prisoner of War.

QM – Quartermaster, a unit's principal logistician responsible for all supplies, stores and equipment. He is supported by a technical quartermaster (TQM). On operations, the QM normally runs B Echelon and the TQM runs A Echelon. This can vary, and sometimes the OC HQ Company or the MTO might run A Echelon.

QMG – Quartermaster general. A four-star general, the head of all logistical and supply matters for the Army.

R&R – Rest and Recuperation.

RAP – Regimental Aid Post. A position at the rear of a battle, commanded by the RMO for first line treatment and stabilizing of casualties, before they are evacuated to a field hospital with surgical facilities and treatment by a field surgical team (FST). Before reaching the RAP, a soldier might receive first aid from his buddy and the company medic, sometimes operating a company aid post.

Rapier – Low-level air defence missile system.

REMF (remf) – Rear echelon mother fucker.

RHQ PARA – Regimental Headquarters of the Parachute Regiment. The HQ responsible then for the Human Resource policy and management of 1, 2 and 3 PARA (the Regular Army battalions), 4, 10 and 15 PARA (then the Territorial Army or Army Reserve battalions) and Depot PARA (the Regiment's training and selection base).

RV – Rendezvous. In military terms can be further defined as, for example, Emergency RV or Final RV (FRV). Has many applications: FRV is often used as a euphemism for death – as in 'he never made the final RV', or 'he's now in the FRV in the sky'.

RSM – Regimental Sergeant Major. A Warrant Officer Class 1 and the most senior NCO of a unit, reporting directly and only to the CO. A company sergeant major is the equivalent for a sub-unit with the rank of WO2.

RTU – Return To Unit, usually used as a euphemism for getting the sack or being fired.

'Rupert' – Toms' slang for 'officer', usually derisory, sometimes affectionate, invariably patronizing.

SF – Special Forces, including inter alia the Army's Special Air Service (SAS) and the Royal Marines' Special Boat Section (SBS).

Sigint – Signals Intelligence. Information gained on the enemy acquired by eavesdropping on and analysis of his radio and other electronic traffic.

SITREP – Situation Report.

SLR – Self-loading rifle.

SMG – Sterling sub-machine gun. A light automatic weapon firing a low velocity 9mm round, carried by signallers and others with heavy equipment not expected to directly kill the enemy.

SOPs – Standard Operating Procedures.

STUFT – Ships Taken Up from Trade.

Sunray – Radio nickname for a commander at any level.

Slidex – Paper-based manual encryption system, very laborious, prone to operator error and time-consuming. Often, by the time a message had been encrypted, sent and then decrypted at the other end, it had been overtaken by events.

TA – Territorial Army.

TAB – Tactical Approach to Battle. An acronym used by Paras for a cross-country march, usually at speed, certainly not a stroll. Can be used as a noun or a verb, as in 'going for a tab' or 'we're tabbing to Sussex Mountain'. The Royal Marine (RM) equivalent is 'yomp' but it somehow seems less purposeful.

Tac – Short for tactical, as in Tac HQ, a commander's easily manoeuvred lightweight HQ from which he can command or direct, as distinct from coordinate or control, the battle. See also Main HQ.

TLC – Tender loving care.

'Tom' – Slang for a soldier in the Parachute Regiment, abbreviated from Tommy Atkins.

Triple A – Oerlikon AA weapon of either 20 or 30mm deployed by the Argentinians. Used also in the ground role they were fearsome.

VT – Variable Time. A VT fuse on an artillery shell enable the time of detonation to be set at a given proximity to the target, thus enabling an 'air-burst' rather than 'impact' detonation. Useful against troops in the open, or where the shell might otherwise land in soft peat.

WP – White Phosphorous, designed to produce an immediate smoke-screen either with grenades or 81mm mortar rounds.

WRAC – Women's Royal Army Corps.

2 Para Group Operations

East Falkland
21 May–14 June 1982

Scale: 10mm of main map = 10km

WR — Wireless Ridge
CCH — Camilla Creek House
SIH — Swan Inlet House
FBP — Furze Bush Pass

x—x — Operations via helicopter
—— — Operations via foot
⬤ — Enemy positions

Wireless Ridge (13/14 June)
Company objectives

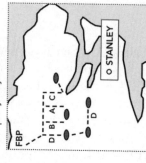

STANLEY

FBP

D C B A

D B A C

D

STANLEY

©pfararhockley

Teal Inlet

San Carlos

Sussex Mts

CCH

Darwin

Goose Green

B Coy Recce

D Coy 3rd June

A Coy 2nd June

B Coy 2nd June

Battalion (-) 3rd June

SIH

Fitzroy

Bluff Cove

Battalion (11th June)

FBP

WR

STANLEY

Chronology of Events
1982

1 April	Argentina invades the Falkland Islands.
5 April	First elements of the Naval Task Force leave Portsmouth.
26 April	2 PARA depart Portsmouth to join Task Force on MV *Norland*.
10 May	HMS *Sheffield* sunk.
20 May	2 PARA land at Bonners Bay, San Carlos Water.
28 May	Battle for Darwin and Goose Green.
29 May	Argentinian garrison at Goose Green surrenders.
2/3 June	Coup-de-main operation by 2 PARA captures Fitzroy and Bluff Cove.
6 June	2 PARA regroup at Fitzroy.
8 June	Argentinian air attacks on RFAs *Sir Galahad* and *Sir Tristram*.
11 June	2 PARA rejoin 3 Commando Brigade.
13/14 June	Battle for Wireless Ridge.
14 June	2 PARA enter Port Stanley. Argentinians surrender.
26 June	2 PARA depart Port Stanley for Ascension Island on MV *Norland*.
6 July	2 PARA depart Ascension Island by air.
7 July	2 PARA land at RAF Brize Norton, UK.

2 PARA Group Roll of Honour

Lieutenant J.A. Barry	D Company
Lance Corporal G.D. Bingley	D Company
Lance Corporal A. Cork	D Company
Captain C. Dent	A Company
Private S.J. Dixon	D Company
Private M.W. Fletcher	D Company
Colour Sergeant G.P.M. Findlay	A Company
Corporal D. Hardman	A Company
Private M.H. Holman-Smith	C Company
Private S. Illingworth	B Company
Lieutenant Colonel H. Jones	Commanding Officer
Private T. Mechan	D Company
Corporal D. Melia	Royal Engineers
Lieutenant R.J. Nunn	Royal Marines (att. Army Air Corps)
Private D.A. Parr	D Company
Corporal C.R. Prior	A Company
Private P. Slough	D Company
Lance Corporal N.R. Smith	D Company
Corporal P.S. Sullivan	D Company
Captain D.A. Wood	Adjutant

Prologue

On 1 April 1982 an Argentinian Task Force invaded the Falkland Islands. At the time I commanded D Company, one of three 100-strong rifle companies of the 2nd Battalion the Parachute Regiment. 2 PARA was on leave, and I was enjoying some ice climbing in the Highlands of Scotland. Five days later I received a telegram with the single word: 'BRUNEVAL'. Whoops of excitement from me, rather less from my wife. Bruneval was 2 PARA's barracks, named after one of its Second World War battle honours. 2 PARA was being recalled to barracks, to play its part in the recovery of the Islands. No planes, no parachutes – instead a journey of more than 8,000 miles to the South Atlantic on a North Sea ferry to get us into battle.

2 PARA was commanded by Lieutenant Colonel H. Jones, who was to be awarded a posthumous Victoria Cross at the Battle of Goose Green. After fighting the first battle of the war, 2 PARA went on to fight the last at Wireless Ridge, the gateway to the capital, Port Stanley. Here, D Company played the decisive role but, in the closing moments, suffered a horrific artillery barrage – and more men lost – from our own guns.

Years after leaving the Army, I was asked to give a lecture on my experiences at the Royal Engineers Depot. As I rose to speak, hands waved from the back of the crowded room. To my amazement, a dozen of those from D Company '82 had somehow learnt of my talk. They had come from across the UK to hear *their* story told.

I told it as it was: how D Company was the Cinderella of 2 PARA, at the back for everything: on training exercises, always starting in reserve; in barracks, the parking lot for those who proved too much of a handful for A and B Companies. I told how, with little recognition, it had, in the view of Martin Middlebrook in his history of the war, *Operation Corporate*, seen 'more action than any other sub-unit in the Falklands war'. Afterwards, I joined them at the bar. Colin Delaney, my erstwhile company medic, put a beer in my hand: 'Phil, didn't you know we were known as Penal Company?' I hadn't, but now a lot fell into place.

Stationed again in the Islands throughout 1989, I was fortunate to retread the ground over which we had fought, cursed and laughed; to discuss 'H's death and whether the battle for Goose Green had even been necessary. Draining my beer, I decided I was uniquely placed and owed it to them to record the experience and privilege of leading *Penal Company* to war.

Mine is a personal view: walking a tightrope between success and disaster, comedy and tragedy, joy and grief, the strength of companionship and the solitude of fear. But above all, it is a tribute to those who helped me through testing but treasured moments in that sub-Arctic winter 'down south' forty years ago.

Chapter 1

MV *Norland*: Midnight, 20 May 1982, Falklands Time

MV *Norland*, an ageing P&O car ferry that normally carried tourists between Hull and Rotterdam, in complete darkness noses gently into San Carlos Water. I hear the distant growl of the anchor chain. Relief. The mines and submarine threat behind us, now is the moment.

Below decks, the dim blue emergency lighting endows everyone with an eerie pallor. Rifle in hands, stooped with over 80 pounds on my back, I compete with the swell to stay on my feet. The smell of sweat, fart and diesel fills the airless Continental Lounge. Dressed for a sub-Arctic winter, the sweat is pouring off me, washing camouflage cream into my eyes. I just wish that 'Wang' Hanley, my company runner, would stop looking at me, his squint further disorientating me.

Looking around, few were talking. I was not alone wrestling with the turmoil in my mind. I had yearned for such a moment for fourteen years. I would not wish to be anywhere else, but … What am I doing here? Will I, can I, do what the Company expects of me?

A sharp click and the PA system hums to life. 'You've been a wonderful bunch of passengers.' The familiar Yorkshire tones of the ship's master, Don Ellerby, sound warm, intimate. 'It's been a pleasure having you aboard. We hope you have a good time ashore, and we look forward to sailing you safely home shortly.'

Don Ellerby's 'passengers' are not his usual tourists going ashore in Rotterdam. They are some 650 young men of the 2nd Battalion the Parachute Regiment. 2 PARA were preparing to leave their home of the last four weeks, to do business with the Argentines.

A love for this man and his ship wells up in my throat. This is our Mother Ship. We'll go ashore, do what we have to do, and bloody well travel home in her.

Happier now, with nothing to do but wait for the landing craft to come alongside and bear us to we know not what, my thoughts drift to how this unusual journey began …

Chapter 2

Penal Company

Any new Army posting starts with an interview with the Commanding Officer. I had recently returned from my honeymoon – three months on the highest unclimbed mountain in China. Now, in October 1981, freshly promoted to Major, I duly entered the office of Lieutenant Colonel Herbert Jones and saluted, to be met by an intense, wiry man with lively eyes and, when deployed, an engaging smile. He reportedly hated his given name, and to everyone he was known as 'H' Jones, or just 'H'. The Commanding Officer of a battalion is God of his domain. I idly mused whether anyone ever commented 'what an unusual name' when he introduced himself, but quickly decided I was not going to put this to the test. A restless, nervous energy, with a suppressed impatience, radiated from his every move and expression. It was like watching a fizzing firework, waiting for the 'bang'.

He pointed me to a chair and, with no preliminaries, said 'You're to take over D Company.' The battalion had recently returned from a two-year tour in Northern Ireland, where it had taken catastrophic casualties in an IRA ambush at Warrenpoint. He told me that he was in the process of reorientating the battalion from counterinsurgency (COIN) operations, where minimum force and care of own casualties were pre-eminent considerations, to 'conventional' all-arms operations, where the violence of the full range of heavy weapons was brought to bear and casualties had to look after themselves until immediate objectives were secured. I listened politely; this was all very obvious.

'Are you clear what I expect?' I gave a sage nod, trying to convey he could rely on me. Then he thoroughly disarmed me: 'Of course, let's be honest, your "Confidential" really all hangs on how well we get on.' Everyone knew this, but no one ever articulated it. The Confidential Report was our annual performance review, on which careers were made or broken. Another nod. 'God' did not need to spell out the one-sided aspect to our relationship. As I left, I inwardly smiled at his brazen confidence to say it exactly how it was. It promised to be an interesting posting. Little did I know.

I headed to D Company's offices. It was time I got to know my 'Toms'. Toms? The name derives from 'Tommy Atkins', the nickname for the British soldier in the First World War, usually shortened to just 'Tommy'. After the Second World War the term fell into disuse, except within the Parachute Regiment. 'Tom' is a term of respect for soldiers in the Parachute Regiment – the Toms refer to themselves as Toms with pride. By comparison, 'squaddie', a term used by 'lesser' regiments to refer to their soldiers, is patronizing and disrespectful. The Toms themselves, however, can also be patronizing, referring to officers, where respect has not been earned, as 'Ruperts' – after the rather hapless Rupert Bear. The Toms refer to these 'lesser' regiments as 'crap-hats'. Strictly, anyone not entitled to wear the maroon beret is a 'crap-hat' although, despite their sand-coloured berets, the term would not normally be applied to the SAS, and the Royal Marines, with their green berets, might be referred to as 'cabbage-tops'. More respectfully, marines were referred to as 'boot-necks', or just 'booties', after the leather neck collars that once formed part of their uniform. Over time, the rest of the Army, tiring of this disrespect, forbade the use of the term 'crap-hat'. The Toms, as ever with orders that they thought misguided, had the answer. 'Crap-hats' instead became 'hats', the tone standing in for the omitted adjective, as in: 'Don't worry about him, Sir, he's just a HAT.' The right provincial accent, say Liverpudlian, makes the comment particularly devastating.

D Company was one of three rifle companies in the battalion, the other two being A and B. Rifle companies were the ones that did the business, dishing out, and sometimes receiving, pain at close quarters to seize the objective, hold ground or sometimes just to notch up enemy scalps and improve the odds. C Company was a specialist reconnaissance and patrols company. Why wasn't the third rifle company C? A fair question – in most battalions it would be – but one that only someone new to the idiosyncrasies of the British Army would ask. I was a newcomer, and did ask, but I never got an answer. Sadly, someone over-obsessed with tidiness and no understanding of the importance of tradition has since undone this anomaly.

I was soon to discover, however, that that was as far as untrammelled thinking went. The alphabet ruled, and D Company was always at the back of the queue for everything. In a plan of attack, for example, it was invariably 'A Company – left forward, B Company – right forward, and (after a pregnant pause as befits an afterthought) D Company – reserve.' The Toms, I found, were philosophical about this. Experience told them that, generally, they ended up doing more than any others. It also added to their resilience. This was to prove the essence of D Company. Reserves are deployed, generally, for two reasons: because the plan is unravelling or to exploit unexpected success. More than most, reserves need the ability to cope with the uncertainty that pervades all military operations – an ability that determines who wins, who loses, who lives and who dies.

D Company also seemed to be the parking lot for other companies' 'HR' problems – bad lads who needed a 'wake-up call'. Because D was the most junior rifle company, it did not seem to work the other way. Either the 'problem' was 're-educated' in D Company or, out of options, he was out. We were the battalion's gulag. Small wonder, perhaps, that the inmates of D labelled their home 'Penal Company'. It was, though, a badge of honour and many a problem Tom arriving on the dreaded 'Three-month Formal Warning' found it was just the rehab he sought, some of them going on to excel.

There were other dimensions. A and B companies shared an office block. Their company commanders were also old friends who had gone through officer training at the Royal Military Academy at Sandhurst together. Both had served in 2 PARA before – 'known knowns'. With them, there was a strong element of a problem shared is a problem halved. D Company shared an office block with C (Patrols) Company, the eyes and ears of the battalion, with whom we had little in common, so buddy-ing up was not as easy.

I was a 'known unknown' when I arrived in 2 PARA. I had not been through officer training at Sandhurst, as I had come in by the back door, via the Royal Air Force. My officer training had taken place at Henlow, an RAF station with no runway, so no aeroplanes except a stripped-out Lightning on a plinth at the edge of the parade square. The six-month course seemed to focus on administration (a glorious catch-all – like how legally to imprison an airman for a month), parade drill and playground-type games (crossing a 10ft ditch with 9ft plank and two rubber bands, with a notional crocodile in the ditch) which were described as 'leadership training'. I suspect it was rather a jolly affair compared with Sandhurst, and I was duly commissioned into the RAF Regiment. It turned out to be the pinnacle of my formal training. On later courses, run by the Army, I was generally a 'could do better if he tried'. The RAF can be a frus-tratingly blinkered and bureaucratic organization, but they seem to run more enlightened courses than the Army.

I still had fond memories of my short six-year RAF career. Like most, I had served emergency tours in Northern Ireland. I had also seen active service in the Dhofar War in Oman, but the RAF Regiment's role there had been purely defensive, involving weeks of waiting for something to happen. One day, out of boredom, I mortared a herd of camels that had wandered into a free-fire zone. Little did I know that they were friendly forces – a bribe to a tribesman to join the Firquats, units of surrendered enemy personnel, to fight on the Sultan's side. I've no idea whether he defected back to the Adoo, as the insurgents were known, but for a while my future hung in the balance. I quickly learnt that officers are expected to exercise judgement, not just follow instructions. After three wonderful years on the RAF Regiment's parachute squadron, I was posted to a head-quarters at Uxbridge to train airmen who would never ever see combat how to shoot.

I had just been invited to join an expedition to climb a hitherto un-climbed 23,000ft peak in the Himalayas. My new Station Commander, however, declared that he could not spare me because of the 'security situation' at Heathrow. The early 1970s was the era when every would-be troublemaker tried his hand at aircraft hijacking. 'I'm sorry, Sir, I thought this was Uxbridge,' I challenged. The look he gave told me it was time to find pastures new. I applied to join the Parachute Regiment, but still wangled my way to the Himalayas, submitting my resignation from the RAF en route. I made my first ascent, but not before two events which might have put paid to all my plans for good, indeed to this Falklands memoir.

The first was an encounter with Air India, a customs officer at Calcutta and a large box. The year was 1974, four years before the release of the film *Midnight Express*, about a young American tricked into carrying drugs into Turkey. Air India had provided the expedition with free flights from Hong Kong to Calcutta. I and one other, a newly commissioned Para-chute Regiment officer, the last two to fly out, went down to their offices to collect our tickets from their country manager. 'Mr Neame, Mr Scott, here are your tickets. It's an honour to help you. We'll pass you through our VIP suite at Kai Tak airport. That way, we can by-pass security for your ice-axes and pass them to you as you get on the plane. Just one thing,' he added, 'can you take a box with you for our staff in Calcutta?'

'What's in the box?' we asked.

'Oh, it's milk powder. Impossible to get in Calcutta at the moment.' Focused only on catching up with the rest of the expedition, we nodded. As we reached the aircraft steps, we were given our ice-axes and a foot-square tin box wrapped in brown paper tied up with string. On our arrival at Calcutta, John was carrying the box.

'Mr Scott, what's in that box?' asked a smug customs official.

'I've no idea,' said John. 'It's Air India's.'

'But it might be gold,' smirked the customs man.

'Oh, no,' John replied. 'But it could be heroin.' I have no idea what impelled John, whom at that point I had only known for two days, to be so helpful, but I suddenly felt an overriding need to disassociate myself from him. Another smirk and a knowing wink, then a wave through. In arrivals, we were met by a sweating and nervy Air India official.

'Mr Scott, do you have the box?' By now, John had entered into the spirit of the occasion, and hidden it behind his back.

'What box?' he asked. The official looked like he could collapse to the floor, before John, with a flourish, passed it to the poor chap with a cheerful 'Oh, this box!'

The second event happened low down on the mountain. Dick Isherwood, a formidable alpinist, and I were pushing the route up to the west col of the mountain. A steep 1,500ft slope needed to be overcome. The snow was like a 45-degree treadmill of ball bearings. After seven hours we made the col – three steps up, sliding two back. The next day we were getting ready to repeat the effort, carrying a load of tentage and other kit, when those below radioed to say they were having a rest day. Dick and I first thought 'what wimps!' Then, 'Sod it, bloody hard day yesterday, we've earned a rest more than them.' We got a brew on instead.

Just as we were taking our first sip of tea, squatting outside our tent, enjoying the warm sunshine, we heard a loud crack. We looked up to see the slope beginning to disintegrate from top to bottom. We watched, mesmerized, as the avalanche grew with a muffled roar, until its snout came to rest a few feet away from our tent. Dick and I grinned at each other. 'Good call today,' I suggested matter-of-factly, taking another sip of tea. In those days our appreciation of avalanche risk was as naïve as that of accepting free tickets from Air India.

Having survived these threats to my future, I was not too worried, on my return, to learn that the RAF was sufficiently upset at my resignation to deny me a reference. The Parachute Regiment, with their own extensive experience of working with the RAF, also took a pragmatic view. I joined 3 PARA but, to escape a tour in Germany, theoretically defending bridges against Soviet armoured divisions, I volunteered for 'Special Duties' in Northern Ireland. There, my claim to fame, during training and selection, was shooting myself in the mirror with a 9mm pistol. Fortunately, the bullet was a blank training round, so the mirror survived. I nearly didn't, expecting to be RTU'd for an ND – which translates as sacked for the negligent discharge of a weapon. Fortune smiled again. The course sergeant major, the renowned Geordie Lillicoe, found it funny: 'Best I've seen,' he chortled as he collected my large fine, 'trying to beat yourself to the draw!' The unit wasn't overtly supposed to exist, so talking about experiences there might anyway have been seen as delusional.

D Company had little interest in such mishaps. The only thing they did know and care about was that I had done P Company – the demanding selection for the Regiment, which earns you the coveted red beret and enables you to join the tribe.

So, I could write my own script. My Toms looked at the blank page expectantly. My company sergeant major, Nobby Clark, of medium build and sharply but softly spoken, was far from the cartoon portrayal of the role. The CSM is the company commander's right-hand man, chief administrator, maintainer of standards and the vital link between officers and non-commissioned officers. A month or so in, we were still weighing each other up, but I could tell he had some concerns. For a start, the length of my hair was pushing accepted military boundaries – an indulgence I carried over from operating in plain clothes on Special Duties. I had a suspicion Nobby saw it as a threat to 'good order and military discipline'. I on the other hand took some delight in the fact that he could order others to get their hair cut, but not me.

With Nobby at my side, I recall a Monday morning inspection of the company, neatly lined up in three ranks. Nobby picked up one or two of the Toms, with just that quiet hint of menace with which I had become familiar, for minor failures of turn-out. Nearing the end of the third rank, he abruptly stopped in front of one neatly turned-out soldier. 'Banks, are you planning to join the Racks?' He was referring to the Women's Royal Army Corps or WRACs. Banks, a fiercely proud Scot, pride only equalled by wearing his red beret, looked from Nobby to me, and back to Nobby. His face spoke volumes, but Banks is a natural survivor. He very wisely said nothing. I also held my peace. 'Report to the company office at two o'clock, looking like a Para,' ordered Nobby. As we left the parade ground, I gingerly said: 'Sergeant Major, are you trying to tell me something?' Nobby just responded with a wintry smile. Banks reported as ordered to the company office after lunch. He and I were both freshly shorn. That evening, when I got home, my wife told me she had had a call from Nobby: 'Mrs Neame, please can you leave your husband's hair to the camp barber, in future?' I started to see Nobby as the 'thinking man's sergeant major', someone I wanted on my side.

In late 1981 the battalion deployed to Kenya for an overseas training exercise, a further stage in 'H's focus on all-arms conventional war operations. I had another agenda – during a short spell of R&R, with three others, I was planning to climb Nelion and Batian, the twin summits of Mount Kenya. As we were packing the company's tropical kit and equipment, the appearance of my extra bag, containing ropes, crampons, ice axes and down jacket, attracted puzzled looks from the company quartermaster sergeant, Bob Powell, and his logistics team. The Toms were still trying to get my measure.

On Exercise Grand Prix, I was also to get more of theirs, and of 'H' himself. 'H' set the company a test exercise. Standing in the shade of a plane tree, looking out over scrubby savannah, he gave me my orders. Some 5 miles away was an enemy camp. I was to destroy it before an attack on their main stronghold beyond. It was known that they undertook aggressive patrolling, so I should expect to come into contact as soon as I set forth. How I executed this task was entirely up to me.

To my left was a prominent bare ridge leading to the objective. It dominated the ground. Straight ahead was a dry scrubby river valley; low ground but offering some cover. Teaching suggested that I should take the ridge. Then, as commanders are also taught, I put myself in the enemy commander's shoes. This of course was 'H', who was directing both the exercise and the enemy. 'H' had been a highly regarded instructor at the School of Infantry. I knew at once that he would expect me to take the dominating high ground, and that would be where he had deployed his enemy forces. I took the valley route.

I had an uninterrupted move to the objective. 'H' was apoplectic. His carefully planned exercise designed to give us lots of practice in exhausting Fire and Manoeuvre had been rendered pointless. In a noisy debrief, within earshot of the company, he told me to sharpen up my appreciation of ground. 'I hope you've learnt something.' I was not sure I had, believing the company had done rather well. 'Yes, but not what I expected,' I replied ambivalently, and returned to the company.

I had of course committed two cardinal sins. (1) Don't fight the Pink. Exercise Instructions were traditionally printed on pink paper. (2) Don't argue with God.

From that moment I had the feeling the Toms had taken my measure and approved. It matched their 'we do things our way in D Company' culture. That suited me, also the outsider. I shamelessly exploited these factors that set the company apart in the training that followed. It proved a vital aspect to our morale and resilience – although I had then no inkling that they were to be so put to the test in the wintry South Atlantic, starting with that brief telegram 'BRUNEVAL' only a few weeks later.

Chapter 3

An Ocean Cruise

Portsmouth Docks, 26 April 1982

MV *Norland*, a North Sea ferry plying between Hull and Rotterdam, was STUFT (Ship Taken Up From Trade). Already on board was a Royal Navy party and a team of engineers fitting a helicopter landing platform to the rear of the ship. A mass of equipment, rations, heavy weapons and ammunition was being hastily crammed, willy-nilly, into her car decks.

The dockside was bedecked with flags. Cheering dock workers mingled with families from Aldershot, waving off their loved ones. There was all the carnival atmosphere of a cruise ship setting off for a holiday in the sun, as we clambered out of coaches to make our way on board. It surely wasn't going to end in mud, blood and bullets – as Wang, ever at my side, succinctly put it, 'for two thousand sheep-shaggers, 8,000 miles away at the arse-end of the world, in some place we've never heard of?' At least we now knew where the Falkland Islands were.

Also on the dockside was the battalion's band. They were our stretcher-bearers in war, but there was apparently insufficient room on board for them – ah, clearly, just a cruise to the sun and back! I glanced at Jim Barry, one of my three platoon commanders. He had forgone a crew place on the British boat competing for the Americas Cup for this trip. I wondered what he was thinking. He was never to get that opportunity again.

The band finished playing 'Ride of the Valkyries', the Regimental March. The ferry let slip, final good-byes were shouted and the odd tear shed. As we cleared the harbour, a cluster of young girls were cheering and waving from the mole. A chorus of wolf whistles erupted from the Toms – their families already supplanted by the adventure to come. Astern, we could still hear the strains of the band's final number – 'Don't Cry for me, Argentina' . . .

We began that afternoon to settle into our new home, and to convert the ship into a floating barracks. As in any barracks, there were separate quarters for officers, senior non-commissioned officers (SNCOs), and other ranks – the Toms. The film *Titanic* shows graphically how this worked. The officers were allocated cabins on the top deck, two to a four-man cabin, and a short stroll to the Snug bar at the stern of the ship, which became the officers' mess. The commanding officer (CO), 'H', and the second-in-command, Chris Keeble, had a cabin each for themselves. 'H's, however, was unoccupied, as he had flown ahead to Ascension Island where the main Task Force was already gathering, and planning, for the recovery of the Islands. The SNCOs were allocated the next deck, with the Forward Lounge as their mess; the regimental sergeant major, to 'H' what Nobby Clark was to me, also had a cabin to himself. The Toms, further down, found themselves below the waterline, four to a four-man cabin, with the Continental Lounge serving as the NAAFI. Below them were the car decks packed with all the battalion's stores and heavy weapons – and the war allocation of high-explosive ammunition that went with them. The Toms took it in their stride – they had long since learnt that life wasn't fair.

We were not alone on board. The battalion had been reinforced with a battery commander and his forward observation parties from the artillery regiment that would be supporting us, a troop from the Parachute Engineer Squadron and an air defence troop equipped with man-portable Blowpipe missiles. We were now the 2 PARA Battalion Group. The Royal Navy party was led by Commander Chris Esplin-Jones, who had taken charge of *Norland* as soon as she had been commandeered, or 'taken up from trade' to adopt the polite Ministry of Defence euphemism. Although he held the same rank as 'H', we were left in no doubt that he was the senior officer on board. He was also responsible for the team of civilian engineer contractors who were still busy fabricating two helicopter landing decks, not standard issue for a car ferry. If nothing else, those heli decks were to prove really useful for team photographs and physical training (PT) areas as we travelled south. And, of course, there was the ship's civilian crew, led by the ship's master, Captain Don Ellerby. Don had been within weeks of retiring before he was obliged to surrender his ship to the Royal Navy, but he remained fully in control of the day-to-day running of the ship – it was just that it was no longer his. However, the Navy can be gracious and he was allowed to keep his own cabin.

With 'H' in Ascension, it fell to Major Chris Keeble to try to integrate 2 PARA into this unusual setting and be amicable cruising companions. This was not a given. Paras regarded themselves, not entirely without reason, some would say, as superior to any other military tribe. We had experience of the RAF, not all of it favourable. They were rather seen as fair-weather brothers-in-arms, with technical problems or the weather itself so often providing them an excuse not to play. But the Navy, variously known as 'fish heads' or 'matelots', were like aliens to us. There was plenty of scope for 'misunderstandings'.

The crew of *Norland* was another matter altogether. Few of us could really get our heads around the idea of going to war with a bunch of civvies but, with a cruise to the sun still the expectation of many, that could be parked for now. A number, however, especially among the stewards, were outright 'queens', and clearly delighted in it. How would this play out amongst a bunch of macho Paras, who were rarely inclined to walk away if provoked or invited to strut their stuff? Among the officers there was a certain anxiety. Stern advice about conduct on board was delivered, and drink was limited to two cans of beer per man per day.

As so often happens, the head-shed's concerns were like an un-zeroed rifle, not quite aligned to its sights. The Toms had long since learnt how to circumvent the two-beers regime from numerous tours in Northern Ireland, and from the team training of which the Army is rightly so proud. A group of like-minded souls would agree no beers for an evening or two, so their mates could get blatted. One solution to this is to supervise the drinking, ensuring each man drank his two cans, thus obliging some to drink who had no wish to do so. Another was to declare the ship dry, with no alcohol for anyone, which would certainly not have suited the regulars of the Snug Bar, the officers' mess. It might have also incited protest from those not subject to military law – a threshold that was yet to come. Wisely, Chris Keeble decided to leave well alone.

He had no need to act on the 'queens', either. The Toms are endowed with generations of accumulated wisdom. They were quick to realize that the stewards could make their lives bearable and better, or a misery. Perhaps the same prescience pertained among the stewards. In any event, a relationship began to develop between 2 PARA and the *Norland* crew which lasted long after the war, indeed until she was decommissioned in 2010. I can put it no better than one of my company's Toms, Tony Banks, who later wrote of Roy 'Wendy' Gibson:

> Among the crew on the *Norland* was a gay steward who would become a 2 PARA icon. He was a big, round-shouldered guy, larger than life, and camper than any row of tents ever pitched in the history of the British Army. At first, he got dog's abuse – every kind of homophobic insult ever invented and quite a few that were invented especially for him. But he just smiled and took it all in his stride. We called him 'Bendy Wendy', which eventually evolved into 'Wendy'. In turn, he called us his 'boys'.

Gradually, he won us over. He looked after us, made sure we were OK, and got extra rations for us. In fact, all of the ship's staff were incredible. They were all volunteers and didn't need to be serving on a ship that had been commandeered by the Royal Navy, so we all respected them greatly for that. But Wendy was more than a brave volunteer – he turned out to be a great entertainer. He was brilliant on the piano and every night in the forward lounge he would hold sing-songs which became legendary affairs and played a big part in keeping up our spirits.

'Wendy', after the war, was made an honorary member of 2 PARA, and duly presented with a battalion tie. Three years later I was working in Regimental Headquarters, which often received letters on all sorts of strange topics from the public. The task of answering these courteously came to me – and often brought a chance for some mischief. A programme following recruits through parachute selection – P Company – was showing on the BBC. One day we received a letter from the Shetland Islands, of all places, protesting that one of the course instructors referring to a struggling selectee on one test as a 'poof' was an insult to the gay community. I refrained from making any judgement on Shetland Islanders but delighted in replying to the scribe that he had misunderstood the context, that the instructor was referring to a weak puff of air so favoured when parachuting, and recounting Wendy's membership of 2 PARA as evidence that the Regiment was, sexuality-wise, completely blind. Strangely, I got no reply.

I shared a cabin with Hugh Jenner. The cabin, an 8ft-square box, had no access to a porthole, but did have its own sink and shower. In this confined space, I was rather thankful that a toilet was not included, but if nature called in the middle of the night, the sink could save a long plod to the 'heads' – a widely used expediency. I was always happy to give Hugh first dibs at the sink in the mornings.

Hugh was the Support Company commander. That meant he was responsible for the heavy weapons: the anti-tank platoon with its MILAN missiles; the mortar platoon with its six 81mm mortars that could launch high explosive bombs over our heads onto the enemy; the machine gun platoon that, with its GPMGs mounted on tripods and using some clever sights, could provide sustained fire effective out to about 1,800 metres by day or night; and the sniper platoon, marksmen with the uncanny ability to turn themselves into bushy-topped trees, so loved by skill-at-arms instructors teaching target indication, and so concealed able to 'slot' selected high-value targets such as officers and radio operators up to 1,200 metres away. The chief instructor of the snipers was not a member of the platoon, but the battalion's padre, David Cooper, who, as well as being an ordained priest, was also a champion Bisley rifle shot. He seemed quite at ease with these diverse roles.

Hugh was another outsider. He was a secondment from a 'hat' regiment, the Cheshires, but – the important thing – he had completed P Company selection. We knew each other well, having shared an office together in the Brigade HQ on our previous tour before joining 2 PARA. That was helpful, as he was used to my occasional histrionic thespianism, such as on certain calls throwing telephones against the wall. He was also quite lucky to be with us at all. Having lost his footing crossing a river in spate on the exercise in Kenya, he was washed hundreds of yards downstream and presumed drowned until he reappeared in the company of two locals who had dragged him, semi-conscious, to the bank.

Bound initially for Freetown, in the Bay of Biscay, *Norland* met up with the MV *Europic Ferry*, another STUFT ship. She was to remain at our heels for the entire journey south, carrying all the battalion's heavy kit: Landrovers, 105 mm light guns, second line supplies of ammunition – and body bags.

We remained ambivalent as to how this cruise would end, but in our minds were stories of long deployments by sea during the Second World War after which troops disembarked totally unfit for purpose, without weeks of renewed training once ashore. We knew we would not have that luxury, should the cruise become something more: never would Paras be unfit for purpose. Our days were filled with an intense routine of training.

We took some things into our own hands. One of the lounges was converted into a gym. The deck below the rear heli platform became a firing range, using as targets the gash bags of rubbish periodically thrown overboard. Every bit of space was put to use for training and briefings. It was like a factory, its well-oiled production line producing fit and well-trained warriors.

The heli deck itself, once completed, was in almost constant use for physical training, but it was also a favoured spot for taking company or other group photos, records of what we desperately hoped would be a historic voyage. Nobby Clark arranged D Company's picture for the history book, the Toms neatly lined up in five rows. Just as well it was done then as the equivalent of one complete row would be absent for the trip home. 'Company Headquarters at the front or the back, Sir?' he asked. I was unable to take all this too seriously, but memories of distancing myself from John Scott at Calcutta airport flitted mischievously to mind. 'At the back,' I joked, 'just how we want it down there.' Nobby gave me one of his thin smiles and took me at my word.

Before leaving home, the battalion's equipment had been up-scaled. Each of a platoon's three sections of eight men was normally equipped with one machine gun, the belt-fed GPMG, affectionately known as the Jimpy. Now they had a second, as some thirty Bren guns, magazine-fed machine guns dating back to the Second World War, had, on 'H's urging, been found from old reserve stocks somewhere. 'H' was a past master at pulling strings, and either cajoling, berating or bullying people into giving him what he wanted – an irresistible force. Likewise, he had arranged for each section to be equipped with one M79 shoulder-fired grenade launcher. Those of us lower down the food chain could only wonder why, if this additional weaponry already existed and was seen as useful, it was not already in our hands. We had also jumped the queue for the brand-new Clansman radios to replace the ancient and hopelessly unreliable Larkspur range, literally the day before sailing. So weapon training and signals training on *Norland* were a high priority.

Signals training rather tested David Benest, the regimental signals officer, as we were forbidden to transmit. David was an earnest young officer and one of the few I knew well, as several years earlier he used to join me climbing, tying onto my rope like an eager young puppy on its lead. We were to be on radio silence until we landed, to minimize the signals intelligence that the Argentinians might acquire on the position and make-up of the Task Force. One day the surreal spectacle of this radio training without actually transmitting absurdly reminded me of a child-hood nonsense rhyme: '*One fine day in the middle of the night/two blind men got up to fight.*'

Time was also given to map reading, Argentinian aircraft and vehicle recognition, and first aid. The last was generally seen as a chore in barracks, compared with more active training. Now there was a damascene conversion. There's nothing like self-interest to concentrate the mind. It was also to prove some of the most entertaining training. When someone is shot, the body goes into shock as it tries to close down activity and divert attention to the wound. The need then is to induce fluid into the body as quickly as possible. To this end each man was issued with a saline drip, to be kept on him at all times on the battlefield – not for him to use on someone else, but for someone else to use on him. Similarly each man had two phials of morphine taped to the inside of his helmet. Thus, each man carried his own pain relief and life support system.

However, finding a vein to insert the fluid into when someone is suffering severe shock is difficult, even for highly trained medics. Steve Hughes, our regimental medical officer (RMO), was freshly out of medical school and his officer training. But he had a wise and forward-thinking head on young shoulders, and quickly understood that in the real world a solution not requiring the skills of a medic had to be found. Short of a vein, he solemnly told us, the next best way of getting fluid into someone is through the rectum. Naturally, we needed to practise how to do this. And so we did. As young fit Paras wandered around the main lounge with bags of saline hanging out of their backsides, for Wendy and the other stewards it was better than a night at the theatre.

There were also at least two sessions of fitness training a day, one on the heli-deck doing an hour of circuit training and PT, and another hour of running in full fighting order around the companion ways from one deck to the other. Activity was ceaseless, and the steady rhythmic drumming of feet a constant.

We reached Freetown one dark night, to let off the engineering contractors, their work on the heli-decks completed. While *Norland* took on more stores, Don Ellerby invited any of his crew who did not wish to continue south towards an uncertain future to leave and return to the UK. This would be their last chance. Only two female members of the crew did so, both with young families. The rest, 'queens' and all, made it clear they were determined to see it through. By now, a real bond was forming between the crew and the battalion. Would they have been so keen had they known what they were to let themselves in for? Probably. As one of the stewards, in a strong scouse camp accent, said; 'You fucking lot need us to look after you!'

Onwards to Ascension, a small volcanic island in the mid-Atlantic. 'Crossing the line' on the way, the Navy, we learnt, like to make a thing of crossing from one hemisphere to another. We had Chris Esplin-Jones's Naval Party to thank for a day off from training and an extra can of beer per man. The 'Fishheads' rose a notch in our estimation.

Ascension Island, a British territory, was the home of a US electronic eavesdropping station. It had become the forward mounting base for the Task Force, most of which was there ahead of us, the 2 PARA Battalion Group being late reinforcements for 3 Commando Brigade, led by Brigadier Julian Thompson. My twin brother was a gunner who had done two tours with the brigade, and before I left he had told me that Thompson was 'OK' in a tone that meant pretty damn good – a promising start. Their three commandos, or battalions, of Marines had already been reinforced by our sister battalion, 3 PARA, as they at the time were on Quick Reaction Force duties. They had sailed south on a genuine cruise ship, the P&O luxury liner *Canberra*, nicknamed the White Whale, reflecting her size and colour – neither a wonderful characteristic if sailing into hostile waters. We were happy on our ferry, which we did not have to share. Our own two up, two down home from Hull felt so much better, and safer, than a luxury apartment in a block of flats from Chelsea.

Ascension was a hive of activity. It had a particularly long runway and its Wideawake airbase was now surrounded by a tented city, like some South American slum. At the height of the build-up, it was reported to be handling more aircraft movements than Heathrow. Around us were anchored dozens of ships of every description, with helicopters constantly shuttling from one to another and to and from the airfield. For the first time, like watching a scene from *The Longest Day*, we felt we were part of a great and bold enterprise. My pulse quickened with a surge of excitement and pride.

Here, the Commando Brigade insisted that we practised amphibious landing procedure. Embarking over the ramp of the bow car doors of the ferry on to Landing Craft Units (LCUs) and then disembarking as it reached the shore over the lowered ramp at the front was, the Marines assured us, an art of almost mystical dimensions needing intense training. We returned to the *Norland* not much the wiser, concluding the process was no different from emplaning an aircraft and jumping out on the command 'Go.' The only difference was that instead of 'Go', the command was 'Out Troops'. It was just a simple matter of detailed planning to ensure the battalion was in good order once its feet touched the ground. The cynics amongst us also observed that we were unlikely to have the same still calm sea, warmth and daylight when going ashore in the Falklands, known as one of the windiest places on the planet. David Constance, our popular Royal Marine liaison officer, had to contend with a fair ribbing in the Snug Bar that evening. To render this exercise's futility complete, when we did go ashore, we left the *Norland* through a side door, not over its roll-on roll-off ramp. However, nothing beats pottering about in boats.

At the end of April, we left Ascension, heading south for our final destination. With 'H' now aboard, the atmosphere tightened. He came with more detail of the Task Force composition and plans. We learnt of a small preliminary operation to recover South Georgia. This was where the whole crisis began to kick off when some Argentinian 'scrap metal merchants' landed at the old whaling station of Grytviken. They had since been reinforced with a small military garrison. He also told us that the brigade was planning an unopposed landing on East Falkland, probably at San Carlos.

We also were joined by a dozen or so RAF fast jet pilots. Their Harrier aircraft, parked on the *Atlantic Conveyor*, a roll-on roll-off container ship, for the trip south were the ground attack/reconnaissance version, the GR3. The Navy's Sea Harriers were to fly combat air patrols to deter Argentinian air attacks on the Task Force, while the RAF chaps flying the GR3 were primarily to attack targets on the ground, which could include close and direct fire support of our own operations ashore. They therefore received a warmer welcome than the Parachute Regiment sometimes accorded the Air Force. They must have suffered a bit of a culture shock, however. There's an adage on the significance of stars in the military. In the Army stars denote how senior a general is – five being a field marshal, reducing to one for a brigadier. The Navy navigate by them. For the RAF it tells them the quality of their hotel. *Norland* was certainly short of their standard four stars. Their habit, while we were still in the tropics, was to take an early morning tea or coffee on the nearest external companion way, enjoying the sun. But being nearly trampled underfoot as one company or other doubled round the decks on their daily 5 mile run in full kit soon deterred this habit. Their presence in the Snug Bar in the evenings, though, perhaps raised the tone a little.

Soon after leaving Ascension, 'H' insisted that the ship be blacked out. This should have been Chris Esplin-Jones's decision, as military commander of the vessel, but maybe it was 'H' letting everyone know he was now on board and not prepared to let the Navy call all the shots. Then, again, perhaps it was his way of calling time on the summer cruise and focusing minds. The battalion set to, taping black gash bags onto every external window or porthole. That job done, someone, I think the RSM, drew attention to *Norland*'s red funnel. Don Ellerby was not happy at having his funnel painted black but, no surprise to us, 'H' got his way. Another work party was quickly assembled to set about this 'Black Adder' task. Fortunately, the expanse of white superstructure on the upper decks seemed to escape 'H's attention.

All the company commanders had secondary duties. A Company's Dair Farrar-Hockley, for example, was responsible for air defence, posting machine-gun and Blowpipe positions around the ship. After a couple of days 'H' felt we needed a break in routine to stop us getting stale. He appointed me battalion sports officer and instructed me to organize an inter-company sports day – good for building up a bit of aggression. This seemed rather a thankless task on a boat, but was certainly better than the tedium of being president of the mess committee, the role which Hugh had drawn.

I set to work. Tugs of war, five-aside football and deck hockey on the heli-deck were predictable fare. I added a shooting match for obvious reasons – and bowls, for the entertainment value on a rolling deck. The latter was perhaps also good training in managing the unpredictability and uncertainty of war, but that's hindsight talking. Something more was needed. I finally presented my programme, with a steeplechase and an orienteering competition as highlights. 'H' gave me a sad look. 'Well, it'll be on your head, Philip,' he shrugged. He didn't need to say that he thought I had lost the plot.

The steeplechase proved more akin to urban free-running, in 1982 an unknown sport. The Toms bounded, bounced, rolled and somersaulted from one deck or companion way to another, all over the top of the ship. The external stairways between decks were entirely ignored except by a few of the more cautious. I held my breath. *Norland*'s crew, the Naval Party and the Harrier pilots emerged on deck, looking on, mouths agape. Part of the course, I hadn't realized, went over the roof of Don Ellerby's cabin. He had been catching up on some sleep, having been up the night before. He emerged, bemused, demanding to know what was happening to his ship. Miraculously, no one was lost overboard.

The orienteering competition took teams to every part of the ship, tip to tail and from its bowels to its funnel. Only one team completed the challenge in the time allowed. Some were lost for so long that the RSM, smiling, considered charging them for absence without leave. I have often thought that there's a long-missed opportunity here for entertainment officers on cruise liners – although perhaps only for Club 18–30 cruises. 'H' never gave praise, but I felt his belief in my sanity was partially restored. Don Ellerby, by now back to his normal good humour, presented the prizes on the rear heli-deck with all due ceremony. The prizes were a slip of paper on which was printed: 'The Bearer of this Token was a member of a Winning Team in the MV *Norland* Sports Competition 1982 and is entitled to goods to the value of £4.50 from the Ship's Shop.' *Norland* was a generous host – there were a lot of tokens.

A happy day was rounded off with news that South Georgia had been recovered with virtually no opposition, and that the force there had also sunk an Argentinian submarine. Spirits were high.

'H's blacking out of the ship was to prove prescient. On 3 May we learnt via the BBC World Service that one of our submarines had sunk the Argentinian cruiser *General Belgrano* the day before, with the loss of hundreds of lives. She was second only to their single aircraft carrier, *25th May*, as the pride of the Argentinian Navy. There was cheering, and we grasped the hands of our Naval Party in congratulations. But the joy was tempered by the waning sun, the cloudier, cooler days, the longer nights and rougher seas as our sunshine cruise sailed on towards a southern hemisphere winter.

Then, late on 4 May, we learnt that the destroyer HMS *Sheffield* had been sunk by Exocet missiles fired from two Argentinian Super Etendarde aircraft. Training had been completed for the day. In the gathering dusk of a gloomy, cloudy evening, *Norland* fell eerily silent. End of fun in the sun. Diplomacy had failed. There was now no going back. *Sheffield* and her crew were, sadly, a secondary consideration.

I saw Jim Barry, who commanded 12 Platoon, in the snug bar. 'Looking like this is going to be better than the Americas Cup,' I offered. 'Good call!' Jim gave a lop-sided grin. Good, he knew he was in the right place. Reassured, I went down to the Toms' deck to see what they were making of the news. Noise was beginning to pick up in the forward lounge. Wang spotted me and, his face full of mischief, made a bee-line for me. 'Sir, sir,' he said urgently, 'what do the *Sheffield* and an old whore have in common?' I looked at him blankly. 'They're both full of dead se(a)men,' he chortled, and rushed off to raise spirits elsewhere. 'No problems, here,' I thought, as I made my excuses and left. The Toms were working this out in their own way. On some difficult days in the mountains humour had been the best antidote to our fears and anxiety – the blacker, the better. The Toms were bouncing back.

To labour the point that we really were now at war, the next day an intense officer of the Naval Party advised that we were now a potential target for enemy submarines. He assured us that we were well protected by the screen provided by the Royal Navy's state of the art frigates, but just in case we were hit by a torpedo we should in future sleep fully clothed. Blank looks from some. He patiently explained that the sea was now getting cold, and we might not have time to get dressed before ending up in the drink. Being fully clothed could delay the onset of hypothermia long enough for us to be picked up, alive. I turned in that night with the best of intentions. The cabin was as hot and stuffy as ever. After half an hour, I decided that this order was more a subject for discussion. Hugh tut-tutted, but I decided to put my full confidence in the Navy's frigates and get a decent night's sleep. For the rest of the voyage I continued to sleep in my 'zube suit', a loose-fitting, black lightweight cotton track suit that many of us had had knocked up by a Chinese tailor in

Singapore for night wear in the Malayan jungle. Dressed as a Kung-Fu fighter, I felt just fine.

The next day, fun in the sun now well behind us, we had the first of many 'abandon ship' and lifeboat drills. The organizing and practice of fire-fighting teams was also added to Dair Farrar-Hockley's growing list of responsibilities. More time was also devoted to briefings and planning for what we all now knew was to come. I spent hours talking through various 'what-if' scenarios with my twenty or so platoon and section commanders. Many had joined since the Kenya exercise. Among my officers, only Shaun Webster, officer commanding (OC) 10 Platoon, had been with me then. Chris Waddington, 11 Platoon, had only completed his officer training at Sandhurst some weeks previously. Our Americas Cup yachtsman, Jim Barry, 12 Platoon, was a Royal Signals officer, who had just begun a two-year secondment to the Parachute Regiment. When not on operations, companies normally managed without seconds-in-command, so Pete Adams, my 2ic, had only joined days before sailing, as had Jonathan (Jacko) Page just days out of Sandhurst. He was sent to me as a supernumerary or spare, so I made him responsible for liaison with the battalion's direct fire supporting weapons – Milan anti-tank and GPMG (SF). Also of concern, Chris, Jim and Jacko had yet to do their Infantry 'Special-to-Arm' training at the School of Infantry. I really did need to get to know them better, and they me, if we were to perform under pressure of the unexpected. These hours were to yield huge dividends.

One thing that became abundantly clear was that the only way to move over the terrain of the Islands, essentially a peat bog the size of Wales, would be by helicopter or on foot. We were going to have to carry everything we needed on our backs. The loads built up. This, now, was going to include ammunition for the support weapons, mortar bombs, anti-tank missiles and the mass of belted 7.62mm rounds for the sustained fire machine guns, which might normally be moved by Land Rover and trailer. My personal on-the-man load, carried in pockets and 'webbing', pouches on a belt and shoulders harness, included:

- Self-loading rifle (SLR) and bayonet
- Identity (Dog) tags worn on a cord around my neck
- 6 magazines holding 120 rounds of 7.62mm ammunition
- 200 rounds of belted 7.62mm – as spare for the machine guns
- My personal radio (PRC349)
- 2 grenades – one high explosive (HE) anti-personnel and one white phosphorous (WP) smoke for concealment, though the burns that the

latter could inflict meant they were favoured for anti-personnel as well, with less risk of collateral damage to your mates
- Pack of mini-flares
- 2 × 24 hour ration packs (stripped down), each with a solid fuel stove – one discarded
- 2 litres water
- 1 litre saline drip bag
- 2 morphine syrettes
- 2 shell dressings
- 1 groundsheet/poncho
- 1 digging tool (entrenching tool (mini pickaxe) or airborne (short-shafted) shovel)
- Binoculars, maps, notebook
- 'Cold/wet warfare waterproofs (smock and trousers)
- Arctic Warfare quilted suit

Also in my bergen rucksack were my sleeping bag, KIP sheet, spare clothing and spare rations. In the platoons additional stuff had to be shared around, including the M79 grenade launcher and its ammunition, the Carl Gustav ('Charlie G') medium anti-tank weapon (MAW) and its 84mm rockets, several 66mm light anti-tank weapons (LAW), night-sights, the 2-inch mortar and its ammunition.

Loads climbed past 80lb. Radio operators and support weapon handlers carried significantly more. In addition, for the landing each man was to carry two 81mm mortar rounds (weighing 13lb each) to drop off at the Mortar Platoon's base plate position.

Thoughts turned to what could be left behind. Into the debate 'H' injected the idea that this was a modern war that would be won by fire-power: bayonets were to be left behind. I relayed this to my company, to be met by looks of dismay. A few days previously they had practised bayonet drills on the heli-deck, with the aid of *Norland* mattresses liberated from unused bunks. Many had clearly acquired a warm machismo glow from this, delivering the coup de grace to the poor mattress with a bellowed 'Haaa …!' The unspoken comment was: 'How can you be a proper paratrooper without your bayonet?' It was like asking Wyatt Earp to take on the OK Corral without his six-guns.

I fed this back to 'H'. Other company commanders had had similar reactions, but, true to form, he was not to be moved. A few days later, with unease among the Toms persisting, I returned to the subject. I suggested that what really bothered the Toms was that they much preferred bayonets as tin openers to the things that came in the ration packs. These were in fact rather neat, and I always had one hanging round my neck with my dog tags. I was desperately trying to keep a straight face. Everyone else was keeping their heads down. There was a long stony silence. Then, 'H', with his best irascible performance, muttered: 'I've had enough of this. They can take their fucking bayonets!' He clearly didn't believe a word I'd said, but had taken the opportunity to resolve what threatened to become a morale issue without losing face. There was more to 'H' than met the eye.

As the situation became more serious, two other changes followed – the second an inevitable consequence of the other. First, the battalion paymaster advised that we should, if we hadn't already, consider making our wills. At the same time he advised we should sign up, at token cost, for a NAAFI insurance policy, known as ADAT (Army Dependants Assurance Trust) sold in units, which would pay out a lump sum within days of our death, no conditions, no questions asked. This concentrated minds. I signed up for the insurance policy, poor value though it probably was, to ease my conscience if I didn't make it back. My mind then flicked back to an Everest expedition six years earlier. Again, we had all been invited to write our wills. Terry Thompson, a Marine, had done so, and had left £100 to the expedition if he died. He did die, falling into a crevasse when, instead of peeing in a bottle in his tent, he decided to go out and water the glacier. That to me was karma. There was no way I was writing my will.

Since the start of our voyage, the padre, David Cooper, had been holding regular Sunday church services. David was much respected by the Toms, not just for his reputation as a marksman, making him potentially the most lethal member of the battalion – a fact that appealed immensely to their sense of irony, but also for his Yorkshire no-nonsense, even earthy approach. At almost every service, you could bank on hearing some irreverent and incisive aside. Now, with talk of enemy submarines and suitably reminded of our mortality by the paymaster's initiative, attendance began to soar. We all saw in David a superb insurance broker for the best policy going – better than ADAT by far. David was under no illusions about the motives of his flock. 'Some of you will not be coming back,' he told them in his final service before we went ashore. 'I can do nothing about that. God won't deflect a bullet. All I can guarantee is He will look after you, whether you do, or whether you don't.' His forthright candour certainly had me subscribing to the aphorism 'there are no atheists in foxholes', rather than the Marxist 'religion is the opiate of the people'. I think most of our Toms felt the same.

Early in the war the British Government had declared a 200-mile Total Exclusion Zone (TEZ) around the Islands, effectively to put them under siege and prevent Argentinian resupply and reinforcement. It was while enforcing the zone that the submarine HMS *Conqueror* had sunk the *General Belgrano*. Now, as we approached the TEZ, we received a signal from Admiral Woodward, the Task Force Commander on the aircraft carrier HMS *Hermes*, pointing out that the crews of all STUFT ships, already under Naval Orders, were henceforth subject to Military Law. That was the Navy's polite way of saying from now on do as you're told, or we'll hang you for mutiny. This was accepted with a shrug by the *Norland*'s crew – there was no real change, just the Navy dotting the i's.

The very next day, however, outline plans for the landing were received. These identified San Carlos, on the west coast of East Falkland, as the area for the amphibious landing, entered via the Falkland Sound which separates East and West Falkland. *Canberra* was to transfer her troops onto HMS *Fearless* out at sea and then scoot eastwards, hopefully beyond the range of the Argentinian Air Force. *Norland*, less of a target than the Great White Whale, *Canberra*, was effectively to be used as an amphibious assault ship: she was to disembark 2 PARA into LCUs in San Carlos Water, and remain there so that her huge volume of stores could then be ferried ashore. Don Ellerby was furious, not with that decision, but with the way it was made. In an uncomfortable exchange he advised Chris Esplin-Jones that he and his crew saw their being placed under military law the day before as a tremendous insult, as if the Navy did not otherwise trust them to undertake this dangerous task. We sympathized with him, knowing his crew well enough by now to be certain that they would be with us through thick and thin. It was a mis-timed, unnecessary and potentially damaging piece of bureaucracy. Not the finest example of Navy communications.

There were similar examples to come. As we entered the TEZ we received the detailed plan for the landings from 3 Commando Brigade. Four LCUs had been allocated for our move ashore to 'Blue Beach' on Bonner Bay, just south of San Carlos Settlement. We were then to secure Sussex Mountain, some 4 miles south, by first light. Military operations are normally conducted on Greenwich Mean Time to avoid confusion over aircraft missions, especially when crossing time zones. Time zones are denoted by an alphabetical suffix. GMT is Z or Zulu time, and British Summer Time (BST) is A or Alpha time. The Falklands were 4 hours behind GMT, so Victor time, therefore 5 hours behind BST. We had the timings for the operation. 2 PARA were to start embarking onto the

LCUs at 0315Z, or 1115V local. At 0515Z the LCUs were to set off for Blue Beach, disembarking their passengers at 0545Z, or 1.45am local, designated H hour.

What we still didn't know was the date. If rough seas were forecast, the date would be slipped. The earliest would be the night of 20/21 May, but was to be confirmed by the Commodore Amphibious Warfare, referred to and pronounced COMAW. The whole fleet was now on radio silence to avoid giving warnings and location to Argentinian electronic eaves-droppers. As 20 May dawned, to the cheerful refrain from a member of the Naval Party on the ship's PA system '*Wakey, wakey, rise and shine/We're off to fight the Argentine*', we waited expectantly. If this were to be the day, we had lots to do by way of final battle preparation – stowing 'leave-behind' kit, final packing of webbing pouches and bergens, breaking out ammunition, loading weapon magazines, issuing rations, camming up (smearing camouflage cream over our faces and hands), final briefings and rehearsals, a last supper followed by a short service conducted by David Cooper, then assembling in the main lounge in the correct groups and order of march for getting into the LCUs – a precise drill to ensure we got ashore from the front ramps in the right order for immediate action. By lunchtime 'H' was all restless energy and busily chewing his fingernails. Mid-afternoon we managed to flash a semaphore signal to a nearby frigate, HMS *Broadsword*: 'Is there anything we should know about?'

'Yes, but it's too secret to tell you,' their lamp flashed back.

The frigate came abreast, and through the miserable drizzle and mist fired a line onto *Norland*'s deck, carrying a copy of the final orders. H Hour, when we were to start embarking into the LCUs, was now only 7 hours away. We discovered these orders had been issued 48 hours earlier, but the Navy had overlooked communicating them to *Norland* despite the vital role for her cargo in the plan.

San Carlos was chosen because it was a sheltered deep-water anchorage, largely surrounded by hills. This, it was hoped, would provide some protection from enemy air attack, especially once the Rapier air defence missile systems were established ashore. It was some 40 miles from Port Stanley, the capital on the eastern shore of East Falkland, around which most of the Argentinian forces were based, and so out of range of their artillery. It would therefore take time before their ground forces could interfere with the landing, by which time the beachhead should be fully secured. The landing could be further protected by the Navy blockading the northern and southern entries to Falkland Sound – what 'H', in his resolute determination not to succumb to Naval domination of proceedings, quaintly called a VCP, or vehicle check point, a term we readily understood from operations in Northern Ireland.

The latest orders, apart from confirming that tonight was the night, contained several changes. Timings for the first landings had slipped by 4 hours. Wags put this down to the Navy and the Marines working to different timings – the Navy on Zulu and the Marines on local or Victor time. Well, with a cocktail of three different time zones, including the UK on BST, anything was possible. On *Norland*, we had stayed on local time within the ship, to preserve some normality around meal and sleeping times. As a result, 2 PARA, along with 40 Commando, instead of being in the second wave, would now be the first – 2 PARA hitting the beach first and 40 Commando 10 minutes later.

One other change was not such good news for D Company. The LCUs were to approach the beach and disgorge their cargoes in stream, one after the other. With D Company, as usual, in reserve, that meant LCU4 for us, and I had been thinking rather smugly that any opposition would be sorted by the time we were disembarked. Now they were to go as a wave, hitting the beach simultaneously. 'Bloody Marines!' I shrugged.

The ship sprang to life. It was 3.30pm local time when we got the line delivery from *Broadsword*. An evening meal in the usual three shifts was eaten between 4.30 and 7.00pm. Following our last supper, Padre David Cooper held his final church service, when we made our peace with our maker and paid our final insurance premiums to the Great Broker in the Sky. Somehow, by 10.00pm we were assembling, fully prepared, if staggering under monstrous loads, in the Continental Bar. All radios were now on, but still on radio silence. This was suddenly broken, as Headquarters 3 Commando Brigade boomed through on an amplified speaker to Battalion HQ on the Brigade net: 'Are you aware that the Brigade is due to start going ashore in 3 hours' time?' Only now, it appeared, had they discovered that Navy communications had overlooked *Norland* and her rather important component in their plans, her passengers. 'H' tersely answered that he was. 'Have you broken out your first line scales of ammunition yet?' There was a note of some panic in the disembodied voice. 'Will you be ready?' By now, 'H' was visibly enjoying the moment, delaying his reply, before a little smugly answering in the affirmative. We all enjoyed it too, as we pictured the sweating watchkeeper in the Ops Room of *Fearless* a few hundred yards away.

The threat of enemy submarines remained, and Intelligence had warned of extensive mining of the coastal waters around the Islands. A note of pessimism had been introduced, as the Naval Party ordered that the lifeboats be half lowered ready for immediate use during the final approach. *Norland*, however, calmly entered San Carlos Water on a now clear, still, dark night on 20 May without incident and dropped anchor off the encouragingly named Wreck Point.

Around 11.00pm Don Ellerby delivered his heart-warming farewell address. And then we waited for the LCUs to arrive. It was not unlike being in the cargo hold of a C130 Hercules aircraft on a long low-level approach for a parachute drop – hot, smelly, bumpy, cheek by jowl. Just wanting it done. For whatever reason, on such flights, most of us, myself certainly, could never keep eyes open and would drift into a deep torpor until the call for 'Action Stations!' The LCUs were late. My chin began to drop onto my chest as I struggled to stay awake, kept upright by the mass of bodies around me. The PA system burst to life again: 'Stand By.'

I shook my head and looked around. I expected some wisecrack from Hanley, but for once even he seemed lost for words. 'OK. Let's get this over with,' I muttered. Slowly the mass began to shift. D Company was at the back of the queue staggering its way down to the car deck. After at least an hour and a half, wondering why things were going so slowly, I reached the car deck with my company HQ. To my surprise the roll-on roll-off car doors were shut. Then I saw a side door on the hull had been opened. Instead of walking down the ramp, we were, one at a time, having to step from the door onto the side rim of the LCU pulled alongside, and then jump down onto its floor. So much for the rehearsals at Ascension.

As I approached the door, I could see that making the step involved a game of three-dimensional chess. In the swell, the step across varied between 6in and 3ft, and vertically between 1ft up and 2ft down. If you missed, the sea was 8ft below, but you'd never get there without first being crushed between the two vessels. Jumping out of a perfectly serviceable aircraft began to seem a doddle.

I gave myself a stern talking-to: 500 others had already made this giant step for man, small steps were for another planet. Fortunately, I did not know that one chap had already failed the test and was now languishing in the sick bay with a broken leg. I shucked my bergen and tossed it to the waiting crewman. But that still left me with 60lb of kit in my webbing and stowed in numerous pockets of my 'cold/wet' clothing. The man stood ready to catch me. I looked back and felt like the man at the airport check-in with overweight bags and a foot-tapping queue worrying about missing their flight behind him. I took my blind leap of faith and fell into the arms of the crewman, who dumped me unceremoniously beside my bergen on the floor of this floating bathtub.

Slowly gathering my wits, I looked for the lifejacket that was supposed to be issued. Nothing. Clearly someone had concluded that peace-time regulations no longer applied – a bit like reserve parachutes being just another needless encumbrance in war. Better there to take the small risk of a failing parachute than being shot out of the sky because the aircraft was high enough to be detected by radar. Here, the only times you were likely to drown were getting into one of these tubs or getting out at the beach if they dropped you too early. At both those moments this lifesaver would not be on you but in the hands of the LCU crew.

The next thing that registered was the three other LCUs circling around waiting for our LCU to be loaded before heading for the beach. There was a lot of shouting from one of them: 'H' expostulating with the coxswain on LCU2. He was with A Company and should have been on LCU1, but they had come alongside in the wrong order. LCU1 was to be at the southernmost end of the wave sweeping onto Blue Beach, ready to lead the way south to Sussex Mountain. As things now were, B Company would end up south of A Company, leading to confusion and last-minute changes of orders on the beach. If we met opposition this could be disastrous. It is rumoured that pistols were drawn to emphasize the gravity of the situation. But the master of a naval craft is the master, no matter the rank of his passengers. The coxswain of LCU2 would not be moved.

It also emerged that I was on LCU3. As we approached the beach, I could see another LCU to my left (or north). There were Intel reports that some enemy might still be in San Carlos Settlement at the northern end of Bonner Bay. The plan had been for D Company to be at the northern end, to protect the rear of the battalion column as it moved south to Sussex Mountain. Instead, in our place were the Support and Headquarters Companies – not the best option for repelling an attack.

As we approached the shore, eyes were peeled for the torchlight Morse code signal from the Special Boat Service (SBS) patrol that had been covertly inserted into the area some days before. Dot – dash was what we wanted: 'A' for 'All Clear'. Dash – dot – dot – dot would have been less welcome: 'B' for 'Beware'. But there was only darkness.

Although the LCUs were supposed to hit the beach in a wave, that proved wishful thinking too. B Company under John Crosland, mistakenly in LCU1, were ahead by some minutes. As they waded ashore, they were reportedly greeted by a call in English: 'Who are you?'

'2 PARA,' John shouted back, 'and who the hell are you?'

'Christ! We weren't expecting you for three days' came the disembodied reply. Welcome to the chaos of war, and we'd barely started …

LCU3's landing proved to be smooth and uneventful. We ground on to the beach, the ramp lowered with only a couple of yards to dry land. Gingerly we hopped off into water up to our knees. Some on the other LCUs were not so lucky, their passengers ending up to their chests in water colder than the North Sea in winter, and wet through as we moved ashore in weather a little above freezing but a forecast windchill of − 5°C.

There was chaos on the beachhead with various companies having to pass through others in the dark, due to the confusion of the LCUs. Just as well there were no enemy in the area. We had been lucky also to avoid a 'blue-on-blue' with the SBS. Coordinating all these moving parts, many of whom had never worked together before, with limited communications or radio silence, was testing resolve and patience. The Toms took it in their stride – for them it was no different from most training exercises. Even those soaking from their chest downwards soon found that they quickly warmed up during what was to follow.

Holiday cruise over. It was about 0630Z, or 2.30am local time.

Chapter 4

Welcome to the Falkland Islands

We had landed 45 minutes late, and the shambles on the beach meant it was a further hour before D Company, at the back, began to move. We still had some 3 hours until daylight at 1030Z, by when we were supposed to be secure on Sussex Mountain – a distance of about 4 miles and 800ft of height gain. One of the tests for P Company selection is to half run and half walk 10 miles in 1¾ hours with 45lb of kit and weapon, in a gait known as 'the airborne shuffle'. So, unless we met opposition, we still expected to breeze it, even though loaded up with twice that. We had barely started when 11 Platoon, in the lead, came across an unconscious and abandoned mortar man. He appeared to have stumbled and knocked himself out as he fell under his enormous load – which included a mortar baseplate, on its own weighing over 25lb. Following a dirt track, we found the mortar line 200 yards or so further on, where we dropped off our passenger and the mortar rounds we had all carried ashore. With 13lb less weight to carry, our spirits briefly rose.

An unopposed move on foot and at night was normally done in file formation, like a long snake. A battalion of 500 souls or so is like a monstrous uncoordinated serpent. The tail is not the place to be. It is impossible for those at the head to keep a constant pace, as they pause to check the route and compass bearings, slow down as gradients steepen or speed up on descents. It is constantly compressing and stretching. Those at the back are in purgatory, one second standing still, the next running to catch up.

Soon the track petered out, and we began to enter the 'Land of Babies' Heads'. 'Babies' heads' referred to the jumble of peat tussocks and bog that covers 90 per cent of the Falklands, of world-beating size, sponginess and saturation unique to the Islands. The lushness of the tussocks conceals the perils that await, as suddenly one leg drops though the cover up to the thigh in black, sour-smelling mire. I was posted back to the Islands seven years after the war with a young family. One day we were all walking over such ground for some sea trout fishing. For the umpteenth time Rachel, with our year-old daughter Jen on her back, stumbled into one of these traps. Our 3-year-old son innocently asked: 'Who put these holes here, Daddy?' I looked at Rachel, muttering crossly.

'God did.'

'Why?' he asked brightly.

Looking at my wife, I could only answer: 'To see if people have a sense of humour, Fred.' But this night, under loads of 100lb, we failed this divine test. We were truly in hell.

As the darkness slowly lifted under clear skies, Sussex Mountain loomed above. We were barely halfway. 'H' ordered us into open formation. We were vulnerable in the light to enemy air attack, and the battalion snake would present a tempting strafing target. At least we now had half a chance of seeing the worst of the giant divots. But there was no relief as the ground began to steepen. A Company was leading, with D Company to their left rear and John Crosland's B Company to their right rear. Between B and us was 'H' with his Tactical Headquarters comprising twenty or so men, including the artillery's battery commander and the mortar officer. With them were their signallers on radio nets forward to the companies, back to Brigade HQ, and to the gun-line and the forward observation officers (FOOs), who spotted for the guns and directed their supporting fire.

We had got used to the buzz of helicopters behind us, ferrying heavy equipment ashore, such as the guns and BVs. (The latter were amphibious tracked armoured vehicles that the Commando Brigade used for their Cold War role of helping to defend Arctic Norway against the Russian hordes.) Suddenly we heard other aircraft approaching from the south, and two Pucara aircraft popped up from behind the ridge of Sussex Mountain ahead, coming straight towards us. These were rudimentary prop-driven aircraft, favoured by the Argentinian Junta for suppressing insurgents at home. Their slow loiter speed made them particularly effective for ground attack operations. Of course, it also rendered them vulnerable to sophisticated air defence weapons, but our Rapier missile system was not yet in place. One detachment was supposed to be located on Sussex Mountain, but not until 2 PARA had secured it. The Task Force, particularly the ships, was now at its most vulnerable.

Nerves jangled.

Our response to the Pucaras was almost comically sluggish. Some dived for the ground, though I did not. The thought of then having to struggle to my feet again, with my enormous load, seemed by far the greater ordeal. Those with GPMGs struggled from their bergens, like beached turtles, to use them as platforms for the guns' bipod legs to get the elevation needed to engage the aircraft. 'H', ever ready to lead from the front, was the first I saw in action, firing with his sub-machine gun at the lead Pucara. The SMG only fired low velocity rounds, so it was but a quixotic gesture.

I could not help recalling a climbing friend of mine who was planning an expedition to Greenland and phoned the bear expert at London Zoo to see if his shotgun would be enough to deter marauding polar bears.

'Have you a piece of paper in front of you?' the Zoo man asked. 'OK, screw it into a ball ... Done that? Now throw it against the wall.' It was obvious that the chap had dealt with many such calls. 'What happened?'

'Nothing,' my friend answered.

'Well, that's what happens if you fire a shotgun at a polar bear.'

It was like a scene from *Monty Python and the Holy Grail*. When the GPMGs finally got into action, the moment was gone. The pilots were already on their way to more tempting targets on the beachhead behind us. Dispersed over some 5 acres of hillside, we were of little interest. We struggled on, too knackered to care that they were a headache for someone else.

A little later we heard the wail of ships' sirens, warning of another imminent air attack. Shortly after, two fast jets appeared from behind Sussex Mountain. These were Mirages, which were only able to operate from long runways on the Argentinian mainland. They had been detected by one of the destroyers on sentry duty out at sea. The Pucara, launching from local airfields on the Islands, arrived with no such warning. As the jets flew over our heads, 'H' again let off with his SMG, but this time those with GPMGs were quicker to react. The chances of bringing down a fast jet with small arms fire are staggeringly slim, but the sight of tracer flashing up towards his aircraft, I am assured, can quite distract a pilot as he tries to identify his target. We watched as they dropped their bombs in the area of the ships in San Carlos Water. There were no reports of hits, so who knows, perhaps we had helped save some sailor's day.

We did have an air defence troop attached to us equipped with Blowpipe missiles for short-range local air defence. These were fired from a shoulder-mounted throw-away canister, but such was their bulk, they could only be moved by being dragged behind the operator like a sled. Because of the missile's slow speed, it could also only engage on-coming aircraft and had to be guided on to its target by the operator. We had little understanding of these limitations within the Company, so during these exchanges with the Argentinian Air Force the Blowpipe troop, who were not airborne forces and wore black berets, were somewhat unkindly dismissed as 'bloody hats!'

It was almost mid-day by the time we stumbled to the top of Sussex Mountain. Well, not quite the top. The plan was to deploy on the 'reverse slope', that is to say concealed from direct view of the enemy by the brow of the hill ahead of us. The 'forward slope', beyond the brow, would be a sucker's spot, enabling the enemy to target us from afar with artillery and other long-range weapons. Instead, C (Patrols) Company sent out patrols and concealed observation posts to warn of any developments beyond the hill.

Had our taskmasters in Whitehall been able to see this exhausted band, the cream of the British Army, staggering onto their first objective almost 3 hours behind schedule, they might have been reminded of their school-book histories of Crimea or Gallipoli. But Paras are made of sterner stuff. Such thoughts did not enter our minds until three days later.

We were, however, cheered by the news that one of the commando battalions, exhausted, had gone firm, or established their defensive position, while still only halfway up the hill they were supposed to secure to the east of San Carlos. Never mind the risk this presented to the beachhead, and our flank; much more importantly, Paras had asserted their superiority over their Marine comrades. Morale thus boosted, we set to, preparing our defences. As ever we were in reserve, with A Company a little way forward to our right and B Company forward to our left.

On occupying a defensive position, the first requirement is to prepare for an attack by 'digging in'. This normally calls for a ditch 6ft deep and 6ft long, at one end of which, using a KIP sheet as the base, the spoil would be placed. This provided shelter, but more importantly some overhead protection from enemy artillery or air attack. Like the rest of the Company, Hanley and I got busy with our lightweight pick and shovel to dig our two-man trench. Six inches down we hit the water table. The deeper we went, the faster our inadequate home filled with water. There was no option but to build upwards, creating igloos, with peat substituting for ice blocks. 'I never signed up to be a bloody eskimo,' I heard Wang mutter. Slowly a small village of igloos took shape, which will doubtless be a subject of deep fascination for archaeologists in centuries to come. This learning on the job proved useful many years later, on an expedition to Mount Denali in arctic Alaska, but that afternoon was a frustrating experience. I had little confidence in the ability of my and Wang's efforts to withstand cannon fire from an aircraft or the blast of artillery shells, but it did provide some shelter from the weather. This had already gone through a full four-season cycle in the short time we had been ashore –

along with their peat bogs, such weather patterns were another of the Falkland Islands' claims to fame.

The next task for defence should have been placing wire and mines to our front to slow down advancing enemy, presenting in the process attractive targets to well-sited machine guns. Laying wire and mines by hand is one of the most laborious and tedious tasks that infantry are called on to perform. Career-minded purists might disapprove, but I confess to being rather thankful that our wire and mines never made it off *Europic Ferry*.

Meanwhile, on the mountain we had circle seats as 'Bomb Alley' began to play out in San Carlos Water below us. Argentinian Skyhawks and Mirages screamed into Falkland Sound from the north at mast height to drop their bombs before climbing desperately to clear the surrounding mountains just feet above our heads and make their escape. We watched some bombs miss a ship, sending up a plume of water nearby. Others hit but failed to explode – the Argentinians had not yet got their fuse settings right for such low-level release. A few succeeded, however, and two Navy ships, *Antelope* and *Antrim*, were hit on that first day. It was grand theatre. We cheered when we saw the odd aircraft depart, trailing smoke. We jeered when a waterspout told of another Argentinian miss. We held our breath as we saw a bomb find its target – exhaling with relief when it failed to explode, gasping with dismay when it did. Like spectators at some gladiatorial games, while wanting them killed, we could not help but admire the skill and daring of the Argentinian pilots.

The Rapier air defence troop had by now been lifted ashore and dropped on high ground to our right, but the Rapier system proved hopelessly unreliable. In the week we were on Sussex Mountain, they never successfully engaged an enemy aircraft. But we did hear of successes by Naval anti-aircraft systems at sea, and by Navy Sea Harriers providing combat air patrols. This news did not come from the Navy, who seemed to treat the rest of the Task Force like mushrooms – kept in the dark and fed shit. The most reliable source of such encouraging, and sometimes discouraging, information on how the war was going was our high frequency (HF) combat radios tuned into the BBC World Service. 'Thank God for Auntie' we thought then – although that charitable view was to change dramatically one week later.

This remained the pattern of events for the time we were on Sussex Mountain. It was not the worst of weather, nor was it the best. Every day brought some rain, usually in sheets, and some sunshine. And always, always the wind, an exhausting wind. But we had an Achilles heel. The issue DMS boot was a comfortable marching boot. They were made of compressed leather shavings and cardboard scrap, however. In the wet – and it was always soaking underfoot – they became like blotting paper. Before long, men were going down with trench-foot, which results in increasing pain and, if left untreated, ulcers and rot. It is certainly incapacitating. There seemed every possibility that the weather and penny-pinching Ministry of Defence procurement policies would do the enemy's work for him.

Robert Graves, in *Goodbye to All That*, told how trench-foot in the First World War was seen as a matter of morale, since only battalions with low morale suffered from it. I suspect the issue boots then were of considerably better quality than the DMS boot. D Company only lost two soldiers to trench-foot, out of more than twenty across the battalion. Of course, I attributed it to Penal Company's unique morale, but there may have been something more to it. Standard operating procedures required everyone to sleep with their boots on, if at risk of contact with the enemy. On day two, however, I instructed the Toms to remove their boots when in their peat sangars and not on stag, the colloquial term for sentry duty or other sort of watch. The prospect of an attack by enemy ground forces seemed distant. Preserving our fitness to fight in the face of debilitating conditions and inferior equipment, in my view, over-rode slavish adherence to SOPs.

It was on Day 4 that the muttering started, and I took up smoking again.

In the middle of the night I was woken by the sound of a huge explosion. I struggled out of my sleeping bag and saw below a mesmerizing firework display erupting from the dark waters of San Carlos Water below. Now and then great sheets of white flame illuminated the hull of a ship in distress. Soon we saw helicopters, their searchlights flashing back and forth, sometimes stopping to winch up a survivor from the inferno. This Dante-esque scene continued throughout the night.

The day before, *Antelope* had received two more direct hits, both the bombs lodging in the hull, unexploded. While a bomb-disposal team was attempting to defuse one, it exploded. This set off the other bomb, then the ammunition magazine. We watched as *Antelope*, her back broken, separated into two. First the stern disappeared beneath the waves, and then, lingering as if for a final farewell, the bow. As I later walked amongst our positions that day, it was all the Toms were talking about, but with the underlying theme: 'What are we doing here?' 'When are we going to give some back, Sir?' And from one: 'Is this another Gallipoli?'

Later, in my peat sangar, I was brewing up with Hanley. I had some porridge on the go on my little solid fuel collapsible cooker, and he was making some tea on his. Puffing on a cigarette, Wang looked relaxed. I was not, the 'Gallipoli' comment echoing my own thoughts. I had not smoked since my first expedition to the Himalayas eight years before, reckoning I needed my lungs to be at their peak in thin air at altitude. Now, looking at Wang, I weakened. 'Hanley, give us a cig.' The risk of lung cancer right then seemed academic. This proved a timely call. The next day we got a message that the Quartermaster, still on *Norland* trying to get all our stores ashore, had 'secured' a special consignment from the NAAFI. On each resupply he would send either a twin pack of Mars Bars or a pack of twenty Players No. 6 per soldier. Wang and I reached a deal – ciggies for him, Mars Bars for me. Win-win all round – we decided we deserved each other.

I'm afraid to admit that I continued with this habit, bumming but never buying cigarettes for the next twenty-five years. It was not unnoticed. On completing my last tour with 2 PARA, as 2iC in 1987, the clerks in the battalion orderly room presented me with one of those red 'In case of emergency break glass' red-painted steel cases, with inside it, a single cigarette and two all-weather matches. I still have it, intact, because the bastards never included the standard little hammer to break the glass. They knew precisely how to wind me up.

There was a further aftermath to this story during the same tour, typical of painstaking British bureaucracy. As 2iC, I was responsible for the battalion's non-public accounts. I got a visit from the Aldershot NAAFI manager – there was an issue of an unpaid bill with the battalion. It emerged that the cigarettes and Mars Bars dished out on the Falklands had not been a gift and needed to be paid for. I told him that our private regimental funds could not possibly pay such a sum. He suggested that we recover the monies from those individuals who had consumed the items. 'That's impossible,' I explained. 'Many are no longer with us.' Not the smartest, he started to protest that we must know where they were. I cut him off: 'Of course. Many are still down there.' The penny dropped. He scuttled from my office and we heard no more about unpaid bills.

'H' was acutely aware of the muttering. If anything, he was even more forthright. It was the job of Paras to close with the enemy, not just hold ground, watching helplessly while the Navy was being obliterated below us. He was constantly straining to be let off the leash. Meanwhile, he tried to maintain morale by appealing to the Toms' professional pride. 'Why are we here – because Maggie says, and she wants it done well,' he would say. Actually, he was spot on. Alongside the stream of dismal news, the one overriding impression we got through the World Service broadcasts was one of resolute leadership from Mrs Thatcher. Whatever our political persuasions, in a simple way we felt she had our backs, and she had our absolute confidence and loyalty. Sure, there was Queen and Country, the just cause, the Islanders. But 'H' echoed the thoughts of most, when he declared: 'We're doing this for Maggie!'

On 22 May one of our forward observation posts reported enemy movement around Cantera House, on the shores of Brenton Loch, 6 miles to our south. 'H' grabbed the opportunity, ordering me to deploy a platoon by helicopter to attack the enemy and secure the tiny settlement. At first light on 23 May Jim Barry's 12 Platoon were picked up by two Sea King helicopters and dropped a couple of miles from the objective. After 4 hours of atrocious going, they reached the house to find abandoned kit but, disappointingly, no sign of Argentinians. They did, though, find themselves under the flight path of the enemy jets making their final approaches to create mayhem in San Carlos Water. Jim Barry called for a Blowpipe missile team to be sent the next day. I was rather proud of his thinking beyond his immediate orders, and indeed his experience. However, other plans were already afoot.

Instead, the next day 'H' called me in to his HQ again. He had got the go-ahead for a raid on Darwin and Goose Green. I was to head off at last light, 2030Z, for Camilla Creek House, some 15 miles away to the south, linking up with 12 Platoon on the way, and secure it as an assembly area for the raid. C (Patrols) Company, which would follow, were then to move forward of the House to a position from where they could covertly observe the isthmus during the next day. The battalion would join me by first light, and half a battery, comprising three 105mm light guns, would be flown in at last light. A and B Companies would conduct the raid, whilst, predictably, D would be in reserve, to cover the withdrawal and protect the gun-line. This was to be a 'hit and run' job. There was to be no direct attack on the two settlements; so the mortars were to be left behind and I would therefore not need my mortar fire controller. We were to move on light scales, so no bergens or sleeping kit.

I had many questions in my mind, not least what exactly was the purpose or objective of the raid? Or, rather absurdly, when would we have done enough hitting before we ran? All would doubtless become clear. Such concerns could wait. Right then I was more filled by the relief, even excitement, that at last we were doing something. I had much to do and little time before we left.

We had been going a little under 4 hours and without bergens had covered close to 6 miles. I was beginning to focus on the rendezvous with

12 Platoon, now not far ahead, as it was too easy for things to go wrong in the darkness. We had already heard of two patrols of 3 PARA shooting each other up, and I certainly did not wish to kick off another 'blue-on-blue'. My signaller on the battalion net or rear link radio, Corporal 'Ozzie' Osborne, grabbed my arm. Abort. Return to Base. No explanation given – not that I expected one over an insecure net. I passed the news on to 12 Platoon. South of us, laden with their bergens, they would also be moving more slowly. 'See you back at Sussex' was the nature of the message. We about-turned, now acutely aware of every one of the 60lb of 'light scales' we each carried, to begin the miserable trudge back. Normally, I would have expected some muttering – 'A whinging Tom is a happy Tom' went the old adage – but there was just a worrying silence.

Nor was I happy. On the way back I started to calculate the impact, mainly in terms of our feet. With the hopeless DMS boot, 'miles-per-foot' was becoming for us as important a calculation as 'miles-per-tyre' for Formula One. We had just wasted 15 miles, some 20 per cent of each of our 'foot-lives', I reckoned. Pathetic – I had never envisaged this being a factor in any military appreciation.

On getting back to Sussex around midnight I reported to 'H', and said as much. Perhaps he thought I was looking for sympathy. I got a look which said: 'like it – or lump it!' Maybe he was feeling a little like the Grand Old Duke of York, who had 'marched his men to the top of the hill, and he marched them down again'. Or maybe his fury at Brigade cancelling the op and denying his battalion the chance to be the first into action had deafened him to the serious point I was trying to make. I certainly wasn't blaming him. And like me, perhaps he could not quite buy in to the reason for the abort – a more urgent call on the limited helicopter lift that we needed to get the guns to Camilla Creek. The helicopters were now required to enable the SAS to exploit an opportunity to seize the vital ground of Mount Kent, dominating the approaches to Stanley. The planning all seemed horribly hand-to-mouth.

About 3 hours later 12 Platoon staggered back into our position, looking like they'd gone fifteen rounds with Mike Tyson. Dawn was a little over 3 hours away. I think Shakespeare writes of those hours as man's weakest moment of resolve. I was at probably my lowest ebb of the campaign. I tried to get some sleep, but Gallipoli kept churning through my mind.

The next day, 25 May, we were briefed about long delays in getting equipment ashore, and were told that no move was planned from the beachhead until the brigade was more logistically settled. Incredibly, we also learnt that plans were being made for one company at a time to rotate through the sheep shearing sheds at Ajax Bay for a spot of 'R&R.' That made it sound as if we could be stuck on Sussex Mountain for weeks. In the next breath, however, we were told that the pace was expected to pick up the following day, with four Chinook and six Wessex support helicopters coming ashore from *Atlantic Conveyor*, a huge container ship taken up from trade. The RAF Harriers had already been flown off it to the aircraft carriers *Hermes* and *Invincible* by our RAF friends from 1 Squadron.

Shortly before nightfall we learnt that *Atlantic Conveyor* had been hit by Exocet missiles launched from Super Etendarde aircraft – with the loss of all the helicopters except one Chinook which had been airborne at the time. Even weeks on Sussex was now looking optimistic.

Who mentioned Gallipoli...?

Chapter 5

The Battle for Darwin and Goose Green: the Prelude

Twenty-four hours later 'H' called me back into Battalion HQ. He was bubbling. 'The raid's back on, only this time we're all going.' He threw a glance towards Hugh Jenner, indicating that this time we would be taking our support weapons. 'Otherwise, same as last time. You're to set off for Camilla Creek House at 1900Z. You'll have the battery on call, and by then the gunners should have adjusted fire onto the house. The battalion will join you there. Off you go.'

The Toms might have asked: 'Isn't it another company's turn?' They had barely recovered from the last foray. They didn't need to ask. They already knew this was what went with D Company. Again, we were to move on light scales, stashing our bergens on the position with the company quartermaster sergeant, CQMS Bob Powell. I hesitated but decided we would go with each platoon's sustained fire (SF) tripods for our machine guns, to give us a little extra reach.

During the first hour, in daylight, we made rapid progress, having picked up a semblance of the track between San Carlos and Darwin. By around 2300Z we had reached a little footbridge where we were to have rendezvoused with 12 Platoon two nights earlier. Camilla Creek House was now less than 2½ miles away. We moved on more carefully, not sure whether it was occupied by the enemy or not. The night was pitch black and the ground devoid of features to navigate by. After 40 minutes I knew we must be getting close, but I did not want to just blunder in. As the gunners had adjusted the house as a target, I got my FOO to call up a prophylactic fire mission onto it – just in case. This would discourage any enemy who might be there, and also show us exactly where the house was. 'Shot. 25. Over' crackled over the FOO's radio. We started to count down the 25 seconds to when we should see the 'splash'. Five – four – three – two – one. Loud crumps 1,000 yards behind us. Blank looks all round. I dug out my map and torch. Crouching down, with Wang shielding the light with his poncho, I anxiously studied the map. My mind flashed to a similar moment in Dhofar. Is it just me, or does everyone in such moments think: 'I've fucked up!' In Dhofar the gunners had used the wrong charge. We were on the track which led directly to the house. There was no way we had gone past it.

I looked at my FOO, aware he was not fully trained: in fact he was the battery's signals sergeant. Traditionally, a battery supported a battalion, which had three rifle companies, so every battery had three FOOs, one per company. A couple of years earlier, to save money, some General or other who had probably never seen action decided to reduce the establishment from three to two FOOs. Last in the queue, as ever, D Company was allocated the 'cheap substitute'. He gave me some blather about 'the met', suggesting changing wind since the target had been adjusted had caused the error. I rather doubted that change of windspeed – it always came from the west – could have accounted for more than 2,000 yards of error, but now was not the time for a Board of Enquiry. I abandoned any thought of fire support.

Preparing for the worst, we moved on, with Chris Waddington's 11 Platoon leading, now in open formation, advancing-to-contact. After a few hundred yards he saw through his night-sight the silhouettes of the farm buildings, some 200 yards away. I told him to get his platoon into a position from where they could provide covering fire if needed, and then got Shaun Webster's 10 Platoon to do a sweep to the right to clear the buildings. They were deserted, but on the kitchen table in the main house were some rations and a half-finished meal. The birds had flown.

We posted sentries around the farm, and I sent a patrol back 200 yards with red and green torches to guide the battalion in. We settled down to enjoy the luxury of a roof over our heads and the comfort of sitting in a chair for the first time in a week.

The luxury was not to last. Too soon for my liking, the rest of the battalion arrived a couple of hours later, and we were obliged to share the shelter. I pulled my company into the downstairs part of the building as other companies found shelter in the outbuildings. Space was tight – the eight men of one of 11 Platoon's sections shared the tiny downstairs toilet.

Battalion HQ was set up in a small upstairs room of the house where I had put my Company HQ. It was then that I learnt from 'H' that the mission was no longer to raid, but rather to recapture the settlements. That did not surprise me. After the earlier aborted raid, 'H' had been scathing about a 'hit and run' raid, dismissing the concept as flabby Marine thinking. Leaving aside my earlier concerns over when we stopped hitting and began running, he did not believe you could expect men to risk their lives for something so unspecific.

Quicker than most, 'H' had also grasped the other perils of such a mission. Following our breaking contact with the enemy, it did not need much to imagine the spin of subsequent headlines: 'Para's attack defeated by Argentinians!' Like Nelson at Copenhagen, putting his telescope to his blind eye and claiming he could see no signal, 'H' was exploiting the woolliness of his orders, superimposing his own objectives for 'the raid'. Good for 'H', I thought, he was going for broke.

The intelligence, when we left *Norland*, indicated an Argentinian garrison of 800 to 1,000, including a battalion of infantry. SAS patrols observing the isthmus and returning via Sussex Mountain had also, we were told, opined that they seemed ill-prepared, with poor field discipline, and were unlikely to put up much resistance. 'We just need to hit 'em hard, and they'll collapse,' 'H' would have us believe. I dozed off with barely a care in the world. Had I known that 'H' had in fact received a very detailed briefing at Brigade HQ of the make-up of the Argentinian garrison at Goose Green, which was estimated to number up to 1,500, knowledge acquired from a mix of SAS patrols and signals intelligence, I might not have slept so well.

I awoke to the squawks, crackles and whistles of an HF radio, with several men huddled intently round it in the dim light of a red-filtered torch. Through the interference I could hear the BBC World Service news. Suddenly I was wide awake: 'In Parliament today, it was reported that there is now a parachute battalion within 7 miles of Darwin and Goose Green,' the voice flatly intoned.

For a moment the room froze in disbelief. If we could tune in to the BBC, so could the Argentinians. 'H' was like a volcano building for its grand eruption. Then it burst. Robert Fox, the BBC's correspondent with the Task Force, who had been embedded with the battalion since we came ashore, was beside 'H'. Earlier in the night I had overheard a surprisingly frank conversation between them, Robert confiding that he was nervous and 'H' agreeing, pointing out that he had never done anything like what we were about to embark on before. Now Robert bore the full blast of his rage. 'We're on radio silence so as not to give away our position, and your bloody BBC goes and tells the whole world! I'll take the governors to court!' I felt rather sorry for Robert. It wasn't his report, and indeed all the BBC had done was to report a minister's statement in Parliament. It was surely there the blame lay. Robert wisely held his peace. Gradually 'H' simmered down, turning his mind to the implications of what had been revealed.

It was now an hour until dawn, and the plan had been for the battalion to stay in the shelter and concealment of the buildings, while C Company went forward to recce the challenge ahead of us. The most likely place, almost the only place, that a battalion 7 miles from Goose Green could be was Camilla Creek. We now had to assume that the Argentinians would have aircraft up at first light, and a strike on the buildings with the battalion crammed into them cheek by jowl would be catastrophic. 'H' ordered us all to disperse into the surrounding 'cuds', or peat bog. The BBC was everyone's enemy as we left the welcome shelter and made our way out into the bleak darkness.

Many theories have been advanced as to the cause of this diabolical security fiasco. Some have argued it was a planned decoy to distract enemy attention from the rest of 3 Commando Brigade as it started its advance east from the beachhead towards Stanley. Clever. But surely our forth-coming attack would have served the same purpose without denying us any element of surprise? At the time I put it down to carelessness and complacency – with Great Britain falling into the error it had been guilty of many times at the start of a war: underestimating the enemy. After all Argentina was just a South American basket case.

In hindsight, I also put it down to desperation. Only years later did any of us learn how anxious Whitehall had become to share some good news with the public, amongst the barrage of bad, as the Task Force was being crucified by the Argentinian Air Force. At the same time Alexander Haig, the US Secretary of State, was still pushing for a negotiated settlement, and every day of bad news was increasing the pressure. The government, however, could countenance nothing but an unconditional surrender of Argentinian forces on the Falklands if it was to survive. Quite simply, under such pressure it was just not prepared to wait 24 hours until the battle started.

Most people recognized that the war was going to be decided by the recapture of Port Stanley, the capital of the Islands. Julian Thompson was clear that his absolute priority was getting his Brigade 40 miles east to where it could start to pick off the Argentinian positions in the mountains defending the approaches to the capital. Concentration of effort is a fundamental principle of war. To Thompson, given his limited resources, particularly logistics, anything that distracted from his main effort was unwelcome.

Darwin and Goose Green formed the second largest settlement of the Islands. With its 1,000-strong garrison and an airfield capable of operating helicopters and Pucara aircraft, it potentially posed a threat to the beachhead less than 20 miles away, and to Thompson's southern flank as he started to push east. Thompson's staff noted, however, the unwelcome burden of dealing with some 1,000 prisoners of war on already stretched logistics if Darwin and Goose Green were recaptured. Describing the twin settlements as a self-imposed POW camp, they reckoned the isthmus could be masked off, with use of the airfield denied by Harrier air strikes.

Enter 'H' Jones, an ambitious officer, desperate for himself and his battalion to achieve at least their fair share of glory, and smart enough to appreciate that one battalion would have to be left to defend the beachhead. His battalion, on Sussex Mountain, was the furthest from Stanley, so might easily draw, in his eyes, that short straw. But it was also the closest to Goose Green. He passionately argued that sitting defensively on the beachhead surrendered all the initiative to the Argentinians. Attacking Goose Green presented an ideal opportunity to unsettle the enemy and start to erode his will.

The pressure on Thompson to compromise his tactical priorities with the government's strategic and political imperatives must have been intense, but in 'H', Whitehall unknowingly had a willing accomplice. This explains the nature and evolution of the operation that was step-by-unplanned-step unfolding.

We now planned to undertake a mission to recapture the settlements with virtually the same resources as for the 'hit and run' raid, although it was a task of immeasurably different scale, risk and commitment. Our only addition was one section of mortars – two out of the six of the battalion's 81mm mortar tubes. As with the half-battery of three light howitzers allocated, the real challenge would be to keep them resupplied with ammunition. Quite simply, it was not worth risking the normal six guns, because Brigade wouldn't be able to get sufficient ammunition to them. This was a far cry from sound, well-proven operational planning. The foremost principle of military planning is identity and maintenance of the aim. Not until you decide what you want to achieve can a sensible estimate be made of the resources required and how best to deploy them. As B Company's John Crosland drily put it, this operation had all the hallmarks of a 'come-as-you-are' party.

Ordered to mount an attack on Goose Green, Thompson had a tightrope to walk. The more effort he devoted to Goose Green, the weaker his push east would become. He was particularly reluctant to risk precious assets like his artillery or light armour beyond the protection of the air defence umbrella, which would be essential for overcoming the strong enemy positions on the hills between him and Stanley, for an operation that he viewed as a distraction. Better, in his ideal world, not to take on Goose Green at all than to fail. But Whitehall had now denied him that choice. Ironically, he was perhaps helped in walking this tightrope by the sinking of *Atlantic Conveyor* and the loss of 75 per cent of his helicopter lift. The resources we ideally needed quite simply could no longer be lifted into the Goose Green operation. It obliged Thompson to place all his chips on 'H' and the fighting spirit of 2 PARA. The BBC World Service newscast had just increased the odds of his bet.

On 27 May the weather was cold and windy, but fortunately dry. Widely spread around Camilla Creek House as daylight broke, we pre-pared for the arrival of enemy aircraft. None. As we dozed, brewed and did a final clean and check of our weapons, I felt we were in a semi-detached bubble, another quiet world, free of the noise of helicopters, enemy jets and the disturbing panoramic view of San Carlos' *Bomb Alley*. Hopes began to rise that perhaps the Argentinians had missed the priceless intel-ligence they had been so freely provided. Or perhaps they could not believe their luck, and assumed it had to be a trap or decoy. Meanwhile, the recce and patrols platoons of C Company were busy around the northern parts of the isthmus, trying to get eyes on the enemy, identify and plot their positions – and also providing a screen in case enemy patrols headed our way to verify the BBC report.

About 1830Z, or 2.30pm local time, Ozzie got a message over the bat-talion net saying that 'H' was to hold an 'O' Group at 1900Z, the occasion for issuing his orders for the attack to his company commanders and other key players in the battalion – the second-in-command, battery com-mander, mortar officer, ops officer, intelligence officer, medical officer and the A Echelon quartermaster – in all twenty or so. I had been closely studying my map, trying to imprint on my mind the ground and the main features that we would have to negotiate that night. The isthmus was around 5 miles long, and a little over a mile across at it its widest point. Little room for manoeuvre. As I got up to go, I remarked to Nobby, sitting beside me: 'Well, if the SAS are right, it could be a cakewalk. But if they've heard the BBC news, and they're ready for a fight, it's going to be a long, bloody do.' Two hours later, just as it was getting dark, I returned. I tossed my map, now covered with red chinagraph, showing enemy positions, down in front of Nobby. 'Well, Sergeant Major, I think it's going to be the long, bloody one.'

Arriving at Battalion HQ, now set up in the open just outside the House, I had five minutes to catch up on the day's events. C Company had been busy. They had picked up a lot of information on enemy positions, called up a Harrier air strike which dropped a few cluster bombs amongst some of the enemy positions, had a dust-up with an enemy patrol from which they had captured a Landrover previously commandeered by the Argentinians from a local inhabitant, and taken a prisoner.

An 'O' Group is a piece of theatre. It is the moment when the commanding officer shares his concept for the operation, his detailed plans, and allocates tasks and responsibilities for its execution. It is, more than anything else, the opportunity for the CO to impose his personality, his values and his determination upon his team. 'H's adjutant Dave Wood, like me a refugee from the RAF Regiment, called us to order in his hard, dry Scottish accent. In front of us was a low bank contained by a low wall. On this, on some old doors, were pinned a map, marked up in red with known enemy positions, and a few aerial photos. The intelligence officer, Alan Coulson, another Scot, and a true eccentric with an impressive 'Pancho Villa' moustache, standing on the wall, kicked off the proceedings. In some detail he described the ground, pointing out the key features (see map, p. 50): Burnside House at the top of the isthmus (possible enemy), Coronation Point (possible enemy company), the Gorse Line (a main feature running across the isthmus from Darwin, where the Falkland Island Company director lived), Darwin Hill, Boca House and, beyond it, an enemy company, Goose Green Schoolhouse (enemy strongpoint) and just beyond, separated by a shallow bay, Goose Green itself, containing most of the enemy force. He then went on to describe the enemy in even more detail.

We could see 'H' fidgeting with impatience. There was just over an hour of daylight left, and 'H' was aware that his company commanders needed time to carry out their own battle preparation – appreciation of his orders, their own planning and then briefing their own men – preferably also in daylight. 'For fuck's sake, Alan. That's enough. They can get it all off the maps later.'

'H' now got up. His plan was for a 6-phase attack, all but the last at night. Phase 6 was the fight through the two settlements, to be conducted in daylight, to try to avoid civilian casualties. It would be 'silent', meaning no use of artillery until contact was made with the enemy to maintain surprise, when it could turn 'noisy'. In addition to the three light guns, we now also had the 4.5in gun of HMS *Arrow* in support, capable of firing twenty-five very large shells per minute. It was, however, only available until two hours before dawn, after which it would have to scoot eastwards

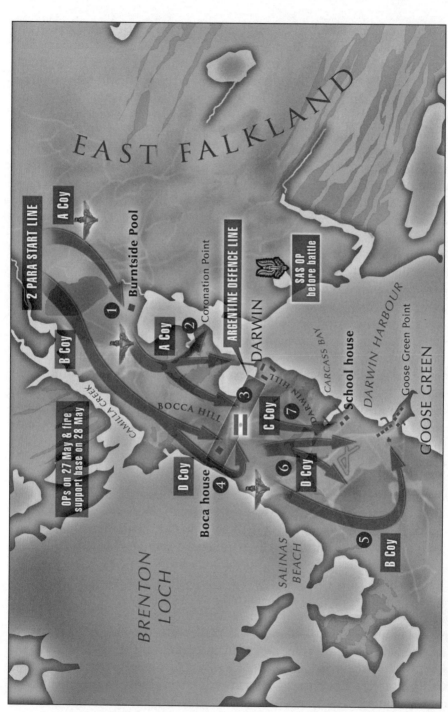

2 PARA manoeuvres at the Battle of Darwin and Goose Green.

to get beyond the reach of Argentinian air attack by daylight. As detailed tasks followed, 'H' exuded confidence and aggression. A Company on the left would kick off with an attack on Burnside House, and B Company would follow on the right. D Company, predictably, would be in reserve. H Hour, when we were to cross the start line just south of Camilla Creek Bridge, 2.5 miles away, was to be 0600Z, leaving us 4½ hours to fight our way to the outskirts of the settlements for the final crucial phase. C Company would leave at last light to mark and then guide the rifle companies to their respective start lines; Support Company would also move at last light to set up a direct fire base of Milans and sustained fire machine guns from the western bank of Camilla Creek. The rest would set off at 0300Z, 28 May. As his orders came to an end, 'H' made a final point: 'All previous evidence suggests that if the enemy is hit hard, he'll crumble!'

Just as well no one asked for the evidence. Really, there was none.

This plan has attracted much criticism since, from General Hindsight, the most common being that it was too detailed and prescriptive, given the circumstances, the incomplete intelligence and an as-yet untested enemy. I had no complaints at the time. For me, he painted a vivid picture of how we might prevail. I could visualize the outcome, as athletes are trained to see themselves crossing the finish line ahead of their competitors. Sure, on paper, it looked prescriptive, but 'H' also emphasized: 'We'll need to be flexible.'

More tellingly, some have argued that it showed little rigorous appreciation. I put this down to 'H's School of Infantry background. I think, then, the school failed to differentiate between battle drills and tactics, and between what was good for training and good for operations. Battle drills are more about doing things right – working effectively as a team at any level to achieve certain things. Tactics is more about doing the right thing. The school, and arguably 'H', never grasped the dichotomy here. On training, troops need practice in battle drills, such as fire and manoeuvre, so a good exercise will ensure as much contact between enemy and friendly forces as possible. In the real tactical world, however, you want to achieve objectives with as little effort and contact as possible. My test exercise in Kenya graphically reflected this dichotomy. For training purposes, 'H' wanted as much contact as possible. Tactically, I wanted to secure the objective that he had set me with as little contact as possible. The objective was not to kill enemy per se, but to capture their camp. So, with his plan for Darwin and Goose Green, its focus was to neutralize every identified enemy position, there was no analysis of vital ground, enemy weaknesses and whether that offered a more economical way to invest the settlements.

To be fair, there are limits to what you can appreciate from a map alone, and the narrow isthmus meant his manoeuvre options were limited. In the end, there probably was no other option than an advance to contact. It was obvious to most of us that the plan was a template to get us over the start line. When I briefed my platoon commanders, it was dark, which made describing the detail off a map they couldn't see somewhat problematic. Having described the plan, my detailed tasking for them was: 'Phase 3 onwards. Wait out,' echoing the standard radio voice procedure for answering a question to which you had no immediate answer.

'Any questions?' I asked. Chris Waddington asked one – sufficiently marginal and unanswerable that I could no longer recall it minutes later – a habit that was to become his endearing stock in trade. Mumbles from Shaun and Jim. Did they understand the challenge that undoubtedly lay ahead? Would they, would we, answer the call when the clarion sounded? As we finished, I tried to scrutinize their faces, but could read nothing in the darkness.

I tried to get some sleep on a cold, lumpy peat tussock in the few hours before we were due to move. It proved elusive. I took some solace from my climbing. I never slept the night before a big route on a steep alpine wall. Why am I doing this? Are we taking on more than we can handle? But, after the first hundred feet or so, with my nose against the problem, the anxieties were soon replaced by the all-absorbing business of solving the technical challenges ahead. This will surely be the same. It's in the quiet moments before action or when confronting danger that the human spirit is truly tested.

Then I thought of 'H', and the testing he must have endured through the day. With his Nelsonian eye to the sensible caution of his brigade commander, he had pushed the mission to a decisive level. As detailed intelligence came in from our patrols during the day, and the map progressively filled with red, he must have concluded that the enemy had indeed taken heed of the BBC broadcast and deployed accordingly. Normal doctrine was that local superiority of three to one was necessary for an attack to succeed against prepared defences. It was already apparent that we were comprehensively outnumbered. 'H', as he prepared his plans before the 'O' Group, must have been beset by similar doubts: What have I committed to? Can we do it? Should I reconsider, discuss with Brigade, maybe abort? I'm sure, as his earlier conversation with Robert Fox indicated, he was far from immune to these 'pre-action siren voices'.

There was not, however, a hint of doubt in his demeanour when he gave his orders. He had clearly overcome the demons of those quiet moments, requiring infinitely more courage than overcoming the physical dangers to follow. The message he conveyed was far beyond 'failure is not an option'. As he finished his orders, failure was quite simply inconceivable to us. We could have taken 50 per cent casualties, and still we would have been pushing forward. We went forth with utter self-belief, with complete faith in the outcome.

That, in the waning light outside Camilla Creek House on the evening of 27 May, was 'H's moment.

Chapter 6

The Battle for Darwin and Goose Green: 'Operation Dinosaur'

Climbers who put up new routes have the privilege of naming the route. Some are very literal – *Milestone Buttress*, for example. One of mine on the Dorset sea-cliffs I christened *Sheerline*. This might seem rather literal, except that it climbed diagonally up and across the crag; it was in fact named in celebration of the 4-litre Austin Sheerline, fully equipped with a pair of flag pennants on the mudguards, that I bought second-hand for £15 when at university. Other names can be more creative. *Pellagra* is a favourite of mine, chosen by the legendary Joe Brown, so the story goes, after he read on the back of a Kellogg's Cornflakes packet that they miti-gated the effects of this disease. One symptom is involuntary shaking of the extremities – a common problem for climbers stretching their limits often being an uncontrollable shaking of the feet on small holds. Brown had a gift for naming routes; another, bold and poorly protected up the steepest part of the Anglesey sea-cliffs he called *Dinosaur*, because it demanded a 'long neck and small brain'.

If John Crosland thought Goose Green a 'come-as-you-are' party, to me it was a 'dinosaur' job. There was nothing very clever or brainy about the planning, but it certainly needed a lot of neck.

Shortly before midnight we set off in file for the start line just beyond the Camilla Creek bridge, some 2½ miles away. D Company, in reserve, was at the back of the battalion snake. At the bridge I was supposed to be met by guides from C Company, to lead me to the start. It was also the same point where the Battalion Main HQ decided to stop and set up shop. As we negotiated our way through this morass of REMFS (rear echelon mother fuckers, who would never be involved in the dirty stuff), we missed both the guides and the track south to Goose Green that we were sup-posed to pick up. 'Great idea putting us behind Main HQ,' muttered Pete Adams, my 2iC. Some 200 yards further on I caught up with Jim Barry, whose 12 Platoon was leading. 'Do you know where you are?' I asked him. Jim looked a little flustered. It was a little mischievous; neither, precisely, did I – but I knew it was not where we should be.

A quick huddle with map and torch under a poncho. Jim set off again on a compass bearing which I knew would at least take us back to the track. It sort of worked. We found the track and waited for A and B Companies to kick off the action. 0600Z came and went. 0630Z, still nothing. Then, over on my left, the silence was broken by the rattle of small arms fire. A Company was finally in action at Burnside House. Shortly after, to my right, the night sky was ripped up by tracer, and then a star-shell from HMS *Arrow*'s 4.5-inch gun burst overhead, throwing a pallid light over the peat tussocks. B Company was in action. Then, looking back, I glimpsed a worrying sight: 'H' and his Tac HQ moving towards me. I knew what was to follow.

'What the hell are you doing here?' he demanded, affronted by his reserve company being ahead of him. 'Waiting for the battle to start,' I answered sweetly, carefully avoiding any reference to getting slightly lost. 'Why drop the C Company guides in the poo?', I justified to myself. The ritual bollocking followed. Then, his dignity restored, 'H' turned conspiratorial: 'I'm thinking of feeding you straight on down the track – maybe we can get in behind them. Wait here, I'm pushing on to see.' Jauntily, off he went, lost to view within seconds.

Around me I saw the odd twinkle of light. Clearly, the odd sinner was having a crafty puff under cover of a poncho or smock. For a moment, I was going to remonstrate about poor light discipline. Then another star-shell popped, lighting up the countryside again. Fuck it, what's the point? I saw Wang was one of the guilty. 'Hanley, you're a disgrace!' More rummaging under his smock, and then a lighted cigarette found its way to my hand, discreetly covered by his beret. Hanley was getting to know me uncomfortably well.

Wang had been Nobby's choice to be my runner soon after I had arrived in D Company. Company commander's 'runner', since the widespread use of radio, is a bit of a misnomer, but it is still a crucial appointment. Wang was also my personal bodyguard, who watched my back when we were in the thick of things; the chap who ensured that I was fed and watered, if busy making plans, giving orders or visiting the platoon positions; and most importantly he was my eyes and ears within the company – in a sense, my barometer of the company's mood. 'Sir,' or if alone in a basha sometimes 'Boss,' he would start. 'The Toms are bit pissed off about this,' in relation to 'H's instructions regarding bayonets on *Norland*, for example. Other times, 'the Tom's liked that one,' as when I explained that their bayonets could be taken only as tin openers. If Nobby, as my CSM, was my right-hand man, Hanley was my left. I would have been lost without them.

I was crouching down, just finishing my cigarette, when, like an un-welcome parent at a teenager's party, 'H' returned. I hurriedly stubbed it out and stood up. 'I've been fired on from a hill over there,' he muttered, indignantly pointing back behind him. 'Go and sort it out.' So much for his bold 'plan B'.

'Where, which hill?' I could see nothing beyond about 20 yards away. This was becoming like some operatic comedy.

'Over there, get moving!' I half expected this to be followed by a theatrical cuff to my head. I shrugged. 'Advance to contact' and hope for the best. I got my FOO to call for more illumination from *Arrow*'s gun, thinking that if we could identify the enemy position, we could adjust some HE fire support on to it from our three field guns. One round, and then nothing. Seconds later my FOO advised me *Arrow*'s gun had jammed. No more 'illum'. Jesus, when is something going to go right around here? The ship had been our only source of light. Because of the lack of helicopter lift, our three field guns had no illumination rounds. We were on our own.

With 12 Platoon leading in an open arrowhead formation, 11 Platoon behind and to their left, and 10 Platoon to the right, we continued south, following the track. About 300 yards further on we came under fire from the high ground ahead and slightly to our right. Or, more precisely, I saw green tracer pouring towards us from the position. We had found 'H's 'hill over there'.

Green tracer. That was new – I had assumed all tracer was red. The air seemed filled with it. It all looked like it was coming at me. I waited for the blow, but strangely was convinced I wouldn't be killed, that I would be telling of this moment in the future. Perhaps the green tracer seemed a little less menacing than the red. I looked around, expecting to see men being scythed down. No, all were still skirmishing forward into the incoming fire. Every infantryman is afforded the experience of live fire overhead during training in controlled conditions. The ominous crack and thump of high velocity small arms rounds now passing us sounded the same. With hindsight, perhaps, as we were coming out of the low ground, the Argentinians were firing high – a known tendency in the dark. At the time I was in fact totally absorbed by 12 Platoon's relentless fire and manoeuvre towards the enemy. Some, lying behind peat divots in the cover of the babies' heads, pouring suppressive fire towards the position; others dashing forward 5 or 10 yards at a time, then dropping to the ground; their turn now to fire and discourage the enemy's enthusiasm to engage, while their comrades leapt to their feet and sprinted forward. All the while tracer was whizzing past through the cacophony of weapons firing. The drill, well-practised, repeated time and again, inexorably closing with the enemy. Exhausting, but effective. An irresistible force.

As we got amongst the enemy trenches, their rate of fire slowed, as 12 Platoon's whirlwind of momentum and aggression seemed simply to over-awe them. Many Argentinians probably ran for their lives. Overwhelming excitement. And relief – not because I was still unharmed, but because D Company was passing its first test. We'd show the rest what we were made of. We started to clear the position trench by trench. I was now thankful that I had won my little tussle with 'H' on *Norland* over bayonets. This was a brutal close-quarter business. Grenade, bayonet or a couple of shots at anything in the trench, move on. Most of the Argentinians had probably given up the fight, but they were still armed. It was not the moment for a discussion. Many of them we found lying in the bottom of their trenches, some with their sleeping bags pulled over their heads, like ostriches with their heads in the sand hoping that they would not be seen. Or perhaps it was a forlorn attempt at redemption: 'Please, Guv'nor, I had no part in this, it's nothing to do with me. No benefit of the doubt was given. Who lives, who dies? It was instinctive: fight or flight? Fight! Kill or be killed.

Once the enemy fire had ceased, our adrenaline rush subsided a little. Jim Barry and his platoon sergeant, Taff Meredith, began to organize a more thorough check of the enemy trenches. No own casualties. I began to relax. This isn't so difficult, I congratulated myself. Maybe the SAS were right. This could be a stroll … Abruptly, the hard clamour of machine-gun fire to my right jolted me out of my complacent drift.

My radio crackled into life, with the soft Scottish accent of Shaun Webster, 10 Platoon's commander. 'Hello 49, this is 41 Alpha. We're under machine-gun fire.' Urgent, agitated. 'We've taken casualties. We're pinned down.'

Pete Adams, perhaps the quickest to recover his balance from this unexpected setback, started letting rip with his SLR, uncomfortably close to my right ear, towards the sound of the enemy machine guns; then a yell,

'Come on, you buggers, get firing!' Ozzie, on the battalion net radio, grabbed my arm. 'B Company,' he shouted, pointing to the earphones on his head. 'We're shooting at them!' 'Tough shit' was my immediate thought, but Pete more sensibly ordered 12 Platoon to check firing. My mind was racing, desperately trying to make sense of the growing chaos. I knew 10 Platoon was somewhere behind and to my right, but exactly where and what their options were, I had no idea. The night was intensely black. We needed some light, but that had gone with the ship's gun. I sensed the company looking to me for directions, but I had nothing useful to offer. There's nothing more unhelpful or demoralizing than an officer uttering nonsense over the radio, I was to learn. I felt uncomfortably inadequate, flatfooted.

Then I got onto Chris Waddington with 11 Platoon, who was at my left rear. '42 Alpha. 49. Anything you can do to help 41 here?' '42 Alpha,' came his reply. 'Already moving across, behind you.' Good for Boy Wonder – a nickname Chris had quickly acquired for his energy and youthful enthusiasm. It was up to 11 Platoon now. The best I could do was make sure we held the position 12 Platoon had won, in the event of a counterattack.

I could only hear the fierce fight that was to follow. I could see nothing. It was perhaps 20 minutes before Chris reported that they had taken out two machine-gun positions and six or so other Argentinian trenches. My guess, later, was that we had taken on two enemy platoons, possibly part of a company position, with B Company having taken on the rest of the company to our right. That moment, in the pitch black, with the need to push on, was not the time for a forensic analysis of the events. War has been described as 'organized chaos'. There was nothing organized about this – just the chaos. it was truly 'come-as-you-are'.

'Re-org on me,' I ordered over the net as I tried to restore some organization to the company. If a true test of simultaneous tasking is to read a map in the dark and fight for your life at the same time, we had spectacularly failed. We were not alone. 'Where are you?' I heard 'H' ask John Crosland at some point on the battalion net. 'Dark side of the moon, for all I know,' answered John. 'H' was slightly in awe of John's 'high intensity' combat experience fighting for the Sultan of Oman in the Dhofar war. Only he could have got away with that response.

Like a pack of hounds, both 10 and 11 Platoons had simply followed their noses from one contact with the enemy to the next. They had pursued the prey to its end but, pulled in every direction, it became clear that they had little idea where they had ended up, or even in which direction to go. Giving them the grid reference for where I was, or at best thought I was, would prove of little help if they didn't know where they were starting from.

Lacking a hunting horn to gather my hounds, I now put up a mini-flare, unsure of what I feared most – letting the enemy know where I was, or a rollocking from the ex-School of Infantry instructor 'H' for poor light discipline. But I could think of no other way to bring some order to the chaos, telling the guys to position on a clock ray method from that flare. Slowly we came together. Nobby began to check ammunition and casualty status with the platoon sergeants. It gradually emerged that we had three injured, one confirmed killed, and two unaccounted for. Lance Corporal Bingley and Private Grayling of 11 Platoon were both injured as they assaulted one of the enemy machine-gun positions, killing its five occupants. Bingley was then shot again, this time in the eye, by one of the enemy as the Argentinian lay dying. There was grit and courage on both sides. Corporal Harley, seeing Bingley go down, finished off the enemy, but too late to save his close friend and section 2iC. His death had been instantaneous. Corporal McAuley and Privates Hanley (Wang's younger brother, Wing) and Francom attacked another position nearby but the enemy were by then running. Private Mort of 10 Platoon had been shot through an arm, and Parr of 11 Platoon was knocked down by a shot to his stomach. Amazingly, the round, perhaps a ricochet, came to rest in his navel, but he had to be casevac'd with suspected internal injuries. All three were walking wounded, able to stagger, with help, to the axis track we'd started from, to find the CSM and surrender to the tender mercies of 'Del' Delaney, the company medic.

There was no sign of Lance Corporal Cork or Fletcher of 10 Platoon, although Cork had been seen to fall when 10 Platoon first came under fire. Eventually we moved on with them still missing. They were not found until daybreak by David Cooper and medics from the regimental aid post. Fletcher was lying half on top of Cork, with a shell dressing in his hand; he appeared to have been trying to give first aid to his mortally wounded section 2iC. The instructions on *Norland* to leave the wounded to look after themselves until the immediate objective had been secured sadly had given way to that desperate desire to care for a close comrade.

Among some of the men, feelings were running high. While we were waiting for those looking for Cork and Fletcher to return, Chris Waddington's began to get the better of him. Barely out of Sandhurst and only 19 years old, he had just been through one hell of an induction programme. He and his platoon's initiative had saved our bacon. I had asked his platoon to do a further check of the Argentinian trenches around us. Looking into one, he began to scream: 'You bastards!' His Toms were looking on, doubtless sharing his feelings after having lost three of their mates. In the dark I could just see the bayonet attached to the end of his SLR flashing above the trench. It didn't look good. I walked up and saw a couple of Argentinians lying at the bottom; impossible to know whether they were alive or dead. I put a restraining hand on his arm. 'Chris, I know you're upset, so are your Toms. But this isn't going to help them. Right now, they want you to lead them.' I said it quietly, for his ears only. Calm returned. Chris rejoined his men. Returning to Aldershot after the adventures that followed, he was possibly the most highly regarded subaltern amongst his peers in the officers' mess. The moniker 'Boy Wonder', richly deserved, stuck, although Chris always credited his platoon's outstanding performance to his platoon sergeant, Pete Light. Honesty and modesty at play there – Sergeant Light was one of the best, but a platoon sergeant can only achieve so much if the raw material lacks potential.

The close-quarter engagement with the enemy, a military term that belies its true violence and brutishness, lasted no more than 30 minutes. The subsequent reorganization took 1½ hours. As we eventually moved on, there was a hint of light to my left where the dark sky met the earth. Slowly, a grey dawn exposed a featureless, sodden landscape – and the single greatest error in our plan: our 'time and space' appreciation. All the ambivalence over the aim of the operation, the consequential under-resourcing of fire support and lack of creativity in the plan would not have mattered one jot had we not got that so drastically wrong.

We had allowed ourselves 4½ hours from H Hour, when we crossed the start line, to surrounding by daybreak the Goose Green settlement almost 4.5 miles away. On a straight march at night, with good going, we might have done it in 2 hours. But the peat bog babies' heads made the going treacherous – and we had to attack and overcome five, possibly more, enemy positions on the way. Throw in the tortuous business of reorganization in featureless terrain on a pitch-black night, with real casualties, and the search for the missing, and the sums were never going to add up. Even on a tightly controlled School of Infantry exercise, with all going smoothly, it would have been a stretch. Here, never. The carefully phased plan was rapidly unravelling.

Much of our training was done at night; amongst our opponents, I suspect, hardly any. Darkness was our friend. It enabled us to get close and, once in amongst them, the irresistible momentum of our whirlwind aggression quickly broke their will. We were like a chainsaw let loose among saplings. So we should have ensured we had plenty of that valuable darkness. Sure, we wanted to fight through the settlements in daylight, but we could have encircled them long before and waited. Starting earlier would, in theory, also have given us more time with the support of the all-important gun of HMS *Arrow*. Most military endeavours stand or fall on detail: the 'big hand on a small map' has been the undoing of many.

Daylight found us not even halfway to Goose Green. The featureless landscape offered us almost no cover but gave the enemy, in their pre-pared positions, huge fields of view – and fire. The boot was now firmly on the Argentinian foot.

For us, back in reserve, the situation ahead was even more discouraging. Some 800 yards to our front was the main feature of the isthmus, a 100ft-high ridgeline stretching west–northwesterly across it from the highest point overlooking Darwin settlement. A prominent line of gorse paral-leled the ridge just on the far side. Some 1,200 yards away, at the bottom of Darwin Hill, on the far side of a lagoon, and some 400 yards west of Darwin settlement, I could see A Company. They appeared to be pinned down by a score of Argentinian positions higher up the hill beyond. In the dark they had been trying to infiltrate along the shore of the lagoon to the settlement. As daylight came up, however, they came under fire from the hill, which now dominated the ground they were on. There was no way they could advance to Darwin without first taking the hill which the enemy occupied.

I could not see B Company, but soon gathered that they had crested Darwin Ridge further to the west. Again, with daylight, they found them-selves on the forward slope of the ridge. They started to come under fire from Browning 0.5-inch heavy machine guns on a knoll 500 yards south of or beyond Boca House, although I was unaware of what was causing them grief at the time. This enemy position was some 1,100 yards ahead of them. The Brownings had an effective range of 2,000 yards; B Company had only their light-role GPMGs with a range of 600 yards. They had a problem. So pinned down, they could also do little about fire they were also receiving from the enemy atop Darwin Hill. Problems seldom come alone. Without help, they could do little than grovel for sparse cover and concealment amongst the peat divots and gorse.

Both A and B Companies had taken casualties and been brought to a standstill. From the radio traffic on the battalion net, it became clear that 'H' and his Tac HQ had joined A Company. He obviously considered that resolving their difficulties first was the key to further progress. It looked like D Company, as so often happened in reserve on exercises, would be needed to bail things out. Comfortably removed from A and B's discomfort, we started to check ourselves over, weapons and ammunition, with eager anticipation.

We were gathered on a low knoll, just west of the track to the settlements. To my right, someone reported trip wires, which suggested a minefield, but the enemy had clearly kept the track open for their own use. Then beyond the minefield I saw twenty or more enemy soldiers moving along a flat part of the western shore, before disappearing behind cliffs. Clearly, we and B Company had missed a few in the dark, and they were trying to rejoin their comrades further south. We tried to discourage them with machine-gun fire, but they showed no reaction. Out of range. We were just wasting ammunition.

I looked towards A Company. Our mortars were now firing onto Darwin Hill beyond them. Just insignificant puffs as the bombs exploded. Most of the impact appeared to be absorbed by the peat, causing little damage. Something of a stalemate. But, if the enemy could move along the coast, concealed from view, maybe we could too. I called 'H' on the radio to share my thoughts and suggested I try to turn their left flank.

'Stop clogging the net,' was his sharp response. 'I'm trying to run a battle here. Stay where you are.'

With nothing else to occupy us, we took closer stock of our immediate surroundings. Around us lay a dozen dead Argentinians – the product of B Company's earlier advance, or perhaps the work of HMS *Arrow*'s gun before she cleared off. Their weapons, FNs, were the same as the SLR, except that the FN was fully automatic rather than semi-automatic so could also fire bursts as opposed to single shots only. The ammunition was identical. Nobby and his team in Company HQ had already started to relieve them of it. Then Hanley and one other started to extend the job to their wrists, some of them decked with watches and jewellery. My mind flashed to a hot evening in Bahrain when I was still in the RAF, where I had had to parade a Guard of Honour for the sheikh's visit to the British air base. I hated that sort of stuff but, told the sheik's sign of appreciation was usually a gold watch, I gave it my best. The inspection over, the sheikh was ushered quickly away by the station commander, leaving me empty-handed. Now I looked at one dead wrist, flashing gold. Well, it's been a long time to wait, but ... Then, thank God, another voice in my head: this is a distraction from what we should be doing – and the start of a slippery slope.

I strolled over. Quietly, I spoke: 'I'm tempted by a gold Rolex too, Hanley, but we need to be worrying about live Argentinians, not dead ones. Leave them alone.'

Wang got it at once. This was nothing to do with sentiment or respect for the dead. It was about being a professional soldier, in the most professional regiment in the world. I looked around. All eyes should have been looking outwards. Instead, they were all looking in, to see how this was going to play out. Looking back, I feel it was perhaps the best, most important intervention I made in the Falklands. It set the tone for Penal Company and the way it would conduct itself for the rest of the war. Tests in battle, I was learning, come in many guises. For a moment I had been a wafer away from failing one.

The odd round of desultory enemy artillery had been popping off around us for some time. Gradually, I became aware of the rounds getting closer. More slowly than it should have, the penny dropped that there was an enemy observer somewhere adjusting for a fire mission on us. He didn't seem very good at it, but when he eventually succeeded, our knoll was not going to be a healthy place to be. Assuming the Argentinian observer was ahead of us, I decided to move forward 400–500 yards into the lee of the closest part of Darwin ridge, hoping we would be in 'dead' ground, invisible to him.

We had moved about 200 yards when 'H' called me on the battalion net: '49 Alpha, what the hell are you doing? I told you to stay where you were.' I took the spare handset from Ozzie. Normally, Ozzie would have answered on my behalf. The tone, however, made it clear that the 'go-between' was not welcome. I explained my predicament, and he reluctantly agreed that I continue, but not before telling me not to move again without first letting him know. I felt inclined to remind 'H' that he had also instructed me to stay off the net but decided the more constructive response was once more to suggest that, as I was already on the move, I go on to recce the right flanking option along the western coastline. 'Stop trying to tell me how to run my battle, out!' The radio clicked. Conversation over. Ozzie shrugged and rolled his eyes.

Ozzie was not part of D Company, but from the Signals Platoon in HQ Company, and was the regular head of my signals detachment for battalion-level operations and exercises. By now, I knew him well, and trusted him implicitly. He was far more than my crucial link to the CO and battalion HQ. The CO, or anyone outside of the company wanting me on the radio, had to come through Ozzie. Like an executive's PA, he was my filter who could keep agitated or irate COs off my back, or for that matter meddlesome 'remfs', allowing me to get on with my job. It was not an easy role, requiring resilience, and sometimes a thick skin, but it was one in which he excelled.

Ozzie was black, and I have little doubt that when joining the Army and going through recruit training and P Company selection, his journey would have been more challenging than for most. Notwithstanding that he had a reputation as a boxer, he would have required, or acquired, that extra element of emotional fortitude. Was it this that equipped him so well to cope with the particular demands of his role, perhaps more acute in Penal Company than in others? Whatever, he was most definitely part of our tribe, widely respected and liked throughout the company. A vital element of my close team, if Nobby was my right hand and Wang my left, Ozzie was my 'top cover', and more.

As I passed the handset back to Ozzie, I was beginning to despair. From where I was, the possibilities for unlocking this stalemate seemed obvious and numerous. Why was 'H' so reluctant to use his reserve? He had not only my company, but also C Company uncommitted, and our long-range GPMG (SF) and anti-tank weapons also available. So immersed was 'H' in fighting A Company's battle, instead of letting them get on with what they knew best how to do, that he had over half the battalion as bystanders. I was just glad I wasn't in Dair's shoes, trying to command A Company with him charging round the place.

My earphone on the company net squawked: '49 Alpha, 49. Under incoming "shelldrake" fire. My "molar" is down.' It's very easy to carry attempts at radio security to the absurd. This was Nobby's signaller telling me that Company HQ had come under enemy artillery fire, and that the company storeman with him had been hit. I cursed myself. Damn! I should have moved us off the knoll sooner. Nobby's Company HQ team, at the back of the company column, had paid the price. Mechan died soon after.

We found a little fold in the slope coming down from the ridge; this was as safe as anywhere. I called a halt and we dispersed in 'all-round' defence. 'OK,' I ordered, 'get a brew on.' The Toms' looks reminded me of one occasion in Aldershot. 'H' had set up an inter-company '10-miler' competition. The 'ten-miler' was one of the key tests for passing P Company selection – marching 10 miles cross-country laden with a 40lb bergen and rifle in under 1¾ hours. As D Company approached the finish line, I wheeled the men away from the barracks and showers, ending up at the assault course. There were puzzled looks all round. 'OK,' I had explained, 'it's never over till it's over. Inter-platoon assault-course race.' Was I now playing another of my little games, they were wondering? A brew mid-battle wasn't standard operating procedure, not what School of Infantry instructors taught. Now, with multi-day routes in the mountains in mind, I explained: 'Look, the last food we've had was 18 hours ago. We're clearly not going anywhere soon. And it looks like we now have a very long day ahead of us. Fuel up!' Out came the brew kits. The smell of burning hexamine soon filled the air, priming expectation of some welcome scoff.

While the battle raged, D Company took breakfast. Julian Thompson, writing the story of 3 Commando Brigade in the Falklands, called his book *No Picnic*. Many years later I was able to tell him of ours.

The best-laid plans of mice and men ... my porridge had just come to the boil, my saucepan a metal mug, designed to fit on the bottom of an issue water bottle, with a bit of masking tape around the rim to avoid burnt lips. Anything to reduce the gear carried. As I took my first spoonful, over the battalion net I heard an urgent: 'Sunray is down!' The CO was hit. Then I thought I heard 'H' gasp: 'No one else is to come up here.' Maybe the fluke of radio waves, or maybe I imagined it, as no one has ever corroborated it.

The death of a commander on the battlefield is momentous. It suggests at once that things have become desperate; morale can crumble and then the battle is lost. Conversely, it can fire up resolve to avenge his death. Such tribal sentiments did not follow 'H's death. 'H' was always highly visible. The Toms all felt they knew him, his impetuosity, his determination to lead from the front – never asking his men to do what he would not also do himself. There was almost an open bet as to whether he would survive his first battle. Now they shrugged. They still had a job to do, and they were just going to carry on with it.

'H' was a classic authoritarian, obsessed with being in control. In that respect, he was a man of his time, and again a product of School of Infantry training that prevailed at the time, and at which he had been an instructor. I remember one course that I attended. On one Command Post exercise, where the aim is to practise commanders and their staff, we were bombarded with events of such intensity and speed that it was impossible to stay on top of the situation. DS would then assail you with questions such as: Where's that unit? What are they doing? What's happening here? The way to game the 'pink' was to limit all initiative and direct that no one was to do anything without your permission. Top marks could be gained for 'control', but no marks scored for achieving objectives nor penalties for opportunities missed. But, here is the irony in 'H'. Some have defined great leadership as building a team that can deliver great performance without you. Well, that is precisely what we went on to do, even as we shook our heads, thinking: 'What a mad way to go.'

There were urgent calls for a casevac helicopter, then Chris Keeble, the battalion 2iC, a mile or so back with Main HQ, came on the net, to assume command. Addressing John Crosland: '29: you have control until I get forward.' Then to me: '49: join up with 29, and see what you can do to help.' Shit! The most untimely order I had ever received. My porridge was barely touched. But I was buggered if I was going to ditch it. We got going, like an army of vagabonds, weapons in one hand, mugs in the other, trying to take the occasional slurp. We would have made Dad's Army look good at that moment. Fortunately there were no witnesses.

Keeble's instructions were, understandably, a little short of design. I had no precise location for B Company, and only the vaguest idea of what situation they were in. At least, though, he seemed intent on getting us into the action. That was enough for me. Ten minutes later, with at least some of my porridge down my throat and quite a lot of it scattered over my arctic smock, we began to crest the ridge. I could see nothing of B Company but could hear the occasional buzz and crack and thump of bullets passing us. A good half a mile or so to our front I could see an enemy position. Surely it was too far away to effectively engage us with small arms. A little nervously we pushed on. Then I saw the side pocket of one of my signallers' trousers ripped off by a bullet. The enemy had something more substantial ahead than our small arms. I twigged that it was a recorded artillery target and got my FOO to call up a fire mission. With dismay, we watched as the rounds, 400 yards off target, plopped uselessly into the sea. 'Left 400, repeat' ordered the FOO, but the rounds again only created some harmless waves. I gave up on the guns.

Infantry doctrine defines effective enemy fire as when it starts inflicting casualties, and to keep advancing to contact until then. Willoughby's ripped trousers was effective enough for me. If we pushed on, we would just end up in the same situation as B Company. We pulled back, in some haste, behind the ridge line. Like Black Adder, I had a cunning plan.

Radioing Chris Keeble, I explained that finding John Crosland was proving difficult. Putting on my long-playing record, I told him I could now see an approach down to the western coastline: 'I think I should go and explore the possibilities.' He quickly agreed. My spirits rose. Chris was freeing up the battlefield, letting those with their noses against the problem, get on with solving it. I was almost drunk with eager anticipation. 'Watch out, 2 PARA. D Company's joining the party!'

Then I sobered up. Chris had backed me, but I didn't quite know where this would lead and I didn't want to let him down. I decided to go down to the shore with just 11 and 12 Platoons, leaving 10 Platoon with my 2iC Pete Adams where we were on the ridge top, to cover us if things went wrong. That proved prescient, because as we got to the shore the steep ground screened my radio signal, and I no longer had direct comms to Chris Keeble, or to anyone else on the battalion net. Pete's ability to relay radio messages in what followed was to prove crucial.

We moved forward along a narrow beach for several hundred yards, until we reached a little stream inlet and, 30 yards away, the ruins of Boca House. On high ground almost 500 yards beyond the ruins, amongst the babies' heads was the Argentinian position that was the source of grief to B Company, their heavy machine guns – now visible – totally dominating all the ground out to Darwin Ridge. Ahead of us, surrounding the ruins, was an extensive closely grazed grass meadow, devoid of any cover. We could get no further but the enemy were at last within range of our light machine guns. I got all twelve of the two platoons' guns lined up behind some dunes on the beach, and we began to have some sport. Best of all, the enemy seemed unaware of where their headache was coming from.

The next forty-five minutes were to change the battle. As we started to engage the enemy ahead, Pete Adams relayed that A Company had finally taken Darwin Hill. In what was certainly the most intense and prolonged single engagement of the day, their guts, aggression and perseverance had won through. Our eventual engagement of the Boca position probably came too late to influence that, but 2 hours earlier, when I first suggested the possibility to 'H', it might certainly have saved time and A Company some pain. Peter Ketley, the anti-tank platoon commander, had proposed to 'H' that he move his Milan wire-guided anti-tank missiles forward to help either A or B Company but, like mine, his offer had also been rejected. Now Chris Keeble had released them too, and minutes after I had started to fire on the Boca position, John Crosland began to use the Milans from the ridge behind him with devastating effect, destroying the Argentinian heavy machine guns' sangars.

I could see the survivors desperately struggling towards shelter in another sangar. Machine-gun fire from our beach made sure they never made it. This merciless scene played out for several minutes, and then white rags began waving from the position.

This presented us with a dilemma. Years in Northern Ireland had made us instinctively mistrustful. Was this a lure, to tempt us into a trap? Should we keep on blasting them until nothing moved? Doing so would remove any risk, and enemy prisoners and injured present a logistics burden that the dead do not. On the other hand, if the white flags were a genuine offer to surrender, we could save valuable time and, more importantly, precious ammunition. We had already expended half of what we had set out with, and still had roughly halfway to go. I shared my thoughts with Jim Barry and Chris Waddington, lying either side of me. *It's genuine, they've had enough – they know they're fucked*, summarizes the brief debate. Taking a surrender, however, would require a unilateral cease-fire on our part. And then, someone to put to the test whether it was reciprocated. That someone, we knew, could only be D Company, leaving cover and advancing across the billiard table between us. The decision was a fine calculation, devoid of any sentiment for the poor souls ahead of us. They still had the capacity to cause us harm. *Who lives, who dies?* We opted for taking a surrender.

So began a tortuous discussion over the radio. I put my proposal to Chris Keeble, knowing John Crosland would be party to the conversation. But all the messages to and fro had to be relayed by Pete Adams, on the high ground behind me. After 20 minutes there had been heaps of debate, but no progress, no OK. Before long the whole point would be lost. Nothing left of the enemy position perhaps, but little ammunition left for us to fight the rest of the battle.

'Hello, 49, this is 49 Alpha. For Niner. If we don't move soon, we're going to be cut off by the tide, over.' There is very little tide in Falkland Sound, but Pete Adams duly relayed the message to Keeble. I could not hear the following discussion on the battalion net. Then: 'Hello, 49 Alpha, this is 49. From Niner. OK. Move. Over.'

'Roger, out.' Our slight deception had worked. The fire from the Milan on Darwin Hill slowly ceased.

I told 11 Platoon to lead the advance, with 12 Platoon and our machine gun fire base standing by to provide fire support if things unravelled. But as the moment to put my plan to the test approached, a flash of doubt. *What if I've called this wrong? It'll be carnage. The blood of my Toms on my hands! If I had doubts, how could I ask others to take the risk on my personal hunch? I had to show belief in my convictions.* 'OK, folks, my call. Sometimes "Ruperts" have to earn their pay. No one moves until I try this out.'

Desperately hoping that Wang, as my loyal bodyguard, was ready to follow and present the enemy with a choice of target, with a silent prayer I began to rise. Before I could get fully to my feet, the firm hand of Corporal Harley, on my right, pushed me down. 'This is Toms' work, Sir,' he chided, leaping forward, his section following, with a speed and enthusiasm that put mine to shame. 'We need you alive to do yours!'

I did not protest. Heart in mouth, waiting for tracer to erupt from the hill ahead, I followed. Seconds passed. Nothing. I began to breathe. So began the longest 500 yards of our lives.

We had covered about 100 yards when one of the anti-tank platoon fired off another Milan missile. 'Check firing!' I heard Pete Adams scream over the battalion net, as we continued to advance, but dreading a response from the Argentinians. We were totally exposed, no cover anywhere. Another 100 yards and Spencer, the left-hand man of 12 Platoon, tripped a wire, setting off a mine a few yards away, blowing both Spencer and his platoon sergeant, Taff Meredith, off their feet. Would this blow the cease-fire? Scrambling to his feet, amazingly unharmed, Spencer saw an irate Meredith bearing down on him. We'd warned them to look out for mines. 'It wasn't me, Sarge, honest!'

With a huge collective sigh, we reached the Argentinian position without further mishap, to be confronted with a scene of pitiful destruction – it would have been shocking, were we not by now becoming shock-proof. Sangars demolished, a dozen or more dead and, from a cursory glance at their blood-soaked bandages, even more wounded. The twenty or more survivors were quickly separated from their weapons and made to lie face down in the peat. I have a picture of that moment, taken by Corporal Owen, who had the fortitude to add an SLR camera to his enormous load. In it, Private Bradford's face says it all: Thank God, we've made it; these poor bastards; keep a grip.

Looking ahead, I saw around thirty Argentinians, perhaps 600 yards away, haring across the airfield towards Goose Green. They were led by a character driving a tractor, who we assumed to be their officer, with some of the men trying to clamber aboard. He was waiting for no one. 'There's leadership from the front,' grunted Hanley. Chortles all round. Whether it was him on that tractor I do not know, but many years later 2nd Lieutenant Pelufo spoke of his experience on the Boca position: 'The Paras got closer and closer. They were trying to outflank us along the beach. They avoided a frontal assault ... However, their fire was very precise. I remember seeing a corporal receive a direct hit from a wire-guided missile.'

D Company, 2 PARA on MV *Norland*, South Atlantic, May 1982. The author is in the middle of the back row. On his right is CSM WO2 Nobby Clark and on his left is company 2ic Lieutenant Pete Adams. On WO2 Clark's right are Lieutenants Page, Waddington, Barry and Webster. On Lieutenant Adams' left is CQMS Colour Sergeant Powell and Sergeants Light, Meredith and O'Rawe. In the front row, to the left of the gangplank, are Corporals Harley (left) and McAuley. My runner, Private Hanley, is immediately behind Harley. Of the ninety-two men in the picture, fourteen (ten dead, four wounded) failed to sail back with us. *(Photo: Parachute Regiment Collection)*

The battalion band playing 'Don't Cry for Me, Argentina' at Portsmouth Docks, 26 April 1982. Our stretcher-bearers in war, it was not considered necessary for the band to travel with us.

MV *Norland* at Ascension Island. This photograph was taken before H. ordered the funnel to be painted black and there was still plenty of white for attacking pilots to spot. The helicopter is about to deliver an underslung load onto the newly completed rear helicopter deck. (*Photo: Parachute Regiment Collection*)

The author compering the prize-giving at the end of the battalion sports day shortly after leaving Ascension Island. The length of his hair continued to frustrate Nobby Clark. *(Photo: W. 'Doc' Owen)*

Standing to against enemy air attack on MV *Norland*. The weapons are GPMGs on their SF tripods. It was more gesture than resolute defence. *(Photo: W. 'Doc' Owen)*

Bomb Alley. San Carlos Water seen from Sussex Mountain. (*Photo: Parachute Regiment Collection*)

A peat igloo on Sussex Mountain. (*Photo: Parachute Regiment Collection*)

The CO, Colonel H. Jones, on top of Sussex Mountain with his Tac HQ.
(*Photo: Parachute Regiment Collection*)

Goose Green 'O' Group. H. Jones is sitting left centre with a pencil in his mouth. The author is behind H. with notebook in hand. Far right is Captain Alan Coulson, the intelligence officer. Alan had a penchant for the heavy and uncomfortable steel parachute helmet in use since the Second World War, and recently replaced by a lighter fibreglass and Kevlar helmet worn by the rest. Half-right with his back to camera, John Crosland can be identified by his iconic black woollen hat that he insisted on wearing in preference to his helmet, and which made him immediately identifiable to his Toms. (*Photo: Parachute Regiment Collection*)

Goose Green

Darwin Hill

Darwin

Boca Ho.

Buntside Ho.

START LINE

Aerial view of Goose Green. Featureless, with little cover, it offered great fields of fire for the enemy defenders. (*Photo: Parachute Regiment Collection*)

An Argentinian 0.5in heavy machine-gun position beyond Boca House. (*Photographer not known*)

Argentinian Triple A anti-aircraft cannon at Goose Green airfield, depressed for use in the ground role. It was a fearsome weapon. (*Photographer not known*)

Approaching the Boca position after the white flags. There was no cover if the surrender backfired. D Company had taken some entrenching tools, although our orders had been to leave them behind to save weight. (*Photo: W. 'Doc' Owen*)

Occupying the Boca position. Private Bradford's face says it all: 'Thank fuck we made it. These poor bastards.' (*Photo: W. 'Doc' Owen*)

The surrender at Boca. The soldier with the head wound was not expected to live but, under the care of Steve Hughes, the RMO, he survived.
(*Photo: W. 'Doc' Owen*)

Captain Steve Hughes at work in the regimental aid post. All the injured were treated equally in the RAP, although one casevac helicopter pilot chose to prioritize friendly forces' casualties despite protests from Hughes. (*Photo: Parachute Regiment Collection*)

Preparing for the surrender at Goose Green. Foreground, left to right: Corporal Elliott (10 Platoon), with his back to the camera; my runner 'Wang' Hanley; Chris Keeble's signaller; CSM Nobby Clark; my signaller Corporal 'Ozzie' Osborne (far right). (*Photo: W. 'Doc' Owen*)

The Goose Green field of surrender covered in downed weapons and equipment. (*Photo: W. 'Doc' Owen*)

Local civilians after being liberated from the Goose Green community hall. (*Photo: Parachute Regiment Collection*)

An Argentinian Skyhawk attack at Goose Green. The aircraft is trailing smoke after being hit, having strafed D Company. (*Photo: Parachute Regiment Collection*)

Chris Waddington at Goose Green, wearing the smock borrowed from one of our dead in exchange for his soaked clothing the night before. He was no longer a 'boy soldier'. The man with his back to the camera is CSM Nobby Clark. (*Photo: Chris Waddington*)

The site of the Argentinian mass burial undertaken by local civilians. (*Photo: Parachute Regiment Collection*)

The burial of 2 PARA men killed at Goose Green and Ajax Bay. (*Photo: Parachute Regiment Collection*)

Argentinian POWs at their temporary camp, the sheep-shearing sheds at Goose Green. (*Photo: W. 'Doc' Owen*)

(*Above*) Rescuing Welsh Guardsmen from the LSL *Sir Galahad*, Fitzroy, 8 June 1982. (*Photo: Parachute Regiment Collection*)

(*Facing, top*) Helicopter move of 2 PARA to Bluff Cove Peak prior to the attack on Wireless Ridge. (*Photo: Parachute Regiment Collection*)

(*Facing, middle*) Wireless Ridge seen from the Anchor observation post on Mt Longdon, looking toward Hearnden Water. The picture shows the NGFO adjusting fire on *Rough Diamond*, with no complaint from C Company, 3 PARA, who were reported to be there.

(*Facing, bottom*) Wireless Ridge. Looking back from *Dirty Dozen* towards *Blueberry Pie* where D Company were shelled by friendly fire. D Company had crossed the col and advanced to about 50 yards short of where this picture was taken, when illumination was set off; only then did the enemy realize where the attack was coming from. It was here that the author lost contact with his signaller, Ozzie, and his FOO. (*Photo: W. 'Doc' Owen*)

Night fire at Wireless Ridge. The exchange of fire between Argentinians on *Dirty Dozen* (right) and our CVR(T)s on *Apple Tart* (left). It was 'like being at the movies'. *(Photo: W. 'Doc' Owen)*

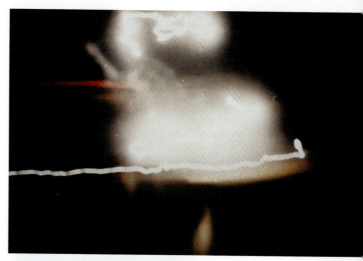

Wireless Ridge. A dead Argentinian on *Dirty Dozen*. *(Photo: W. 'Doc' Owen)*

'Endex' Wireless Ridge. Helmets off, red berets on! Private Delaney, the company medic, is in the foreground. *(Photo: W. 'Doc' Owen)*

Corporal Owen's section celebrating their success at Wireless Ridge. Port Stanley is in the background. It is just possible to see smoke coming from the racecourse after the attack on the Argentinian guns there by Scout helicopters equipped with SS11 wire-guided missiles. (*Photo: W. 'Doc' Owen*)

D Company on the road to Stanley. (*Photo: W. 'Doc' Owen*)

D Company returning from the battalion thanksgiving service in Stanley Cathedral, tired after a job well done. They were boys no longer. (*Photo: Parachute Regiment Collection*)

The British cemetery at San Carlos. (*Photo: Author*)

The three rifle company commanders on Darwin Hill for the thirtieth anniversary return to the Falklands. Left to right: Dair Farrar-Hockley (OC A Coy), author (D Coy), John Crosland (OC B Coy). (*Photo: Author*)

The Argentinian cemetery near Goose Green. (*Photo: Author*)

Unaware of Pelufo's sentiments at the time, the phases of war flashed into my mind. Exploitation? Hot Pursuit? They're running. Don't let them reorganize. Keep them running. We had to grab this moment. Hot pursuit!

Pete Adams and Shaun Webster with 10 Platoon joined us. I told Shaun to leave one of his sections to look after the prisoners with Company HQ and the medics. Letting John Crosland know what we were doing, we set off, almost at the trot, 12 Platoon in the lead. Five minutes later Chris Keeble, trying to catch up with developments, got me on the radio: 'Push ahead to Goose Green.'

'We already are,' I replied, trying not to sound smug.

We gained the northern edge of the airfield. Suddenly we were engulfed in a terrifying cacophony of staccato thumps. On the hill behind us the ground was being pockmarked with small eruptions. We were under direct fire, but what the hell from? We swung left to seek the shelter of a shallow valley between the airfield and Darwin Ridge. The fire ceased. As our heart rates steadied, I recalled from the 'O' Group that the Argentinians had a number of Oerlikon 20mm and 35mm anti-aircraft guns, known as Triple A's. We realized that we had come under Argentinian anti-aircraft fire. I could not tell, nor was I very interested in, the calibre, but the Argentinians' ability to depress the barrels and use them directly against us had brought us back to earth after the elation at the Boca position. Maybe exploitation, rather than hot pursuit? Regrettably, I was not quite that analytical – I just knew we had to keep the pressure on, and not do anything stupid.

The valley now led us to a bridge on the main track into Goose Green, about half a mile north of the settlement. Soon after, we passed what looked like an Argentinian command post to our right. I got Shaun Webster and his two remaining sections of 10 Platoon to check that it had been abandoned. I didn't want any bypassed enemy soldiers shooting us up from the rear. The plan was good, but it was to get them into all sorts of trouble, and not just from the enemy.

Clausewitz, the renowned Prussian military philosopher, in *On War*, wrote of the fog and chaos of war. In the next few hours we were to discover how right he was.

Shaun and his men found the position was deserted but as they checked it, they came under fire from the south side of the airfield. They moved forward to try to sort this, but as they did so, came under fire from behind. This was probably from our own machine-gun platoon with their GPMG (SF)s, now ensconced on Darwin Ridge, trying to engage the same enemy position or, perhaps, still trying to catch up with the accelerating speed of events, thinking 10 Platoon were enemy forces. They briefly also came under fire from their right. This turned out to be B Company, now undertaking a wide right flanking move to seal off Goose Green from the south. Fortunately both these misunderstandings were resolved before any harm was done. 10 Platoon decided to withdraw and try to rejoin the company.

Meanwhile, I pushed on in the cover provided by the little valley, which led towards the area of the schoolhouse, 600 yards north of the settlement. There, we had been told at the previous evening's 'O' Group, were perhaps a hundred enemy. The main objective at last was looking seductively within reach.

Ahead of us now was the main vehicle track crossing a small stream and, about 350 yards beyond, the schoolhouse. 12 Platoon ground to a slow crawl. I went forward to see what was holding them up, and found orange tripwires across their path. We were in another minefield. 'Better than Triple A fire,' I encouraged. 'Just avoid the wires.' After Spencer's earlier experience, I felt 12 Platoon weren't convinced. I was desperate to keep the momentum going. 'Jim, work your way up to the higher ground on the right, somewhere you can provide covering fire. It's time 11 Platoon took a turn at the front.' I pushed the ever-willing 11 Platoon into the lead. I didn't think it would help to tell them about mines. In their enthusiasm they didn't seem to notice. Mad buggers, they must surely have wondered why I was walking on tiptoes. The pace picked up ...

As we got to the track, a drainage ditch provided a little cover. An Argentinian tent and a sangar lay some 50 yards away, between us and the schoolhouse – possibly a command post. It looked deserted, but better safe than sorry. I called a halt. Corporal McAuley was nearby. 'Stick a rocket into that,' I called. McAuley delegated the task to one of his Toms carrying a light anti-tank weapon, or LAW. A 'throw away when used' recoilless weapon, fired from the shoulder, it projected a 66mm armour-piercing rocket 200 yards – ideal for busting defensive sangars in close-quarter combat – as long as no one is behind it when fired. The back-blast could spoil their day.

Private Dixon drew the short straw. Lying alongside him in the ditch, we watched as he took aim. Boom – a lick of flame flashed out behind him, and the rocket sped towards the enemy CP. It flew well above it, exploding out of sight. We'd missed the barn door at fifty paces!

Another Tom, who I think may have been Hanley's younger brother Wing, stepped up with another LAW. I now took a closer interest – taking nothing for granted. It proved instructive.

We had just covered some 1,500 yards, heavily laden, almost at the trot. The last 200 yards had seen the added excitement of skipping over mine tripwires. We were panting like horses at the end of the Grand National. As he lined up on the target, the muzzle of the rocket launcher on his shoulder was waving about like an agitated water divining stick. Ear drums rattled once more as the rocket left the launcher. Even as I saw him squeeze the trigger, I knew it was going to be another miss. 'Blimey, fuck!' I yelled theatrically. 'Call yourselves bloody trained soldiers?' I could have done no better, but I needed to appeal to their professional pride – and besides, I was getting pissed off.

Corporal McAuley, suitably stung by the rebuke to his team, now grabbed the section's last LAW. A little older and experienced, he took cool aim and calmly squeezed the trigger. Bullseye! The Argentinian shelter disintegrated. We cheered. With much laughter, part embarrassment, part relief, at the satisfactory conclusion of this little farce, we gave Corporal McAuley a polite round of applause.

With 11 Platoon, I now moved on towards the schoolhouse. We stopped behind a low rise on which stood a tin shed, apparently a dairy, to call on our artillery to soften up the schoolhouse before we assaulted it. Fifteen or so rounds of high explosive should discourage opposition. 'Battery unavailable, counter-battery fire' came the reply over the FOO's radio. The response reflected the prevailing doctrine for defending Germany against the Soviet hordes – that the priority of our own artillery was first to neutralize the Soviet artillery. This was enabled by sophisticated radar that could track where enemy shells were launched from. Only here, we did not have the sophisticated radar. Counter-battery fire was like looking for a needle in a haystack – with your eyes closed. We began to come under artillery fire ourselves from the enemy's three guns, those very guns that ours were supposed to be neutralizing. Doctrine had become mindless dogma – our battery commander was on another planet.

It could have been worse. The enemy were using impact fuses. Had they had variable time (VT) fuses that could be set so that the shells exploded as air-bursts 30ft or so above us, it would have been a different story. As it was, the soft peat soaked up most of the blast. Even a metre away, we could be showered by clods of peat, but nothing life-changing. A few rounds, however, were landing on the hardened ground of the track, now 20 yards or so to my right. Then the whistling buzz of shrapnel had us all twitching. If Dixon had been thinking he was having a bad day for missing the barn door 20 minutes earlier, it now got tragically worse. A round detonated on the track, which I dismissed as harmless. Then, crouching a couple of yards away, I saw him clutch his neck and collapse with a shriek of pain. 'Wing' Hanley, the ever-steady Sergeant Pete Light and Private Sharpe went into lifesaving first aid drills: applying shell-dressings to his wounds to staunch the bleeding from a hole in his back; removing his morphine syrette from inside his helmet and injecting into his arm; then using the infamous anal drip. All to little avail.

'Del' Delaney, our company medic, was still to catch us up after dealing with the Argentinian wounded back at the Boca position. The regimental aid post, with Steve Hughes the doctor, who might have been able to do more, was on Darwin Hill, separated from us by a forward slope raked by Argentinian Triple A fire – effectively the other side of the world. It probably would have made no difference. Dixon's screams subsided into a whimper, and then a deafening, over-whelming silence. The noise of shells exploding around us, the whizzing of shrapnel seeking another fortuitous target, the shower of dirt falling amongst us, all became 'noises off'. At that moment Dixon, who until then had for me been little more than a name on the company roll, took over my world. The hilarious first aid sessions on *Norland*, the recent banter around missing the barn door moments before, when we seemed to be sweeping all before us, now were a lifetime away. Even hardened Paras find it hard to laugh, watching a comrade die.

Meanwhile we had unexpectedly been joined by parts of C company. They had, confusingly, also been ordered forward towards Goose Green by Chris Keeble, choosing to do so down the forward slope of Darwin Hill and, like the Light Brigade, charging straight into the fire of the enemy guns – in this case Argentinian Triple A fire. Their Company HQ took the full force of it, their company commander and his signaller both wounded, but most had pushed on albeit in some disarray. Their recce platoon joined me in the now very unhealthy forming-up point for the attack on the schoolhouse, which the enemy guns had clearly registered as a defensive fire target.

Moments later one of their soldiers also fell to the incoming artillery. I saw his platoon commander visibly shaken. This could be contagious. I consciously closed down my feelings and steeled myself. Dixon was history. My responsibility now had to be to the living, those still with a part to play in this unfolding chaos. We had to move on, get out of this killing zone. But chaos was not done with us yet.

My radio earphone crackled. It was Taff Meredith, platoon sergeant of 12 Platoon. 'Hello 49 Alpha, this is 43. There's a white flag flying from the high ground to our south. 43 Alpha has gone with a section to take a surrender.' This, I reckoned, would have been the southern edge of the airfield.

Jim Barry, the platoon commander, had been beside me on the beach before Boca, listening to my debate on the radio with Chris Keeble on the merits of taking a surrender under the questionable protection of a white flag. We had only taken that earlier surrender after lengthy preparation for a cease-fire with the rest of the battalion; even then, things had been messy. I felt that cold cramp in my stomach which warns of something very nasty about to happen. 'Stop him,' I screamed into my microphone.

Meanwhile enemy shells continued to explode amongst us. We could not stay in this position, hoping for our artillery to do something useful. We had to attack, with or without their support.

'49 Alpha, it's 43, I can't raise 43 Alpha. He's talking to the enemy.' Meredith again. A rattle of small arms fire penetrated the call. Then, more urgently, 'They're down. 43A is down, and others with him.' Fuck, fuck, fuck! Why the hell did I share my thoughts about surrenders back at Boca?

12 Platoon now could no longer provide direct fire support onto the schoolhouse; down to two sections, they had enough problems and un-certainties of their own. 10 Platoon were still involved with their fun and games on the airfield. Yes, we had a gaggle of C Company with us, but they were as unbiddable as a pack of wild dogs – they were on a separate company radio net and, with their Company HQ out of action, there was no one on the battalion net to communicate with. Life was getting tricky. 'Unbalanced' might be the military euphemism for our situation.

I was unsure what to attend to first. My eyes alighted first on C Company's patrols platoon further to the left scrabbling along the shoreline behind us, also apparently heading for the schoolhouse, then on my ever-cool 2ic, Pete Adams, previously himself a platoon commander in C Company. Help was at hand. 'Pete, over to you with this mess here. See what you can do with 11 and C Company. Sort out the school,' I shouted. 'I'm going to see what's going on with 12 Platoon.' I had no idea what con-fronted them on the southern edge of the airfield, directly ahead. My other big fear was a counterattack on them, after their setback, from the settlement itself, now just 600 yards away. With my two shadows, Ozzie my signaller and Wang my runner, I went in search of Taff Meredith; I also badly needed to know how far off 10 Platoon still were in case my fears of a counterattack started to materialize.

I need not have worried. I found Taff, with a GPMG crew, pouring fire towards an enemy position with a flag flying above it, 75 yards along the track that led directly into Goose Green. A few yards beyond and to the right, there was a dramatic firework display – bangs and flashes in all directions. This turned out to be an ammunition dump set alight by 12 Platoon's response, and it continued to entertain us throughout the night. Near Meredith were three survivors of the section that had gone with Jim Barry to take the surrender that never was. I momentarily listened to a clearly agitated but, given what he had just experienced, surprisingly coherent Private Godfrey trying to explain what had happened.

The gist of his blurt was that Jim had started to parley, in sign language, with an Argentinian officer facing him 2 or 3 yards away. Both were gesturing to the other to put down their weapons. Suddenly a sustained burst of machine-gun fire sprayed the area. The Argentinians opened fire and dived back into their trenches. Jim Barry and Corporal Sullivan, the section commander, were killed instantly, and Shevill was wounded. Lance Corporal Smith, Sullivan's 2ic, was killed whilst trying to launch a LAW rocket into the position. Knight, Barry's signaller, was able to shoot two Argentinians before he too sought cover, and Carter despatched another. Godfrey himself, Barry's runner and platoon medic, leapt for cover in some wheel ruts. Then he, Carter and Mountford, under covering fire from Sergeant Meredith and Corporal Kinchin's section, managed to rejoin the platoon. Poor Godfrey could not be stopped, but little at the time penetrated. As he finished his tale, Knight appeared, and much later the badly injured Shevill. It was only after nightfall, hours away, that we were able to casevac him.

Meredith had impressively restored control of the situation. Taff had only joined the company after the Kenya exercise, looking a little over-weight from his previous tour away from the battalion. I had harboured some doubts about him. Now this short stocky man was showing me never to judge people on their first appearance. He was 'hell-on wheels', a fear-some scourge of any Argentinians who got in his way.

Over to my left sounds alone told me that the attack on the schoolhouse was under way. Soon flames erupting from the area suggested it was going rather well. What next? I was pushing Meredith to exploit his advantage and advance to the flagpole. They had already tried, Taff explained, but the position was still strongly held. They had also come under fire from Goose Green itself. I was persuaded. We needed to regroup, get orga-nized and take a more considered approach to cracking this last nut.

I got news from Pete that the school had been destroyed, set alight by white phosphorous grenades. The Argentinians had fled into Goose Green, although many were believed to have perished within the building. 11 Platoon had then come under intense fire from the settlement itself, so were withdrawing to rejoin me. Behind, I could see 10 Platoon approaching the bridge on the track where it had all kicked off, followed by the CSM and Company HQ. Some order began to return.

Before I could think how to set about the enemy still ahead of us, Chris Keeble came up on the battalion net. I was not to exploit further as the fog at sea had finally cleared and there was a Harrier air strike in-bound in around 15 minutes. Much encouraged, we settled down to wait for the Royal Air Force to show us how it's done.

Approaching the time-on-target, I heard the roar of approaching jets from the south. All eyes were fixed on the horizon, keen with anticipation. Then we saw it. A long way off and low. This was going to be something. I had once flown as a passenger in a Strikemaster on a live sortie in Dhofar – a vivid experience, but that was over 10 years ago. On it came, seeming to head straight for us. What was the forward air controller up to?

Then I saw the flash of its guns opening up, and the track to our front stitched with a ribbon of cannon fire, its pattern moving inexorably closer and closer. Reality belatedly dawned. This was no Harrier, this was an Argentinian Skyhawk. We all tried to shrink into the tiniest ruts of the hard stony dirt of the track – a perfect aiming mark for the pilot. I cursed my carelessness. The entire company had by now regrouped on the track, presenting a perfect target.

The Toms recovered with impressive speed and in seconds were firing into its path with everything they had. The ground came alive just a couple of feet to my left, so close I felt I had only to stretch out my hand and I would lose it. Then the jet banked away to the west. As it did so, we could see smoke trailing from the rear of its fuselage. A great cheer went up. News later that the Blowpipe team attached to the battalion firing from Darwin Hill also claimed the jet got short shrift. As far as we were concerned, it was our scalp.

Miraculously, no one had been hit. Someone up there was looking after us. We breathed again. Then we heard the sharp whine of more incoming jets. I was shrieking to the Toms to disperse off the track. There was little enthusiasm: there was a minefield on our right, and small arms fire from Goose Green was able to engage the ground to our left. The jets appeared from the north-east, three of them – Harriers. Thank God! We settled down to watch the display. Although it remained in dead ground to us, we saw the flashes as cluster bombs exploded at either end of the settlement. We were on our feet, cheering them on.

Now that I had the whole company to hand, I again turned to working out a plan for the enemy still to our front beyond the flagpole and the exploding ammunition dump. Ozzie's radio crackled: Keeble on the net again. I took the handset from Ozzie. As Keeble began to speak, I heard aircraft again. Shit, now what? I hung up, quickly.

This time a pair of Pucaras approached from the south. One veered off to the west, the other headed straight for us. Again, we poured lead into its path but it flew on and then dropped a canister in the area of the bridge over the inlet behind us, where Nobby and the company aid post had set up shop. A ball of flame erupted. Napalm. Blimey! It all happens at Goose Green. I radioed: '4, this is 49 Alpha. Send sitrep.' With relief, I heard Nobby's voice: 'We're fine' – he even managed to sound slightly bored. Later, I learned from Delaney, our medic, that this was not quite the case: Nobby managed his first crap since coming ashore shortly after. This may also have been because, as darkness fell, Company HQ realized they were in a minefield.

The aircraft wheeled away, also streaming smoke. Another cheer of self-congratulation. Then we saw the pilot eject and descend to earth 300 yards away. A section of 12 Platoon were off like a pack of wolves. Fifteen minutes later they returned, their prisoner unharmed but looking a little green about the gills. His parachute was retained by 12 Platoon, so a couple of Toms at least had a slightly warmer night than their mates. They handed the pilot over to the care of Nobby, his erstwhile target – a denouement I had to smile at.

Back to the battalion net and Chris Keeble once more. 'Go firm, reverse slope to Goose Green in the area where you are,' he said, before adding enigmatically: 'Do not push on. There are other plans in hand.' I had not the faintest idea why we should not exploit, nor what his other plans were, but he was obviously feeling constrained by the fact that there are no secrets on an open insecure radio net. I duly complied.

With these instructions, I suddenly began to feel very tired. I was glad to obey; I was ready for a breather. I did, however, want to get away from our vulnerable position on the track. I got Taff Meredith to recce the situation to our right, where further back, near the bridge, it was mined. Up ahead, just reverse slope, it was clear. We spread out in a defensive position in the peat.

The light was starting to fade, and the odd snowflake began to fall. As we dug out shell-scrapes for meagre protection, some 1,500 yards beyond the settlement a Chinook appeared and landed. Ours, or one of theirs? Reinforcements for us – perhaps the other plans Keeble had referred to – or for the enemy? In truth, I barely cared. B Company was down there somewhere – it was their problem. We were exhausted, hungry and down to our last rounds of ammunition. Had the enemy decided to counter-attack, we had little other than unconsumed rations to throw at them, and our bayonets. However, I felt relaxed. Maybe it was the adrenaline subsiding. Since the RAF firepower demo, the enemy artillery and Triple A fire had ceased. In my gut I felt the day was ours.

As night fell, we were at last able to recover the bodies of Barry, Sullivan and Smith from where they had fallen at the white flag incident to the company aid post and lie them with our other dead and wounded. I did a tour of the platoons and learnt a little of 11 Platoon's battle for the schoolhouse. It appeared to have been a chaotic combined effort by 11 Platoon and C Company's patrols platoon. An assault with WP and HE grenades had set the building on fire, and it quickly burned to a shell. We never knew how many Argentinians burnt with it, but there was still opposition from defenders in the surrounding trenches. Most of these fled along the shoreline towards the settlement as the final attack went in. At that point the enemy guns began to shell the school and surrounding area, and 11 Platoon then came under small arms fire directly from the isthmus on which the settlement sat. They leapt for cover in the deserted trenches, but soon realized they could not stay.

It was now bitterly cold. Poor Chris Waddington, 11 Platoon's fearless leader, was unlucky to discover the trench at the schoolhouse into which he had dived on coming under fire from Goose Green was filled with water. Soaked to the skin from head to toe, he realized he was starting to suffer from hypothermia, its onset speeded by his utter exhaustion. Determined not to become a casualty himself, or even die of cold, as night fell he stole away to swap his upper garments with the dry ones of one of his dead soldiers. Leaving his own smock to cover his comrade, he thanked him quietly for saving his life, and then made his way back to his platoon. Chris spent the rest of the war in a smock still stained with the blood of its original owner. It was a pragmatic decision. Once, in the mountains, I had 'borrowed' a dead man's mittens for a mate whose hands were turning white. Had it been me, I might have gone public, and joked with Nobby whether the new smock was a good fit. However, as a 'boy soldier' newly arrived and still feeling his way, he felt somehow ashamed. It took years before Chris shared this with anyone. Later, as Chris's feet were going dead with cold, his radio operator, Maclean, swapped his still dry socks with his platoon commander's, to help keep him operational.

Under cover of darkness, teams came forward from Darwin Ridge with ammunition resupply. They then evacuated our dead and wounded, after hours on the battlefield, to the regimental aid post.

News also came in of Keeble's plan. Communications had been established with the farm manager in Goose Green, Eric Goss, via Brook Hardcastle, the Falkland Island Company's director in Darwin, now under A Company's control. We learned that the rest of the civilian inhabitants, some 120 all told, were in the community hall, where they had been imprisoned for the previous four weeks. Arrangements had been made to send two prisoners into the settlement bearing an ultimatum for the Argentinian commander. It was blunt, but with help from Robert Fox, our embedded BBC reporter who had spent many years working in Italy and South America, it was designed to appeal to the Latino sense of honour. It could be précised as follows: 'You are surrounded. Our Air Force has already shown what awaits you should you not surrender. In that case, the blood of any civilians will be on your hands – and seen to be in law.' Given the state we were in, this was a weak hand of cards masterfully played. The prisoners returned with a message that the terms were accepted. The Argentinians were to form up on a meadow on the outskirts of the settlement at 09.00 local time for a formal surrender.

I received orders that D Company was to move covertly, an hour beforehand, to a position from where we could dominate the field with our machine guns – but we were to be discreet. At the appointed hour a party of perhaps two hundred Argentinians walked from the settlement and formed up on the field. From side left, Keeble's party of around ten appeared. I could see discussions taking place, agitated gesticulating. We readied ourselves, weapons cocked. Then one of the Argentinians drew a sword and ceremoniously passed it to Keeble. It was like we were in the front seats of the stalls, watching a carefully choreographed scene from an opera.

But where were the rest of them? Two hundred was clearly not the whole garrison. Minutes passed. Keeble seemed relaxed. Then hundreds of soldiers began to pour out of the houses and sheds of the settlement and form up on the field. Probably close to a thousand. Orders were barked, an anthem was sung, weapons were laid on the ground. We looked at each other, mouths agape, unable to believe our eyes at the numbers. Keeble withdrew. We moved forward, to shepherd them away from their weapons and stand guard over them. I wondered briefly what they were thinking, as our little band of ninety, staring-eyed after virtually no sleep for three nights, and doubtless looking like unkempt brigands, took over their future. Were they glad that 'for them, the war was over'? Were they angry when they saw what a small force they had surrendered to? I looked at their faces. I could read little there, not even apprehension – just a blank numbness or maybe a sullen dejection.

C Company moved past us into the settlement to free the locals from the community hall. I watched as two ladies emerged, proffering packets of cigarettes in gratitude, although knowing the reprobates in C Company of old, Pete Adams volunteered these were probably a fee they had charged for unlocking the door. 'Bastards!' we muttered jealously, enjoying the moment.

It was 29 May 1982. The day indeed was finally ours, but what the hell were we going to do with 1,200 prisoners?

Chapter 7

The Battle for Darwin and Goose Green: the Aftermath

The immediate solution to 1,200 prisoners of war was to usher them into the cavernous black corrugated iron sheep-shearing sheds on the outskirts of the settlement. It now being the onset of winter, there was little shearing to be done. On the roof, for the benefit of the Argentinian Air Force, we painted in large white letters: POWs.

At the request of one of their senior officers, we allowed their officers to retain their pistols, fully loaded. In an interesting insight into the nature of the society of the invaders, and the culture of their army, they claimed that they feared for their lives if stuck amongst their soldiers with no weapons for self-defence. The Argentinian dictatorship's 'Dirty War' of repression on its own people had, it seemed, infected the way its army conducted business. My guess is that I was not alone in harbouring a little pity for these poor soldiers who were now our prisoners. Certainly, we treated them with at least a common decency, even a little kindness. I saw them no longer as enemy meriting no quarter, as I had the day before, but more as hapless souls in the wrong place at the wrong time.

I do not think the locals felt inclined to be as generous. While they were incarcerated in the community hall for four weeks, the Argentinians had helped themselves to their houses, where they seemed happy to defecate anywhere. Many houses had been seriously trashed. The locals helped us recover the dead from the battlefield. Ours were flown to Ajax Bay, the logistics area at San Carlos. They buried the Argentinian dead in mass graves just outside the settlement. One I saw was marked with a simple cross made of old planks, on which had been stencilled, with no sentiment, '39 ARGIE BODIES'.

The rightness of our cause had not hitherto been a major factor in our thoughts. Mine were rather that we were professional soldiers as ever clearing up a mess created by politicians, or, as 'H' had put it so succinctly: 'We're doing it for Maggie!' Now, with these insights into the Argentinian army, coupled with the warmth of the Islanders' gratitude for their liberation, I began to think 'doing it for Maggie' was one and the same thing as doing it for the Islanders.

The locals opened their houses to us. By good fortune, my Company HQ of fifteen or so was taken in by Eric Goss, the local farm manager, and his wife Shirley. Good fortune, because Eric was the one person who had not been held in the community hall, the Argentinians considering that they needed one person to deal with on the outside. His house, therefore, had not been trashed. Food was scarce, so we continued to live on 24-hour ration packs. But there was an abundance of peat around – fuel for their cooker and boiler. This meant that we could dispense with our rather pathetic solid fuel stoves, and enjoy a hot meal and a hot drink simultaneously, rather than consecutively. I had a shave, the first in four days, in hot water for the first time since coming ashore. There was a roof over our heads, and there was warmth – from their stove, yes, but much more, from their companionship, their concern, the sharing of their story with ours. We'd by-passed purgatory and gone straight from hell to heaven.

We even had the offer of a hot bath. Some of my crew grabbed this. I declined. I had spent ten days getting acclimatized to the dismal weather and hardened to my sweat, smells and general discomfort. This was not the end, and I knew I did not want to go through that acclimatization again. At the end of some animated debate, with each making their own choice, and amidst banter of who was a wimp and who was anti-social, I sided with the unwashed.

Much as I wanted to in this transitory bliss, I could not escape the fact that although the company had taken everything thrown at it in fine style, we had suffered. In measurable terms, eight dead and four injured, some 13 per cent casualties. There was an anomaly here. Historically, the proportion of casualties is one dead to two wounded; ours was the reverse – two dead to one wounded; and our casualty rate had also been twice that of any of the other companies. Why? It nagged at me. Was this down to me? Had I been careless? One third of the losses – three dead and one wounded – were from the 'white flag' incident with Jim Barry. Gradually I became aware that I was not the only one engaged in these unproductive ruminations.

In simple terms, it was obvious was that if we were to remain operationally effective as a unit, we could not afford to lose many more. Battlefield casualty replacements, or BCRs as they are comfortingly called, were not available at the end of our long and slender lines of communication from the UK. So, when three or four Toms reported sick to the medical officer, Steve Hughes, the day after the surrender, I was alarmed. Sick with what?

If the RMO pulled them out of the line, we might never see them back. Then it occurred to me that what they were really seeking was some sort of reassurance. I didn't want to second guess the Doc, but these young chaps, all aged between 18 and 20, had come through a traumatic experience. They had lost mates, delivered death, been strafed, shelled and walked through minefields – a big call on young men. I ordered that no one was to see the RMO without first seeing the CSM. I trusted Nobby, the thinking man's sergeant major, to deliver the appropriate advice or reassurance – for some an arm round the shoulder, for others perhaps a sharp pencil up their nose. We had only one man see the RMO after that, one of 11 Platoon's section commanders, who was reluctantly packed off to Ajax Bay with pneumonia.

Nevertheless, there was a lot to reflect on, and time for all of us to do so. I worried about the white flag incident, and the deaths of Jim Barry, Sullivan and Smith. Jim would never fulfil his America's Cup dreams now. I had already arranged for Jacko Page to take over 12 Platoon. But it had been an avoidable waste of life. Many were inclined to blame the Argentinians for a breach of trust, or trickery. Maybe, but we'll never know. The Argentinians involved all died in the immediate aftermath, as far as we could establish, and in fairness they would also have been on edge. With machine-gun fire coming into the area, they may well have thought they were victims of a double cross. Some have argued there was genuine confusion, each thinking the other was surrendering, though I find that hard to accept. Others have sought to blame our machine gun platoon and their propensity to engage anything that moved, but they were working with the best of intentions and the battlefield had become intensely fluid and confusing in a very short space of time. I still curse myself for sharing the pros and cons of taking a surrender with Jim at Boca House. He had only taken on board half the lesson, the benefits, but not the other half, the risks. I should perhaps have taken more account of his inexperience, and of his abundant enthusiasm and courage. Or perhaps I had over-played the 'hot pursuit, we've got them on the ropes' message I had sent out. It was, I think, over-enthusiasm that actually did for Jim at the white flag, and that I have always found difficult to fault or regret.

Dixon's death preyed on my mind more than the others, and still does – perhaps because I was so close and the memory is so vivid, but more because of the helplessness those of us nearby felt at our inability to make a difference. Had we been able to get him to the doctor in our RAP, might he have been saved? I was also angry, however – angry at the pitiful mismanagement of our artillery and the farce of counter-battery fire, while suffering casualties like Dixon from the enemy battery. 'H' had made it clear that the guns would be at priority call to the company in contact. Had they been, we might have launched our assault on the school before the enemy guns were directed onto us.

I thought a lot about 'H'. Impossible not to – he was an enigma. Few within the battalion referred to him as 'H', a term of endearment they did not perhaps feel; for most, he was simply the colonel or the CO. A number saw him as a tartar and would go out of their way to avoid him in any coincidental crossing of paths. But no one could ignore him. He was a dominant factor in the life of everyone from private to major to an extent that I have never seen remotely replicated anywhere before or since. His values were crystal clear and respected. His manner, towards anyone, could be endearing one minute, over-bearing, even bullying the next – not I felt by design, but through his impatience to get things done, and perhaps because of an arrogance in his abilities. But that is belied by the almost intimate sharing of his anxieties with Robert Fox that I had overheard in Camilla Creek House. Was his manner a sort of over-compensation for the doubts, insecurities and uncertainties that can beset us all? After all, many have observed that authenticity is vital, but there is also a thespian dimension to leadership. His aggressive mind-set was con-tagious. Equally, most could see that it bordered on a rashness that some-times needed to be questioned and not followed blindly. He lacked guile or circumspection although, as illustrated by his conspiratorial exchange with me before D Company's first engagement early in the battle, he was not inflexible or unimaginative

As to his planning, the only serious criticism that I think holds up is the time and space appreciation. The time allowed to achieve what we had to do before daylight proved hopelessly naïve, but no one challenged it at the time. Perhaps his style and the moment discouraged that, but it's also very easy to be wise in hindsight. I feel we all should bear some responsibility for that critical miscalculation. Some would argue that his deployment of the battalion's long-range direct fire weapons like our GPMG (SF) and Milan anti-tank missiles was flawed; true, but this would have been of little import if the time/space appreciation had been sound, and we had got to the settlements by daybreak. The other limitations, like the limited and inept fire support from the artillery, were frankly largely beyond his control.

On the day, on the ground, however, some aspects of his performance are perhaps open to question. This derives from his becoming too involved in A Company's battle for Darwin Hill. This might have been partly down to misfortune, stuck there with his lead company as the arrival of day-light put a very different complexion on the battlefield. But he became immersed in their battle at a section commander's level, and was probably more hindrance than help. In so doing, he lost perception of the wider battle, much, I must admit, to my own frustration. Perhaps, in the stress of the moment and what he had committed to with only the ambivalent support of the Brigade, he focused too much on what he felt he was best at: getting stuck in and leading from the front. He demanded boldness, aggression and commitment, and died leading by example, demonstrably not asking anyone to do anything that he was not prepared to do himself. The battalion widely respected that; nevertheless, they also asked whether that was what they needed from him. Perversely, perhaps it was, as it rendered the battalion well-prepared for his death, and able to carry on and fulfil his mission without him.

Nevertheless, I can conceive of the battle at Goose Green being fought and won under no other commanding officer that I have known. Nor can I think of any other whom I would rather have had in his stead to commit us to such a task. His ability to instil a faith (that is not too strong a word) in us that we would prevail was remarkable. Had he or we worried that we might fail, I suspect we might have done; but all we thought about, all we could see, was winning – and so we did. If ever there was a man for the moment, 'H' was that man.

Keeble's picking up of the baton, mid-battle, brought with it the real risk of losing momentum, as he was nearly 2 miles behind the action. Normally control should have passed to the battery commander until the second-in-command could get to a position from where he could assert control, but Keeble could not contact him. Very sensibly, therefore, Keeble consciously passed control to John Crosland, who at this point was close to but not immediately engaged in the action. In effect, he also 'freed up' the battlefield by letting those closest to the problems get on with resolving them. It brought some difficulties, for example C Company being caught on a forward slope by Triple A fire and the muddle with them around the schoolhouse. He was also not helped by the gunners, who conspicuously failed to contribute meaningfully. But Keeble was at last able to get close air support from our Harriers, which in turn provided the key to his masterfully executed plan to negotiate a surrender.

With hindsight, it was a serious oversight that the conflict termination aspect of this battle had not been considered at the outset of planning the Goose Green operation, but, given the ambivalence that beset the mission, perhaps it was not surprising. The order from London 'to capture Darwin and Goose Green' came with no limiting direction. No one, until Keeble developed his plan for the surrender, seems to have asked: what would success look like? The mission might have been achieved by comprehensively bombarding the Argentinian garrison into submission. Or it might have been, as 'H's plan envisaged, by fighting through the settlements, a potentially very bloody business. Either would most certainly have involved civilian casualties in possibly significant numbers. Under pressure from the United States for the UK to negotiate with the Argentinians, it could have handed the Junta a monumental propaganda advantage. How about: 'Islanders slaughtered by "rescuing" British?' Militarily, mission accomplished; but would Whitehall have seen that as a success? Keeble not only played his hand well to bring us victory, but his prescience also avoided that victory resulting in outcomes that could have been far from what was required or expected.

Ultimately, however, any glory belongs to our Toms. Through the chaos and the cock-ups, the hardship and exhaustion, the setbacks and the loss of comrades, they kept pushing, pushing, pushing. Such was their aggression, that the Argentinians, questioned after the battle, believed they had been facing a brigade – three times stronger, numerically, than the six hundred who actually defeated them. Robert Fox, the BBC reporter embedded with us, put his finger on it in his despatch after the battle:

> The odd sort of thing I've found about the Paras and they've had a fearsome reputation I know, but amongst the officers and many of the men, I have found some of the most civilised men that I have ever been in a tight corner with in my life. The standard of personal generosity, of kindness, of respect ... strange to say, of respect for human life is of a very very high degree indeed and I think that says a lot for their efficiency. That is why they are such good fighting troops because they're fighting troops who care about each other desperately as individuals.

Meanwhile, there was more to do than just reflect. The settlement itself was a mess. After setting up a skeletal perimeter defence, we were called upon to provide work parties for that most detested of military duties, area cleaning, under the RSM. We could have been back in barracks were it not for discarded Argentinian weapons and ammunition all around. These were collected first for heli-lift to Ajax Bay. Near the sheep-shearing sheds housing the POWs was a huge pile of mixed ammunition simply dumped in a comprehensive mess. There was some concern about how to tackle this. How stable was it? Had it been booby-trapped? The prisoners, so close to it, were also concerned. In their own interests, twenty or so volunteered to help move the ammunition to the outskirts. Two hours into the job there was a massive explosion. It appeared it had indeed been booby-trapped. Half the work party were killed instantly, others injured. As the sound of explosions abated, I heard a single shot. One of our medics reportedly had pulled an Argentinian from the flames but, finding him beyond treatment, had done the only thing possible and put him out of his agony. Area cleaning became a little more circumspect thereafter.

On 1 June we were told that our dead were to be buried at Ajax Bay. Keeble insisted that we would bury our own dead. A Sea King helicopter was tasked, and twenty men, including the most senior members of the battalion, duly emplaned for this. I heartily supported Keeble's position. Only later did the huge risk occur to me. If anything had happened to that helicopter – we had already lost one during the battle to a marauding Pucara – then the battalion would to all intents have been rendered non-operational. Sometimes there is no perfect course of action.

I was not sure what to expect, but was a bit taken aback by what I saw. A huge divot, some 6ft deep at one end and a similar width had been gouged into the peat by a mechanical digger, the soil thrown up to the sides. The machine itself stood a few yards away, the engine still steaming in the cold damp air from its evidently recent efforts. A few yards from the shallow end lay our eighteen dead, eight from my company, but also Dave Wood, 'H's adjutant, and Dair's company 2ic, Chris Dent, both killed on Darwin Hill shortly before 'H' himself. I had liked them both, and of course Dave and I had in common our RAF Regiment background. They were tidily laid out with labels in white body bags. Soldiers from the logistics area were lined up around this mass grave, officers overlooking the deep end. David Cooper started the service. Then, working in teams of six, as David intoned the names in alphabetical order, we felt for the handles thoughtfully designed into the bags, and carried our dead one by one through the mud into this gaping gash in the hillside, laying them crossways, neatly side by side, under a dismal grey sky. We formed up at the mouth. Prayers were said. A bugler thinly played the Last Post, most of the sound whipped away in the biting wind. We saluted and turned towards our waiting helicopter. Behind me, I heard the mechanical digger roar into life. I felt devoid of emotion, empty inside, detached. Another job done. On with the next.

No one said much on the way back to Goose Green. That evening it began to snow, covering the ugly scars of the battlefield and evidence of the settlement's occupation under a thin pristine white cloak.

By now we had become aware of reaction back home to the news of our victory via the BBC on our HF radios, but also from telexes of congratulation received at Brigade. These came from Prince Charles, our Colonel in Chief, the Chief of the General Staff, and many other lesser mortals. I'm not sure we fully believed the view of the CGS that 'the Battalion has executed a feat of arms and gallantry probably unsurpassed in the glorious history of the British Army'. But it was still good to hear it. Whilst gratifying to bask in this glory, it did perhaps distract us from a rigorous analysis of what had gone well, and what could have gone better. Or perhaps the experience was all still too close, too raw to probe the poor performance of our artillery, the parlous time/space appreciation, the poor deployment of our direct fire support weapons, the variable effectiveness of our command and control, the implications of not identifying and maintaining the aim.

The debate as to whether the battle needed to have been fought at all still rumbled on, however, now with the question: precisely what had it achieved? Tactically, whilst Goose Green presented a theoretical threat to the beachhead at San Carlos, in reality the risk was remarkably slim. Julian Thompson's staff were probably right: it could have been masked off and would have avoided the burden on already stretched logistics of 1,200 POWs to be guarded, fed and sheltered. Nevertheless, General Menendez had deployed part of his strategic reserve in a last-ditch attempt to save his garrison from defeat in the final hours of the fighting, only for them to join the garrison in captivity. A marginal benefit. Our victory, together with the arrival of 5 Brigade, did enable the opening of a southern flank approach to Port Stanley, although the wisdom of this has also been widely questioned. In theory, it gave the Argentinians more to worry about. However, 5 Brigade, equipped and deployed primarily for post-conflict garrison duties, lacked its own logistic resources and capability for supporting any operational manoeuvre. 3 Commando Brigade's logistic units were already suffering from lack of heavy helicopter lift caused by the sinking of *Atlantic Conveyor*. With these limitations, the demands of supporting the manoeuvre of two brigades was bound to mean compromise. Concentration of effort is a key principle of warfare, so opening a southern flank undoubtedly diluted 3 Commando Brigade's efforts. Opening the southern flank was probably a zero-sum benefit. The tactical justification for the Goose Green operation remains therefore highly questionable, and Julian Thompson's reluctance to undertake it well judged.

On a strategic level, however, the picture is rather different. In London the view was that with nothing but a string of naval losses since the recapture of South Georgia, public support for the war could start to waver. American pressure for a cease-fire and negotiations was also becoming increasingly acute. Even if negotiations achieved nothing, they would drag subsequent military operations, at the end of an 8,000-mile supply chain, deeper into the hostile southern hemisphere winter. That alone might scupper any chance of victory. The government was thus desperate for a military success, and Goose Green was the only meaningful and feasible prospect. Sometimes tactical priorities and strategic needs do not align, and tactics inevitably must defer to strategy.

We were only vaguely aware of these considerations. There were, however, other important positive but hard to quantify operational outcomes from the battle that we were acutely aware of. First, going on the offensive is always good for morale. The attacker has more of the initiative and control. It is so much more uplifting to be delivering shit than to be receiving it. We'd had enough of defending the beachhead, and for all the nagging fear before battle was joined, we were buzzing at the prospect of getting stuck in. Then, to win against such odds on such a scale was like walking with the Gods. No one could stop us now. We felt that, but so I think did every part of Julian Thompson's army. We had secured moral ascendancy over the enemy. Few conflicts are won by physically destroying the enemy; they're won by destroying his confidence and his will to fight. We felt we had started that job in spades. The battles to come would be that much easier. Of course, that had depended on us actually winning. But that comes back to 'H's clear-sighted philosophy: if we're going down to the isthmus to fight, we fight to win, not to raid, and we have to win at all costs.

I never for a moment thought that we would lose the battle. It was won ugly. We made mistakes. We could have done many things better. However, we ground out the result. Was it, all things considered, worth the cost? Absolutely.

Chapter 8

On to Fitzroy and Bluff Cove

Soon after returning from the burial service, the battalion was told that it was to be transferred from 3 Commando Brigade to 5 Brigade. Back in England, 2 and 3 PARA had been part of 5 Brigade, along with a Gurkha battalion. With both parachute battalions deployed already, 5 Brigade had been reinforced with the Scots Guards and the Welsh Guards. To pluck two battalions off public duties, guarding the Queen and Buckingham Palace in fancy uniforms in London, and send them hurriedly off to war seemed an odd decision. It did, however, mean that the government did not have to breach its NATO obligations in the Cold War by taking troops from Germany. So 5 Brigade was now an ad hoc organization thrown together, but at least capable of garrison duties once the war was won. They travelled south in a manner befitting the Guards on the luxury liner *Queen Elizabeth II*, transferring to *Norland* at South Georgia, on which they arrived in San Carlos Water.

It was clearly something of a culture shock. The Welsh Guards set off to march to Goose Green. It soon became clear, however, that they would never make it, and they were withdrawn back to San Carlos. One company commander was heard to ask: 'What on earth are we doing here?'

Their new brigadier, Tony Wilson, arrived at Goose Green by helicopter. He soon became known as the Man of Many Hats, but he clearly had bolder ambitions than acting as a garrison commander. Our capture of Goose Green had provided him the opportunity. He briefed Chris Keeble on his intention to open up a southern flank on the approach to Stanley. This involved a complex seven-day 3-phase plan to advance the 30 miles to the settlements of Bluff Cove and Fitzroy on foot over desolate bog and ankle-breaking stone runs, prepared for contact with the enemy every step of the way. Given the experience already of one of his battalions trying to march from San Carlos to Goose Green, the plan had only the most tenuous connection with reality. That day Wilson was wearing the green beret of the light infantry.

Keeble, I got the impression, was a little nonplussed. Fortunately, ABI (airborne initiative) was about to come to his rescue. The next day John

Crosland strolled from Goose Green to Darwin to see how his old friend Dair and A Company were doing. They had a chat with Brook Hardcastle, the resident director of the Falkland Islands Company, which then owned almost all the farms on the Islands. Hardcastle informed them that he thought the enemy had pulled out of Bluff Cove and Fitzroy. A call to Ron Binnie, the Fitzroy manager, could confirm this, but unfortunately, his phone line to Fitzroy had been cut. Maybe there was still a link from Swan Inlet, 10 miles to the east, Hardcastle suggested.

John rushed back to Goose Green and gate-crashed a conference at 5 Brigade HQ. Wilson today was sporting the red beret of the Parachute Regiment but, horror of horrors, on his feet were a pair of green wellie boots. No self-respecting Para would ever be seen in such footwear – even though, given the conditions, they were truthfully rather sensible. Undeterred by this vision, John relayed his news, and suggested a quick visit by helicopter to Swan Inlet to make a phone call. Wilson reacted enthusiastically, summoned three light Scout helicopters and warned Chris Keeble to prepare the battalion for a short notice coup-de-main operation. I only learned of all this at Keeble's hastily summoned 'O' Group. It all sounded a little cavalier, but infinitely better than Wilson's original plan. The pace picked up. Our days of relaxation were coming to an end.

An hour later John was on the radio: 'Fleet and Balham clear.' Fleet was where John lived; Balham, as those of a certain age and fans of Peter Sellars may recall, was the 'Gateway to the South'. He had spoken to the Fitzroy manager, Ron Binnie, on the phone. The Argentinians had indeed pulled out of Fitzroy and Bluff Cove. John ended the phone conversation with 'Thanks, Ron. Be with you soon.'

By now, an advance party of Gurkhas had been flown in to take over the defence of Goose Green. The one remaining heavy lift Chinook helicopter that had brought them was commandeered to fly B Company and Chris Keeble's Tac HQ into Fitzroy and A Company into Bluff Cove by nightfall, before returning, low on fuel, to San Carlos. The rest of the battalion would be flown forward the following day.

Early the next morning, 3 June, three Sea King helicopters arrived. On one was Wilson, today sporting a pilot's flying helmet, his wellies a less incongruous mix than the day before. With him was another man – short, slim and older but also wearing a comical hat which looked to me like an Afrika Korps kepi. This turned out to be Major General Jeremy Moore of the Royal Marines, sporting a Norwegian arctic warfare ski cap. He, I was told, was the new Commander Land Forces, or CLF, also arrived aboard the *QE2*, and now the overall commander of both 3 Commando and 5 Brigade.

I made my way with a score of my Toms to the first helicopter, its rotors spinning. I got that distinctive smell of burnt avtur. Ever since lining up to emplane a C130, engines running, for my first parachute exercise, the smell still gives me an adrenaline surge. It did so now; I felt ready for anything.

The roar of the engines and beating rotor blades making conversation impossible, I showed the crewman our destination marked on my map, a low hill 3 miles east of Bluff Cove. The crewman turned away for a quick discussion over his intercom with his pilot in the cockpit. Rumours abounded that it was Prince Andrew. I really have no idea, but whoever he was, it transpired the pilot didn't have maps going that far east. A quick sucking of teeth. Clutching my map firmly to avoid it being whipped away in the rotors' downdraft, I signalled that the pilot could borrow mine, as long as I got it back. Sadly, I lacked the presence of mind to insist that the pilot autograph it before returning it, just in case the rumours had been true. Another lost opportunity, but the pilot not having the right maps had wound me up. I just wanted to get going.

Twenty minutes later we piled out onto our destination, Bluff Cove Rincon, a desolate flat-topped hill, followed in the next hour by the rest of the company. The two settlements were separated by a large inlet but joined by a rough track and a bridge that had been partly demolished by the Argentinians. This was checked for more explosives by our attached troop of Royal Engineers and soon repaired. Overall, it had been an outstandingly successful coup-de-main operation, a great opportunity boldly seized. Launching the southern flank advance to Stanley, whatever its merits, was well and truly under way.

The settlements also provided shelter for the rest of the battalion, at least for those not on-stag. Bluff Cove Rincon lay 3 miles east of Bluff Cove settlement, separated by the cove and a narrow channel of water leading to the open sea, Fitzroy a further 4 miles to the south. We were in the middle of nowhere, completely on our own. Some later claimed the pilot dropped us in the wrong place, so absurd our destination turned out to be, but in fairness it was within 400 yards of the spot I had marked on my map. This small error was just as well, as it was reverse slope and out of sight to the Argentinian positions around Stanley; our eventual position, we were soon to discover, was not.

Some 3 miles to our north was Mount Challenger, which overlooked us. This was still under enemy control, and almost certainly the home of an enemy artillery observation post. Within an hour of getting established on the Rincon, we started to come under periodic harassing fire. The explosions were significantly larger than we had experienced at Goose Green – 155mm medium guns. We started to dig in with a rare enthusiasm, but the ground here was even more sodden than on Sussex Mountain – it was peat igloos or sangars again. This time they went up impressively quickly, and not just because of our increased expertise. The incoming shells, however, were impact fused, so the blessing of occupying a bog was that they were 2–3ft down in the ground by the time they exploded. If anyone had been unlucky enough to get a direct hit on their sangar, it would have spoilt their day but, well spread out as they were, these incoming shells were more like wasps at a picnic – you either give up or learn to live with them. Sadly, here, we did not have the luxury of the first option.

Neither, anyway, was it picnic weather. That night the weather turned. Instead of the four seasons in a day that we had become used to, the rain set in. The water level rose, so that even within our igloos the ground on which we lay was constantly awash. On day two I began to wonder what on earth we were achieving. Keeble's intention had been for us to provide an outer defensive screen for the two settlements, but the cove and the sea provided a natural obstacle to an attack from where we were. The enemy's only option, if they wanted to recover them, would be to advance along the main road from Stanley towards Bluff Cove, and we were too far from that to play any part in preventing any such attack. In any event, the Argentinians' attempt to demolish the bridge between the two settlements suggested they had no intentions of doing so. We were a completely wasted resource, engaged only in a struggle for survival.

There was more discouragement on that first night. To our surprise, we heard aircraft flying overhead in and out of Stanley airfield. It appeared that the TEZ that Britain had declared around the Islands was not as total as we had assumed. The Argentinian Air Force was still in the game. Ozzie spent half the night composing this information into Slidex code for passing over the radio to Battalion HQ. 'Can't be' came the reply, after more laborious decoding by Ozzie; 'it's probably Navy ships out at sea.' As paratroopers, we were familiar enough with the noise of C130 transport aircraft to know at once what they were. An unamused Ozzie got his head down, with nothing to show for his labours. Years later, I was to learn that the Navy in fact sent a frigate close in to try to enforce the exclusion zone more effectively – some other unit must have independently corroborated our report, or maybe someone in Battalion HQ thought twice and decided to pass on the intelligence. At the time it just underlined the pointlessness of our existence on this sodden hill.

On day three I got a call to say that 'Niner' – nine being the call-sign for the CO – was coming to visit. As I heard his helicopter approaching, I left my sangar to greet him, asking Hanley to get a brew on for our guest. We might be on the arsehole of the world, but D Company would still provide due hospitality. The rain had briefly let up a little. Out climbed a man I had never seen before, accompanied by the RSM. He must have seen the puzzlement on my face. Striding towards me, looking fresh and sprightly, he introduced himself: 'I'm David Chaundler, your new CO.' I managed a belated salute, struggling to keep up with the 'changes of the Guard'. New brigadier, and now our third CO in a week. He got quickly down to business. 'What are you doing out here?'

'That's a good question, Colonel,' I replied, and took him briefly through my view of the situation. As we toured the company's sangars, it was clear that Chaundler knew several of my NCOs. I learned that he had previously been a company commander in 2 PARA, and that he had been selected to take over from 'H' in due course. 'H's death had brought forward that event, so he had been flown down to Ascension Island. From there he had hustled a lift on a Hercules C130 transport, was parachuted into the South Atlantic, picked up by a Navy frigate, and dropped off at San Carlos. In between telling of this adventure as if it was just a normal day at the office, the new CO was keen to get across the reaction to the Goose Green battle back home. He even showed us a copy of the headline in *The Sun* that he had brought with him. Despite the dire conditions, he quite cheered us up.

Then came the sucker punch. We needed to get ready for another major battle. Nothing certain, but what he would promise was that if it were to happen, we would be properly supported by abundant artillery support. I interpreted that as 'no more dinosaur jobs'. As he prepared to get back into his light helicopter, he told me: 'You're achieving nothing out here. I'm going to get you back to Fitzroy. Essential, if these chaps are going to be fit to fight again.' Then he was gone. I was encouraged. I'd had enough of strength through gloom.

His visit had created a good first impression. There were a few mutterings among the Toms along the lines of: 'Why us again, haven't we done our bit?' But this was rhetorical. They already knew the answer, but just to be sure, I quoted Carly Simon: 'Because nobody does it better.'

Nevertheless, we were all a little surprised at the change of command. We had assumed that Chris Keeble would remain CO, possibly promoted in the field – a normal practice in time of war. He had certainly met the call when it came at Goose Green and was a known quantity with 3 Commando Brigade. It was never great to change jockeys in mid-race. What it said to me was that the army did not see this as a serious war, just a Navy operation. Keeble had not been listed for promotion or for command. Chaundler had. The HR plan must go on regardless. Even so, we still expected Keeble to remain in command until the battalion returned home, especially given the extraordinary challenge of getting the new CO into theatre. The classic film *Tunes of Glory* suggests, however, the invidious and unenviable situation that Chaundler might have faced, assuming command over Keeble on the battalion's return after a successful campaign under him.

That afternoon Ozzie got a long message in Slidex. After almost an hour of tortuous decoding, we ended up with brief instructions to rendezvous with an LCU that night on the eastern shore of Bluff Cove inlet. It would ferry us the 11-mile sea journey round to Fitzroy. The whole move was to be undertaken by night to avoid tipping off the Argentinian observers on Mount Challenger and to avoid exposing the LCU to risk of air attack. After stand-to that evening, we vacated our sangars, packed up and departed. The rain had returned with a vengeance, the night was as black as pitch. Stumbling the 2 miles through the peat bog to the shore with 100lb each on our backs took us nearly two hours. The LCU was there and waiting. We must have presented a pitiful sight, for as we waded aboard we were greeted by the crew with a tot of Pusser's Rum. A final headcount to ensure we were leaving no one behind, then the engines revved and we backed off from the beach. The 2½-hour trip seemed never ending, as the cold and wet seeped into our bones. Hanley tried to keep our spirits up with an incessant stream of chatter and jokes. I wondered how many swigs of rum he had managed before passing the bottle on.

Reaching Fitzroy in the early hours of the next day, we were led to the settlement's sheep-shearing sheds and shown to a small corner of the massive corrugated iron building. A Company, also pulled back by LCU that night, got there before us. I learned that they had handed over responsibility for the Bluff Cove settlement to the Scots Guards, who had arrived the previous morning. They had endured a horrific journey of ten hours in LCUs, with 'green' – a Marine's term for sea water – constantly washing over the side and drenching all within the open-topped hull. Were we being regrouped together for a purpose? The technical quartermaster's staff revived us with a brew of tea. We crawled thankfully into our soaking sleeping bags to grab a couple of hours' sleep before dawn stand-to.

Stand-to is a time-honoured British Army tradition dating back to Wellington. The most probable time for an enemy to attack was at first light or last light, according to centuries of evidence. Therefore all positions are manned and ready from 15 minutes before to 15 minutes after first light. Then admin can be undertaken, such as getting a brew. Similarly, all admin and feeding should be completed 15 minutes before last light in the evening, before stand-to until 15 minutes after last light. Then, those not on-stag could get their heads down – brewing up being forbidden to avoid the risk of give-away light.

Of course, in the position we were now, there was no risk of attack by enemy troops at first light. Neither, with the limited night capability of the Argentinian Air Force, was there any likelihood of attack from the air at that time. Nevertheless, it is considered good for the soul and discipline to adhere to such routines, regardless. So, we duly piled out of our green maggots and deployed outside the sheds ready to repel the Argentinian hordes or, maybe, an enemy Pucara. It was not such a hardship compared to being inside a sheep-shearing shed if an aircraft dropped its load upon it. Sometimes the old ways are the best ways.

Stand-to that morning, 6 June, proved uneventful. It had even stopped raining. No need to bother with a brew, we were now on 'central feeding', the battalion's cooks having set up a field kitchen in one of the outbuildings. We set to work in drying out all our kit – a refreshingly simple task in brighter skies and the ever-present Falklands wind. In the meadows around the settlement, devoid of babies' heads, even our boots began to dry and our feet to recover. Mishaps still continued to stalk us, however. That afternoon, while cleaning their weapons, one of my FOO's signallers accidentally fired his SMG, wounding the FOO's assistant. The signaller was duly charged under the 'catch-all' section 69 of the Army Act for conduct prejudicial to good order and military discipline in that he *negligently* discharged his weapon. The army has always refused to acknowledge that such errors are accidental. It was a pretty academic exercise in the circumstances, as punishment could only be a few extra sentry duties. My bigger concern was that not only was my FOO not trained for the job, but he now no longer had an assistant to help him. My faith in our artillery support dwindled further.

The next day, the weather continued to be kind. The Argentinian Air Force began to get busy again, and we had several Air Raid Warnings 'Red'. This meant bursting out of the sheep-shearing sheds to pre-allocated positions, putting some distance between ourselves and the most obvious targets – and standing by to put up a wall of small arms fire for the enemy pilots to fly through. All we saw, however, were friendly Sea Harriers overhead, their patrols seemingly deterring the Argentinians. A Rapier air defence battery had been lifted by helicopter onto Fitzroy Hill to the north, but as yet their missile launchers were still not operational.

5 Brigade's headquarters had also been flown into Fitzroy. At that evening's briefing the CO told us of their early plans for the battle for Port Stanley. 3 Commando Brigade would attack the northern hills protecting the capital, Mounts Harriet, Two Sisters, Longdon and Wireless Ridge; 5 Brigade would follow up with the Scots Guards and Welsh Guards taking Mount William and Tumbledown. 2 PARA would be the 5 Brigade reserve, prepared to exploit on to Sapper Hill, just south-west of Stanley.

In the early hours of the next day two Royal Fleet Auxiliary ships, *Sir Tristram* and *Sir Galahad* appeared offshore in Port Pleasant water. These 'Landing Ships Logistic' (LSLs) had sailed from San Carlos south around East Falkland, bringing forward the Welsh Guards and much-needed combat supplies – rations and ammunition. Also on board was 16 Field Ambulance comprising the brigade's field surgical teams.

The Royal Marine LCUs immediately got busy, but to our surprise there was no sign of troops coming ashore, just loads of supplies. This made little sense. The ships were extremely vulnerable, and in full view of the Argentinian OP on Mount Challenger that had previously bothered us on Bluff Cove Rincon. I envisaged the uproar that 'H' would now be making if priority was being given to off-loading supplies ahead of his precious battalion. It was a calm clear almost balmy day, the sunshine glinting dazzlingly off the sea, as we watched what was going on a short way offshore.

In the early afternoon over our radios came another Air Raid Warning Red. Rushing to our designated positions, we heard jets approaching from the south-west, and then four Skyhawks appeared flying low, heading straight for us. A deafening cacophony engulfed the settlement as the battalion's sixty machine guns opened up. The rest of us tried to lose ourselves in the dirt. We prepared ourselves for grief. The aircraft scorched overhead, seemingly undeterred by the hail of lead that we put in their path. A Blowpipe missile careered around hopelessly before disappearing uselessly behind a hill. Nothing at all from the Rapier battery.

No grief descended. We were not their intended target. They flew north-east before taking a sweeping turn to their right. A minute later they were heading back, now going straight for the two ships, perhaps a kilometre out to sea. Massive explosions and two palls of black smoke told of direct hits on both. The aircraft were gone.

Soon we could see that at least one ship had managed to launch some lifeboats and rafts, although the rafts seemed to be struggling to get clear of the blazing hulls. Then, Sea King helicopters appeared. Spellbound, we watched as some appeared to be trying to blow the rafts away from the flames using the downdraught of their rotors. Others were busy winching survivors from the icy waters. Lifeboats started to reach the shore. We gathered on the beach and jetty to help their pitiful occupants to dry land, many of the Toms wading out up to their chests to support the most hideously burnt.

Steve Hughes, David Cooper and our RAP team bore the brunt of the moment, triaging the survivors, providing first-line treatment and organizing casevac to the field hospital at Ajax Bay. The scale and suddenness of this disaster was something impossible to train for. The speed and efficiency with which they brought some order to the chaos, treatment for the most seriously injured, and succour and comfort to the traumatized was simply inspiring. I was a mere bystander seeing these heroes at work. But in whatever lay ahead, if the worst should happen to me, I'm sure I was far from alone in taking comfort from what we witnessed, knowing I would be in the best of hands. While putting on an appearance of being ready for anything, that thespian element to leadership, I, like most I am sure, was not really jumping for joy at the prospect of another battle; I needed all the encouragement I could find.

Those Welsh Guardsmen who were not injured but were doubtless in shock were farmed out to the companies in the sheep-shearing sheds until they could, in one way or another, be taken care of. It took me back fifteen years to the day that I helped rescue a climber, Tony Toole, who had fallen 80ft from a climb in the Lake District called Dovedale Grooves. I and my mate, another Tony, had gone up to attempt the same route. Toole had been belayed to an old steel piton hammered into the rocks, feeding rope out to his partner who was leading. His partner had fallen, and, as he tried to check the fall, the impact had pulled Toole and the old piton to which he was tied from the rock. Toole joined his partner accelerating at 32ft per second per second onto the scree below. His partner, amazingly with just a broken wrist, we had met on his way down to get help. Toole, however, lay alive but badly broken. The piton, in which he had placed too much faith, was still clipped to him alongside. Some of his mates appeared. 'Tony, you won't be needing this any more,' they chuckled, like vultures, stripping him of all his climbing gear for themselves, before joining us in carrying him down to a waiting ambulance.

It was déjà vu. We looked at these poor guardsmen. We looked at their pristine boots. We looked at ours, near to falling off our feet. 'Taffy, you won't be needing these anymore.' Numerous boots changed feet, their original owners too traumatized to protest. Some might deduce that 'war brutalizes.' My view, that evening, was 'pragmatism rules. They'd failed the course, we had to pick up where they had failed.' In truth, we were desperately searching for the bravado to take us forward from this sobering event.

Disasters on this scale invariably need a scapegoat. The Man of Many Hats, Brigadier Tony Wilson, Commander of 5 Brigade, drew the short straw. The concept of the operation to exploit 2 PARA's successful coup de main was his. Certainly it was risky but boldness has its place, even if perhaps driven by an element of vanity. Something of a laughing-stock though he was, and inept though his headquarters were proving to be, to dump all the blame on him, however, has always struck me as rather harsh. Surely it could not have taken place without the support of the COMAW, the overall commander of the two ships, or indeed of the CLF, Jeremy Moore. The fact is many mishaps beset the operation which led step by step inexorably to disaster. The two LSLs were late loading their cargoes. The five-hour delay made it impossible to complete their tasks and return to San Carlos under cover of darkness. The option of transferring at least the Welsh Guards into LCUs halfway round East Falkland, as was done with the Scots Guards three nights previously, seems to have been rejected after their appalling 10 hours in open boats before arriving at Bluff Cove. It had arguably rendered them non-operational for at least 24 hours. In any event, that had been attempted the previous night, but the rendezvous at sea with the LCUs had failed.

The Masters of the two ships must have been aware of the risks they were taking. Perhaps they were unaware that the Argentinians had eyes-on from Mount Challenger. They may have reasoned that there was a Rapier battery already ashore to provide air defence, unaware that it was still non-operational. Perhaps they assumed that CAP from the aircraft would justify the risk. But there was no CAP in the area, apparently lured elsewhere by a carefully planned diversionary raid by other Argentinian aircraft. Maybe, also, a degree of complacency had crept in – no enemy aircraft had been active for several days during the bad weather. Or, maybe, after a couple of false starts to the move, an element of desperation had corrupted the calculation of risk.

It still begs the question, why had priority not been given to getting troops ashore before stores? Ewen Southby-Tailyour, the major in charge of the LCUs, reportedly beseeched the two Welsh Guards company commanders to let him get their men off first. Their orders were that their destination was Bluff Cove. They were unaware that the ships had been diverted to Fitzroy to try to make up at least two of the five delayed hours. They refused to disembark until their orders were countermanded by their superiors. The comfort of the ship, in comparison to marching the 6 miles from Fitzroy to Bluff Cove, might also have seemed attractive. They, so far, had not witnessed the capability and determination of the Argentinian pilots to inflict terrible damage to those afloat. Their CO and brigade commander, ashore at Brigade HQ, meanwhile remained blissfully unaware of the situation.

The disaster was a result of misjudgement on the part of many, compounded by poor communications and some misfortune. Meanwhile, in the Argentinian pilots they faced an enemy of determination and guile, still ready to stick a spoke in our plans. As we tried, that night, to make sense of what had happened, we were largely unaware of all this. What we did know was that we would not still have been sitting on those ships. Indeed, a dozen of our HQ Company with the battalion's first-line logistics echelon had bulldozed their way on board the first LCU that arrived to unload the *Sir Tristram*. Forty-eight lives and more than a hundred wounded – many with life-changing burns – might have been spared, and the Welsh Guards would still have been an operational unit, even if the ships and their crews might still have perished.

Behind every cloud, however, there is a silver lining. With the Welsh Guards now largely out of the game, it became necessary to reappraise 5 Brigade's capability, and the part they were to play in the final push on Stanley. The momentum was with 3 Commando Brigade, and greater emphasis was now placed on the northern thrust. As a result, on 10 June we received the news that 2 PARA was to switch from the hapless 5 Brigade back to 3 Commando Brigade as the brigade reserve. This was welcome news. Marines, we may have considered a little ponderous by airborne standards, but we respected Julian Thompson and his Brigade HQ as thoroughly professional. There was another unspoken reason why morale rose. Even though we had been designated 5 Brigade's reserve, given what we had seen we had become convinced that we would end up coming to the rescue and bearing the brunt of their operation. With the Commandos and 3 PARA, there seemed every reason to hope that the reserve might not be needed. After Goose Green there was undeniably a feeling that we had done our share and more; we had no burning desire to stretch our necks again.

Chapter 9

The Battle for Wireless Ridge

'Going into battle a second time is like someone who has just had a severe electric shock being invited to stick his fingers back into the socket and to flick the switch again.' [Padre David Cooper]

On 10 June the CO flew up to 3 Brigade's HQ, on the flanks of Mount Kent, where he learnt that its attacks on Mounts Harriet, Two Sisters and Longdon were to commence the following night. 2 PARA were to 'yomp' from Fitzroy to concentrate at Bluff Cove Peak, just to the west of Mount Kent, by last light and stand-by for further orders. This was over 12 miles. Chaundler politely pointed out that only Marines yomped, and Paras tabbed, explaining that TAB stood for tactical approach to battle. More seriously, he protested that there was no way he could do that and have his battalion in a condition to fight by the evening of 11 June. Maybe Thompson was engaged in a quiet wind-up, as he immediately relented, and four Sea King helicopters were quickly found to lift the battalion and its first-line equipment the following afternoon.

By now there was in Fitzroy a troop of CVR(T) from the Blues and Royals, comprising two Scorpions, each with a 76mm gun, and two Scimitars, each with an automatic 30mm cannon. All were also mounted with GPMGS. Under Captain the Honourable Robin Innes-Ker, they had driven over from San Carlos and were desperate to get into the action. Chaundler well understood the difference these vehicles could have made at Goose Green. He invited Robin to join us, provided he could drive over the bridge to Bluff Cove, and then on to Bluff Cove Peak. Besides, the Household Cavalry would surely bring a touch of class to the Battalion Group. The offer was accepted.

The next day, after we made preparations for the move, our cooks served up lunch. This was to be our last meal before we went back to 24-hour arctic ration packs. To mark the occasion, Ron Binnie, the farm manager, had thoughtfully donated several of his sheep to the 'airborne stew' – a staple diet of airborne forces whose ingredients could be anything, availability of resources being the determining factor. The helicopter lift went smoothly. We spread out in company leaguers and erected bashas. These were generally two-man shelters, one soldier's Australian lightweight jungle warfare poncho serving as a groundsheet, the other's as overhead protection from the weather. In such snug shelter most crawled into their green maggots and tried to sleep. A busy night lay ahead.

Late in the afternoon the CO called a brief 'O' Group. We were to move off in a little over three hours. It was thought 3 PARA had the toughest objective: the capture of Mount Longdon. Our likely task was to reinforce them, or to exploit past them towards Wireless Ridge; less likely, we could divert south to support 45 Commando on Two Sisters. We were to head round the northern flanks of Mount Kent to Murrell Bridge and hold until our task could be confirmed. This was about 6 miles, the last 4 miles along the track connecting Estancia House and Port Stanley. We were to move on light scales, our bergens to be stashed on our present position. B Company would lead the move and D Company was, predictably, to bring up the rear.

We had, however, something far worse to contend with than the forthcoming stop-start frustrations at the end of the battalion 'snake'. A dozen or so of the company, including myself, were starting to suffer from severe squids. After two weeks of living on the dehydrated food of arctic ration packs, the diet of tinned food prepared by the cooks had been a little testing for our digestive system, but Ron Binnie's sheep were proving the final straw.

Two hours after last light we were formed up, ready to move. Ensuring that all 600 men got to the right place at the right time, in the dark and on radio silence, was a tortuous but much practised procedure, involving the extensive use of 'Easco lights'. These were battery-powered low-wattage lights that we clipped to our smocks if parachuting at night. If you were injured after hitting the ground, you turned it on by removing one of the jacks from its dead socket and inserting it into a live one, so that the medics could find you. If you were unconscious, you hoped someone landing nearby would see and turn your light on for you – otherwise you were running out of chips. Their more widely used application was as reading lamps under bashas in the field when 'light discipline' allowed or was covertly being ignored.

Little information percolated to the end of the snake – we were on radio silence. Hoping we would have enough time before the man ahead disappeared into the night, indicating that we were on the move, I stepped out of line, along with several others, and lowered my trousers for a quick prophylactic dump. It did not help that the toilet paper in composite ration packs, or 'compo', was that old-fashioned crisp non-absorbent stuff. God, I was not looking forward to this tab.

Slowly the snake, in fits and starts, began to move. It was a clear night and fiercely cold, so I had my arctic quilted jacket on. By the time we joined the Estancia–Stanley track, I was sweating freely. The snake stopped, whispered word came down of a 10-minute break. The ground was glistening with a thick layer of frost. Once again, I felt compelled to step out of line and drop my trousers. To perform satisfactorily, I found I had to get my webbing off with its 60lb of ammunition, rations and water – further adding to the effort. Ahead, to judge from the numerous twin mounds, those parts of the body that camouflage cream rarely reaches, glistening under the moonlight, every other man seemed to be doing the same. The affliction, quickly named 'Galtieri's Revenge' after the head of the Argentinian junta, threatened more harm to us than his armed forces. What a state in which to do battle. Like going on a date, you want to feel and look your best at such moments. Instead, I had visions of the medics, should they have to pick me up and seeing me in soiled underpants, laughing: 'Looks like you were shit-scared, Sir!' Why the hell hadn't we just stayed on the 24-hour rat packs? I cursed Ron Binnie's generosity. The Falkland sheep were known to be riddled with liver fluke. The 'airborne stew' was now referred to as 'liver fluke stew'. In the end, I had to laugh.

By the time we set off again the battles to our east had been joined. The sky ahead was lit up by flashes of exploding shells, the dull crump of explosions following, with a mix of star-shells. A compass was becoming superfluous – head towards the sound of the guns. The track proved more in the imagination as we had to negotiate two of the large ankle-threatening stone-runs that punctuate the normal peat-bog Falkland landscape. Heavily laden, my radio headset over my ears, weapon in one gloved hand, and tottering drunkenly from one slippery boulder to the next in the dark was more punishing than anything dreamed up on P Company selection.

We reached Murrell Bridge. A long stop followed. Eventually whispers came down the snake: 'Minefield ahead.' Fifteen minutes later more whispers: 'Waiting for orders from Brigade.' But what about the bloody minefield? I no longer cared. The sweat under my quilted jacket felt like it was turning to ice. I was desperate to get moving.

Dawn was approaching when we finally received word from Brigade that we were to move up to the north-west of Mount Longdon. This meant leaving the track and passing left of the minefield. With daylight, we heard that all that night's objectives were now in friendly hands, but we now began to be harassed by enemy artillery fire. John Crosland, leading the snake, reasoned this had to be registered defensive fire (DF) targets, and skilfully gave these areas a wide berth, leaving us largely untroubled, although at the cost of some extra distance. It was a bright dry day, my bowels seemed to be settling, my spirits were rising. Life at the end of the snake also improved, with daylight enabling us to see what was going on and anticipate the constant stopping and starting. Even the news that we might be attacking Wireless Ridge that night helped, bringing some relief to our burden of uncertainty. We tabbed on.

We reached Furze Bush Pass, in the lee of Mount Longdon, which John reckoned would provide a measure of protection from the enemy artillery. The CO agreed that it was an ideal lying up position for whatever awaited us. We dispersed in all-round defence, dug shell-scrapes and offered thanks for the end of a long night, although it was by now after midday.

We were roused from our torpor by the arrival of a light helicopter. Out of it leapt Hector Gullan, a Para serving a tour attached to 3 Commando Brigade. He also had a pedigree at least as long as John's in the Dhofar War, which is where I had first come across him. He had been Julian Thompson's liaison officer with us during Goose Green. He waved a map above his head. 'Wireless Ridge tonight, chaps.'

I can't say I felt the same thrill that he exhibited. We had no idea at this point what Wireless Ridge entailed – ground, enemy. I hadn't yet even found the right map sheet. Although the CVR(T)s were with us, our 81mm mortars, Milans, GPMGs (SF) and their ammunition were still back at the previous day's landing zone on Bluff Cove Peak, requiring heli-lift forward. There was a lot to do in the four remaining hours of daylight. Chaundler got busy planning, while Keeble and the Tech QM chased the heli-lift for our support weapons.

Later that afternoon Chaundler held his 'O' Group for the attack. The information was worryingly sparse. Before the CO could get into the detail, Hector Gullan, listening in to the brigade net, interrupted the proceedings. The attack was to be delayed by 24 hours. 5 Brigade had just advised that the Scots Guards would not be ready to attack Mount Tumbledown until the following night. Tumbledown, about 1,500 yards further south, was higher than Wireless Ridge and totally dominated it. To hold it, with Tumbledown still in enemy hands, could be very costly. Indeed, the news was a blessing because it was hard to see how we also could be ready in the time left. Moreover, as was later to emerge, many of the reported dispositions of even friendly forces, let alone enemy, proved to be woefully misleading. The makings of a potential cock-up were thankfully avoided by the Scots Guards. We, however, were in the nice position of smugly allowing responsibility for the delay to rest squarely with them and 5 Brigade. The CO pragmatically dismissed his 'O' Group until the next day.

There is always a downside to such good fortune: we would have to weather another night in the open on light scales with no sleeping bags. As we got further into winter, it was getting colder by the night. Few slept. Most of us counted down the hours until daylight, some even volunteering for an extra stag on sentry duty rather than dozing off and turning into ice. I couldn't quite bring myself to hug Hanley for warmth that night, but we still had a pretty cosy arrangement.

Stand-to that clear morning of 13 June was for once welcomed as men got moving into their defensive positions, some even engaging in doubling on the spot and other physical training to bring life to frozen limbs. The 30 minutes to stand-down crawled by, filled with visions of the hot brew to follow.

Mid-morning, the 'O' Group reconvened. Intelligence now confirmed that we faced the Argentinian 7th Regiment, reportedly manned principally with regulars rather than conscripts, and comprising four companies and various attachments. The main ridgeline immediately north of Moody Brook and Stanley Harbour was thought to be defended by at least two companies. Beyond, in the area of Moody Brook, was believed to be a squadron of Panhard armoured cars. On the racecourse just west of Stanley was a battery of the now respected Triple A anti-aircraft guns, probably just within range of the main ridgeline. On a broad squat hill north of the main ridge was thought to be the regiment's headquarters, another company, and other supporting troops.

Chaundler kept to his first plan for an initially silent attack from the north starting from the area of the Murrell river. However, A Company would now lead and seize this position, which was defined by a 250ft contour. It would be supported by direct fire from 3 PARA's C Company, on a hill half a mile to the west. B and D Companies would then move forward to attack the main ridge, B taking the western part, D the eastern. Arrangements had now been made to helicopter forward all the battalion's support weapons from Bluff Cove Peak over the course of the day. We had also been allocated not one but two batteries of guns, and 3 PARA's 81mm mortars in addition to our own. Also, of course, we had the four CVR(T)s to shoot us into our respective objectives. Their second-generation night-viewing aids would make them especially valuable for pinpointing and neutralizing stubborn points of resistance. The plan now felt more robust than it had done the previous night. As a final bonus, two light Scout helicopters had been allocated to take the CO, the battery commander and the three rifle company commanders to the top of Mount Longdon, to view the ground over which we would fight.

While waiting for our helicopter, I prepared and gave my orders to my Company 'O' Group – comprising the company 2iC, platoon commanders, FOO, MFC, CSM, signaller. They seemed a little quiet and reflective, memories of the Goose Green neck-stretch dampening their mood perhaps. As I described how the CO was at least delivering on his promise with details of the fire support we would have, spirits appeared to lift a little, but still it felt a sombre occasion. I got to the end and asked if there were any questions. By now, a pattern had been established. No 'O' Group ever seemed to finish without at least one question from the ever or over-eager Chris Waddington. This time, a worrying silence. I began to wrap up with some final words of encouragement, but Nobby interrupted. 'Hold on a minute, Sir. We haven't had Mr Waddington's question yet.' Chris blushed. No question, but much laughter all round. The tension was broken, nerves calmed. They dispersed, appearing ready for anything; I felt that there was no one I would rather have in their places.

It was mid-afternoon before a Scout arrived to lift John, Dair and myself up to Mount Longdon. The CO met us at the landing site and led us up to the 'anchor OP', so called because the naval gunfire observer (NGFO), Willy McCracken, manning this static observation post, would be helping control our indirect fire support throughout the battle, while our own FOOs would be moving with us. Chaundler bounded ahead, like a spring chicken, with John wondering what the CO had had for breakfast as we struggled to keep up. Our additional two weeks of privation was taking its toll, I reasoned. Examining the forthcoming battleground, the CO and the battery commander had already agreed key objectives and other artillery targets that Willy would register and adjust fire on before the battle began. Willy had also confirmed that he would have the 4.5in gun of HMS *Ambuscade* available for the battle. We had already been impressed by HMS *Arrow*'s gun at Goose Green. Until it jammed, it had proved to be hugely more effective and accurate than the army's 105mm pack howitzers. Assuming the gun remained trouble free, we now had around three times the indirect fire support than on the previous evening.

Our deliberations were suddenly interrupted by the appearance of six Argentinian Skyhawks below us, flying westward down the valley of the river Murrell, towards Mount Kent. Their targets were obvious: Brigade HQ and the gun-lines nearby. Our machine gun platoon, still waiting to be flown forward, claimed the scalp of one aircraft as it flew away trailing smoke. However, it proved a nil-all encounter: no damage was inflicted by the jets and no aircraft crashed. Once the excitement died down, the CO and the battery commander were plucked away for further discussions about our plans with the brigadier. John, Dair and I continued to inspect the ground and our forthcoming objectives.

I was challenging Willy as to why he had called me Nigel. I already knew the answer, as my identical twin was also a gunner who had served with Commandos, but I was enjoying winding him up by playing 'confused from Aldershot'. Interrupting this silliness, Dair then got our serious attention. Pointing to a knoll below, he declared: 'Look at those, they're not 3 PARA.' He was pointing to the position that we had been told was occupied by 3 PARA's C Company, who were supposed to provide fire support to Dair as A Company attacked the first objective. The lack of field discipline was the give-away: no sentries, weapons lying around, helmets discarded. Where C Company should have been, there was in fact an Argentinian company.

Quite how such an error occurred we never discovered, but it now required a fundamental change to our plans. However, the CO was gone and could not be raised, presumably locked in deep discussion on plans with 3 Brigade that were now academic. While waiting for our helicopter to take us back to the battalion, John, Dair and I reviewed the options. 'Welcome back to the confusion of war,' I thought, with memories flashing through my mind of the friendly air strike on Goose Green that was so unexpectedly pre-empted by an enemy Skyhawk attack. It was John who came up with a 'make-and-mend' plan which not only addressed the need to take care of this 'new' enemy position, but also exploited the increased scope for manoeuvre on our right that this discovery now gave us.

Shortly before nightfall, after losing his helicopter to a casevac mission, the CO managed to get back to his battalion. John gave him our news. All the battle procedure had meanwhile been completed, the support weapons were in position and the anchor OP had been busy adjusting the artillery targets, but the plan of manoeuvre needed a radical overhaul. Considering this was the third plan he had had to develop, the CO took it remarkably calmly. 'Go away and have your suppers. Come back in forty-five minutes, and you'll have a new set of orders.'

Time was now the enemy. When I got back to the company, Hanley kept me supplied with tea, while I quickly cooked a freeze-dried compo stew of meat and veg. At the same time I held a Company 'O' Group, to tell them about the discoveries from our recce, and that we now also had a ship's gun in support. The more I could tell them now, the less time we would need when the new plan was divulged.

Back at battalion HQ, it quickly became clear that the CO had bought into the Crosland concept, but with a few other changes to take into account the latest facts. The first was that enemy troops had been reported near the head of Hearnden Water, to the east of the enemy regimental headquarters. The second was that the SAS were undertaking an operation in the area of Cortley Hill, some 1.5 miles further east along the main ridge, so we were not to exploit beyond a line of telegraph wires running north from Moody Brook Camp. The third was that, after seeing the ground and holding discussions with anchor OP Willy McCracken, the CO had decided that, with this weight of fire support, the attack would go 'noisy' from the outset. It was obvious that little element of surprise would be achieved by a 'silent' start. The enemy knew we were coming, but surprise could now be achieved by exploiting our increased scope for manoeuvre; better by far to make sure that all their positions had been adjusted by our artillery, harassed until the battle began and, with the fire support now available, their positions saturated with high explosive before each position was assaulted. Away with stealth and subtlety, we were now to play to our strength: an overwhelming weight of firepower to break the enemy's will before we closed.

As to manoeuvre, the plan was much as John Crosland had suggested to Dair and I on Mount Longdon. For once, D Company was to kick off the action in phase 1 by taking the newly identified enemy position that was previously thought to be occupied by C Company 3 PARA. No explanation or assurance on this confusion had been forthcoming, but by now the location had been adjusted by our artillery, with no objections from 3 PARA. This objective was to be known as *Rough Diamond* (see map, p. 113). Some wag interjected that D Company was the rough diamond, but for once I was too focused on what lay ahead to play their game. A and B Companies, in phase 2, were then to take out the large enemy position with the suspected regimental headquarters on the squat hill to the east, nicknamed *Apple Tart*. C Company, in phase 3, were to sort out any enemy on the Northern Spur near Hearnden Water. In phase 4 D Company was to sweep round to roll up the enemy on the mile or so of final ridgeline, from west to east. A shallow col, over which ran the Estancia–Stanley track, divided this ridge at the halfway point. The western half was named *Blueberry Pie* and the final objective *Dirty Dozen* – cue for more comments about D Company. The troop of CVR(T)s were to join the

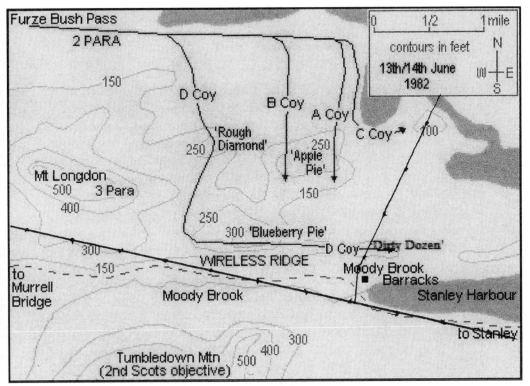

2 PARA manoeuvres at the Battle for Wireless Ridge.

radio net of the assaulting company for each phase, to provide it direct fire support from the flank – known as enfilade fire.

My biggest concern was the limit of exploitation (LOE) imposed on us – the telegraph wires running north from Moody Brook. There was a lot of ridgeline beyond, on which, from Longdon, we had seen enemy soldiers, but we knew nothing about SAS plans in the area. My other unease concerned what was beyond the ridge. I fully agreed with the instruction not to exploit south of the ridge into a potential hornet's nest in Moody Brook, and on to ground dominated from Tumbledown, but until it fell, any amount of mischief could come from there. It was more a matter of faith that it would have fallen to the Scots Guards by the time we secured the ridge.

Nevertheless, it was an elegant solution to the confusion inflicted on the CO's earlier plans, building on the preparation that had already been done, while exploiting the additional firepower and room for manoeuvre. The 'O' Group was wrapped up within half an hour. I had the same amount of time to brief my platoon commanders before we had to move out at last light. By now we were all becoming rather adept at coping with uncertainty and sudden change, and were light on our feet. We had 4 hours left to cover the 3 miles and be ready to cross the start line.

Learning from the events at Goose Green, the CO had allowed a full further 10 hours of darkness from H Hour to achieve our objectives.

D Company was in unusual territory – we were in at the deep end, rather than rescuing others from it as the battalion reserve, then with the lion's share of the rest of the battle to follow. Anticipating the unspoken question – why us?, I felt a little encouragement was called for. I finished the briefing by again quoting Carly Simon, this time in respect of D Company in relation to the rest of the battalion: 'because nobody does it better!'

As we set off, on time, eastwards towards our start line, the moon was out and the wind was whipping up scurries of snow. I fancied for a moment I was Doctor Zhivago, until, heavily laden, I stumbled, cursing, as we got among the peat 'babies' heads'.

A little before H Hour we had shaken out into assault formation on our start line, with 11 Platoon as left forward and 10 as right forward, and 12 Platoon behind in reserve. Conscious of the role that normally befell D Company, I made a point of ringing the changes amongst the platoons, but it was 12 Platoon's turn in reserve. The CO came up on the battalion net. I expected the word to go. The Blues and Royals were already on my company net. Their principal task was to keep an eye on the *Apple Tart* position with their good night-sights and protect my left flank from any interference from there. Instead, the CO spoke to John Crosland, still heading to B Company's start line. 'Stay where you are. There's something we need to discuss.'

'Now what?' I thought. 'Surely not another postponement!' Each delay allowed more time for nerves to gnaw away like rats at our intestines. Time for a last covert cigarette. Hanley, as ever, fulfilled his most important responsibility without prompting. I heard someone muttering: 'No prisoners!' I paid no heed – some poor soul desperately trying to stop his courage seeping away. In 11 Platoon the younger Toms naturally looked to the rock-like Tom Harley: 'Are you scared, Corporal?' 'Of course I'm scared,' came his reply, 'now get ready to move.' With the young Tom reassured to find himself in such august company, I gave the hand signal to fix bayonets, passed on, in the moonlight, along the line.

The cause for the delay, I later discovered, was the arrival of a captured Argentinian map showing a minefield between B Company's start line and their objective in phase 2. John laconically dismissed the news: it was too late to worry about such detail. Come the time, they set off but encountered no mines. Perhaps, like 'JC', John Crosland's whole company walked on water.

After 15 minutes I got word from the CO to crack on. I repeated the order over my company net. The FOO called up thirty rounds 'fire for effect' on *Rough Diamond* from each of the six guns: 180 rounds of airburst high explosive on the objective, a little under 800 yards to our front. Our second battery repeated the exercise on *Apple Tart*. That should discourage any interference in our attack from there.

With the fire mission complete, we were still over 400 yards from the objective. I took a calculated risk and told the FOO: 'Add 100 [yards], repeat.' We now had a spectacular view of the artillery appearing to remove the enemy position from the map. We adjusted our rate of advance accordingly. This had its challenges as the ground was littered with small ponds which in the snow and the dark were easy to miss. Creaney in 11 Platoon and Fergusson in 10 both took involuntary baths. The artillery fire lifted and we readied ourselves for the inevitable fusillade of tracer coming at us – every round with a name on it. But there was little more than a few desultory shots. The two leading platoons poured fire ahead of them and, as they got into the enemy sangars, all resistance ceased. It was a mopping-up job, rather than a fight through. The artillery had done the work for us. Most of the enemy had fled. Those we encountered were either injured or again doing their 'ostrich head-in-the-sand trick' that we had encountered at Goose Green – lying in their sangars, sleeping bags pulled over themselves, pretending they weren't there.

Our orders had been to reorganize on the position and wait until A and B Companies had completed the phase 2 attack on *Apple Tart*, when the CO would give us permission to move to our next start line. Following our experience at Goose Green, a small team from HQ Company, consisting of clerks, drivers and storemen, had been attached as stretcher-bearers, and for POW handling and ammunition resupply. However, barely had we finished rounding up the remaining enemy to hand over to this team than we began to come under heavy enemy artillery fire. The Argentinians clearly followed the same practice as we did, registering their own positions as artillery targets, in theory to support counterattacks to recover lost positions.

Private Godfrey, his instincts for survival sharpened by his experience of the white flag incident at Goose Green, dived into one of the many peat puddles that littered the area. From the smell of him afterwards, the Argentinians had evidently been using this as a latrine. Rumour has it that Sergeant Meredith subsequently exploited his services as the platoon HQ runner, to collect some more Schermuly flares from Company HQ ... anything to get him elsewhere. There, Nobby, getting a whiff of the problem, kept him at a distance, tossing him the flares like feeding an animal at the zoo. For years I had believed every organization needs a Godfrey. In the RAF Regiment his name had been Marsh – someone whom misfortune always seemed to target first, to the relief of his comrades, but also their gratitude and admiration. Godfrey had a strength of spirit and humour that others envied.

This position was not a healthy place to linger – in more ways than one. Abandoning our prisoners to the approaching HQ Company team, I moved the company forward 300 yards. The CO was fully engaged in directing A and B Companies' attack on *Apple Tart*. There seemed little point in distracting him with this infringement of his orders.

We fetched up in a shallow bowl, its features cloaked by a chilling mist covering the ground. It was, however, a bright night, not the dense darkness of Goose Green. Some 500 yards south, above the mist, we could just discern our next objective, *Blueberry Pie*. The cold was penetrating. The sweat generated by the effort of the previous few hours began to freeze on our backs. Those who had blundered into the ponds would, before long, be casualties – although someone volunteered that Godfrey was probably already one, infected with leptospirosis, a disease spread by rat-piss that we had learned about during our earlier training for Belize. The propensity of the Toms to mine humour in every situation never ceased to amaze me, but these were serious concerns. We had to keep moving.

As the fire died down on *Apple Tart*, it was clear that A and B Companies had, like us, found the artillery had done the job for them, meeting little opposition as the enemy fled. Ozzie relayed that C Company was on its way to Hearnden Water. I decided to set off straight away to our phase 4 start line. I had by now put 12 Platoon in the lead. Not, I assured them, that I was influenced by their leading us astray on the way to the Goose Green start line, but I was keen to orientate precisely where we were in relation to our next objective. Five rounds fire for effect on it served that purpose and would hopefully start to unnerve the enemy. We crested the ridge about 400 yards west of where the rounds were landing and after perhaps 50 yards were confronted by a 5ft-high peat wall – presumably a favoured spot for the locals to mine their household fuel. Thus concealed and protected from any alert enemy sentry, it was an ideal spot for a start line – and for another covert ciggy for the desperate. I now told the CO we were ready for phase 4 as soon as he was.

With no news from C Company at Hearnden Water, we faced another long wait before all the fire support could be made available to us. Away to the south, I could hear the constant drone of C130s still flying in and out of Stanley. So much for our warning of this from Bluff Cove Rincon. The cold continued to penetrate, but I felt that we were sufficiently safe here for those who had taken swimming excursions in the ponds to take the chance to dig out their quilted liners from their bum-rolls and get them on under their smocks. This was now as much an exercise in beating the environment as beating the enemy.

Finally, we got the word. I called for the FOO to order a ten-round fire mission on the objective and off we set to roll up the enemy along this half-mile stretch of rocky ridge. 11 Platoon took on the northern slope and 12 the crest of the ridge, with 10 behind in reserve. The CVR(T)s were back on my company net, but I had no targets to offer them. Instead, they focused their efforts on the second part of the ridge, *Dirty Dozen*, directly to their front. As we advanced, the FOO set up a rolling barrage, adding 300 metres after every five-round fire mission (thirty rounds in all). As on the first objective, this did the trick. We met no serious resistance, but each trench or sangar encountered received the same treatment: a grenade, either white phosphorous or HE anti-personnel sufficed, and a burst of fire to make sure. Then quickly on to the next. 10 Platoon, following up, cleared the enemy sangars more thoroughly, winkling out and despatching a number of enemy soldiers from foxholes among the rocks. Most appeared to have fled, however and what we most encountered was abandoned weapons, including a heavy recoilless anti-tank gun, which earlier had been firing at the CVR(T)s on *Apple Tart*. Keeping up this fire and manoeuvre for the whole kilometre was hard physical work, but it was proving a cakewalk. I sensed that the Toms were actually enjoying themselves. It was going like a dream.

We got to a point overlooking a shallow col, about 250 yards across. Beyond it was the final objective, *Dirty Dozen*, another half-mile-long rocky ridge. It was a lively place. Judging from the mass of green tracer, a lot of small arms fire was erupting from it; it was clearly still strongly held and the enemy there still full of fight. Thankfully, it was all being directed towards *Apple Tart*, to our left, now held by A and B Companies. From there, a mass of stuff was being fired back at the enemy – red tracer from our machine-guns, cannon fire and 75mm high explosive shells, most of it from the four CVR(T)s. The only thing missing was artillery fire onto the position, which I had expected the second battery to be engaging. The enemy seemed quite unaware of our presence a few hundred yards to their left. We were detached spectators as multicoloured flashes of tracer criss-crossed the darkness ahead of us, with explosions and sound effects to match. It was like watching a movie. I could have spent the night mesmerized by this display, but we still had work to do.

Beguilingly, to my half-right, we could also see the lights of Stanley 3 miles away across the dark, still water of Stanley Harbour. That surprised me: I had assumed the town would have been blacked out, but leaving it lit up was presumably to avoid civilian casualties. A hint of mutual trust, or secret dialogue, between both sides, perhaps?

The last kilometre had been a bit of a headlong dash, so we stopped to quickly reorganize and recharge our magazines with ammunition. I had a quick chat with Robin Innes-Ker and the tank crews about where we were and that we were about to attack. I had seen enough of their firepower demonstration to want to be sure he realized it would be us and not fleeing enemy coming into his right-hand arc. Then I got my FOO, now a Warrant Officer Class II, having been promoted from sergeant while at Fitzroy, to call for twenty rounds fire for effect on the final objective. 'Shot. Two-five. Over' came over the gunners' radio. Once the rounds started to fall, we would be on our way. I began mentally to count down the 25 seconds.

I was at 24 when suddenly we were deafened and rocked by shells exploding right overhead, and the shrieking whistle of shrapnel all around us. Fortunately we were all still prone on the ground. It took me two or three seconds, possibly more, to realize this was our own guns. Argentinian airburst, with its primitive fuses, was hopelessly imprecise. 'Check firing!' I screamed at the FOO. He looked at me blankly. 'It's our guns!' I screamed again. By the time his order to check firing got through to the gun-line, there were another four rounds per gun already in the air. We lay there helplessly for almost another minute, hugging the ground, trying to disappear into every nook, cranny and peat divot, while a total of thirty rounds exploded above us, raking the area with shrapnel. It was the most shocking and terrifying minute of my life. I was sure I was going to die.

Talking later, we all did. It was a salutary lesson on the power of artillery to undermine the will to fight. Another three or four similar salvos and I think our will, let alone our capacity, to operate would have been close to shredded. I think about my father on the Western Front in the First World War, and wonder.

The cacophony stopped and we took stock. Miraculously we had taken only two casualties, both in 11 Platoon. Corporal McAuley had been thrown against a rock and a back injury left him unable to stand. Private Parr, a member of McAuley's section, however, was dead – killed instantly by wounds to his chest and torso. 11 Platoon had been more on the open northern slope of the ridge, slightly away from the rocks on the spine that had provided some cover and undoubtedly saved us from more casualties. Parr had only rejoined us at Fitzroy, following his injury at Goose Green. Determined not to let his mates down, he had effectively discharged himself from the field hospital at Ajax Bay to be with them.

Shaken though we were, we still remained an effective force. Much was still expected of us. The FOO, clearly in a state of shock, was still telling himself it had been enemy artillery. I was already halfway to working out what had happened. I told him to tell me what target number he had called. I made him get his map out, and find it. His finger went to where we were. He still didn't get it: he clearly had no idea where he or we were. For a moment I wanted to shoot him on the spot for dereliction of duty, or anything – it would probably also have gone down quite well with the company. But anger gradually gave way to pity – he was not a qualified FOO and he was going to live with this for the rest of his life.

The pieces of the puzzle fell into place. We had not called up this target during our earlier advance, instead just adding 300 yards to the previous target number, and repeating, for our rolling barrage. When I instructed him to call for fire on the final objective, unthinkingly, and with no idea where we were, he had called up the next target on his list, not the one marked as the final objective. Now at least we understood the problem. I pointed out the correct target to him and ordered him to call for fire for effect on that. With much of our earlier confidence gone, we reluctantly readied ourselves to give the attack another go.

'Shot. Two-five. Over.' I started my mental countdown again. On time, I heard the shells exploding – but way over to our right in the area of Moody Brook, again not on our objective. My anger started to resurface: 'What the fuck is going on?' Urgent exchanges followed on the gunner net. It appeared this target had not been adjusted. Having been assured that all targets had been both adjusted and harassed prior to us crossing the start line, I was more than a little disturbed. No wonder the enemy on this final and crucial objective still seemed full of fight. However, there was a quick answer. 'Call up the last target which landed on us. Add 350[metres], and the rounds will land just where we want them. Let's go.'

More gunner murmuring over their net. 'No. I can't do that. We have to adjust the target,' the FOO stated. I could see no reason for this and wished later that I had taken his handset and spoken directly to the gun-line. So began the exhaustive process of adjustment, using one gun. 'Add 300, left 500. Fire.' Wait for the gun-line to do their calculations and adjustments. 'Shot. Three zero.' Wait another thirty seconds' time of flight. 'Splash' – beyond and to the left. 'Drop 200. Right 200. Fire.' More adjustments on the gun-line. 'Shot.' Wait thirty seconds. I was getting twitchy. How long before the enemy realized we were up here, and started to give us their attention, making the move across the col without surprise a hair-raising proposition? Thank God for the Blues and Royals' fire-power demonstration from *Apple Tart*, which seemed to have the enemy spellbound.

After about 20 minutes, on the fourth iteration, the FOO had rounds on target. 'Twenty rounds fire for effect,' I ordered. Over the radio I warned off the company. Rounds started exploding over the enemy, and we began to move. We'd gone barely 20 yards when the firing ceased. Apparently one of the guns was out of alignment, and its stray rounds were exploding uncomfortably close to C Company. This was not our night. We went to ground again. 'Get the other battery onto it,' I suggested. More discussions over the gunner net.

The other battery was almost out of ammunition came the reply. The only answer was to fire each gun individually until the rogue gun could be identified. Into this unfolding farce the CO now entered, calling me on the battalion net. I took the handset from Ozzie, expecting support or hoping that he had some means of helping up his sleeve. 'When are you going to attack?' he demanded impatiently, sounding somewhat rattled by the chaos that had descended on his plan. Until the blue-on-blue it had gone like clockwork. 'You can't sit there all night!'

I was taken aback. It was certainly not helpful. Had the battery commander not told him of the problems with the guns, or better still not offered a solution? It would be foolhardy to attack without artillery: the four CVR(T)s could only achieve so much. All I could find for an answer was: 'When we get the artillery support we were promised!' Over an open, all-ears net, it was probably not the most diplomatic response. What I did not know then was that at some point during the attack on *Apple Tart*, he had lost contact with his battery commander, so was probably unaware of the cause of the delay. What I did know, having now experienced first-hand the effect our artillery could have, was that I was not going ahead without it. I was also buggered if I was going to see D Company beaten by these setbacks. If we had to do it on our own despite the 'slings and arrows' from our own side, so be it.

I persevered with the guns, the Toms lying patiently around me. Over an hour had now passed since our first attempt to attack the objective and the 'blue-on-blue'. We had got four guns on target when harassing fire from enemy 155s began to fall around us. I'd had enough. We had to move, or we would have another problem. Four guns would have to do. Fewer guns, more rounds. I ordered the FOO to start with thirty rounds fire for effect. The rounds began to come in on target. Sweet relief. Gingerly, D Company once more started to advance.

As we got onto the col separating the two parts of the ridge, 11 Platoon, still left forward, saw orange cord around them, a tell-tale sign that they were among mines. Trying to negotiate a way through these, they then found themselves in a low barbed-wire entanglement, the first wire we had come across. Had they used that at Goose Green, our task would have been many times harder. 12 Platoon, on the right, seemed to be having a clear run, so the wire and mines had probably been sited as an obstacle against attack from the north. That, at least, was encouraging for our attack from the west, but the platoon had come to a standstill, leaving 12 Platoon ahead on their own.

Leaving 11 to extract themselves from the mines and wire, I brought 10 Platoon forward behind 12 and pushed them out to my left with a word not to go too far left in case they also ended up in obstacles. Rapidly reorganized, we were now perhaps 100 yards from the nearest enemy positions. Fortunately, the enemy had remained fully fixated on the Blues and Royals, assisted by our machine gun platoon and Milans, to the north. Time to get the guns to add 200 yards and repeat, and for us to end the cat-and-mouse stuff and get stuck in.

As the guns lifted, we continued to advance. I was beginning to think we would get right on top of them with complete surprise, but our luck was not to hold. With just 50 yards to go, a flare burst into life on my left. Life was too short to worry about whether one of ours had fired a Schermuly, or whether someone had hit an enemy trip flare. The penny dropped horribly quickly with the enemy. Within seconds, they had turned their attention from what was going on ahead of them to us on their flank. We found ourselves under intense small arms fire from six or more positions to our front. The sky filled with tracer, the rounds kicking up dirt behind us. Every single man dived for cover. Across the col, the ground was pock-marked with peat ponds or possibly water-filled shell-holes. Some ended up in these, a distinctly mixed blessing, while others found themselves eating a peat tussock. I chewed peat.

Our situation could only get worse, so we had to move. But after the cock-ups of the previous hour, the company seemed to have lost its chutzpah. Slowly, the Toms started to return fire. Some used M79 grenade launchers to lob grenades into the enemy a little above and ahead us. But no one wanted to be the first to move. There was plenty of fire – but none of the manoeuvre that was supposed to go with it. I started shouting across to the platoons, probably gibberish, in a bid to get some movement going. The shouting was picked up by others, like some desperate banshee war cry. Still no movement. Eventually I began to scramble to my feet, imagining a round tearing into me, with Hanley firing madly beside me. As I looked left and right, there were section commanders and Toms doing the same. Seconds later the D Company I knew was back into their well-practised fire and manoeuvre, one fire-team sprinting forward while another poured lead towards the enemy. I was vaguely aware of Ozzie stumbling and going down. But I couldn't stop; we had to get through this killing ground.

As we closed, the enemy, seemingly overawed by this irresistible momentum, began to cut and run. The Toms started to clear the initial enemy positions, but I felt we had to keep pushing forward. If we stopped to reorganize, then so might the enemy. I didn't want to repeat the excitement of the last few minutes all the way along to the telegraph wires still 800 yards away. 11 Platoon, following on, could do the detailed clearing. I urged 10 and 12 Platoons on. Getting ready to follow with my team, I could only see Hanley. There was no sign of Ozzie – had he just fallen and was desperately looking for me or had he been hit? I had no idea. I looked for the FOO – no sign of him either. After all the gunnery mishaps, he was no longer on my Christmas card list, but I was concerned for Ozzie. I also needed him, but spotting him in the dark presented a particular challenge. We'd gained a foothold on the ridge, but it was still alive with the crack of small-arms fire and machine-gun tracer. My mind was racing:

> Maybe, we do need to reorganize, take stock. But the enemy are still engaging us ahead. We can't stop here. I'll have to communicate with the guns or the battalion through Pete Adams. Right here, we're hanging on by our fingernails. We have to push on now and get a proper grasp on this blasted ridge. Sorry, Ozzie, you're on your own. I've got to keep the pressure on with 10 and 11.

So we did, and the enemy continued to cut and run. Before long, fire and manoeuvre was barely any longer necessary. As we appeared out of the dark, the enemy melted away or we found them in the usual 'ostrich posture', hiding at the bottom of a sangar. Maybe I was getting carried away with maintaining the momentum, for at one point I heard Sergeant Meredith shouting to one of his sections on my right: 'Get a shift on, the OC's getting ahead of you.'

After what I guessed was 500 yards, I stopped 10 Platoon, while 12 pushed on, largely unopposed, alone. We deliberately had not ventured onto, and therefore cleared, the south side of the ridge and we needed to make sure we didn't get a nasty surprise from there. There were some deep rocky defiles along this part of the ridge, which I thought would be ideal for the Company HQ when Pete Adams and the CSM caught up. Once I was happy with Shaun Webster's deployment of 10 Platoon, I radioed for situation reports.

11 Platoon were just extracting themselves from the wire and mines, but only after Pete Adams had called for the help of our attached engineers. The CSM's team had been busy with the casualties. Parr and McAuley were now away with the stretcher-bearers. This had taken longer than expected as they had to contend with small arms fire from Tumbledown and Moody Brook. At one point they heard Argentinians shouting on the far side of the ridge and had thought they were going to be counter-attacked. The enemy, however, had moved off towards the old Marines' barracks. The CSM's team was now dealing with Slough from 12 Platoon. He had been shot in the head and chest and was in a bad way. Colour Sergeant Powell, the company's quartermaster sergeant, was about to get him stretchered back. Slough survived the pitching ride to the RAP, but sadly was to die later in the field hospital. So far, however, he was the only known casualty from the hair-raising initial assault. I had been expecting worse. There was still no news of Ozzie and the FOO.

Across the Moody Brook valley I could hear the Scots Guards' battle for Tumbledown in progress, but it still seemed to be in Argentinian hands. We could worry about that come daylight. Then I got a call from 12 Platoon. They were going firm at the telegraph wires, our limit of exploitation. *Dirty Dozen* was now ours, with 1½ hours of darkness in hand, despite the time lost with the gunnery fiasco. Jacko Page, however, could see enemy further along the ridge and feared they might counter-attack. This was just what had worried me ever since the 'O' Group. Elsewhere, things seemed to be under control. I decided I needed to see for myself.

I told Shaun that I was leaving him in charge of defending this part of the ridge until he was joined by Pete Adams. Shaun, a modest and un-assuming soul, seemed to grow in stature. Good. I set off confidently with the trusty Wang. But my confidence was soon to prove misplaced, the calm before the storm. What was to follow was perhaps our most un-settling and confusing 2 hours of the war.

Wang and I had gone barely 100 yards when enemy artillery began to harass the ridge. Not heavy or constant, nothing remotely like the thirty rounds we had endured from our own guns, but with an insistent, nerve-testing 'where's-the-next-round-going' Russian roulette uncertainty. We dropped over on to the northern side of the ridge where it seemed a little quieter. Out towards 12 Platoon it had now gone quiet. Was this good news or bad? I radioed Jacko but got no response. A little worried, I tried Shaun and 10 Platoon. Again nothing. Either my radio had gone on the blink, or the feeble signal of my PRC 349 personal radio was screened. Shit! Right then, I was commanding nothing. I had also begun to realize that there was an awful lot of undefended ridge top between 10 and 12 Platoons, with little idea of what was on the far southern side. I began to feel rather less confident than I had 30 minutes earlier. I needed to share my concerns with my platoon commanders but had no comms. I decided to go on and speak directly to Jacko, and to send Hanley back to brief Shaun. I needed to make sure he was aware of the need to cover the risks further to his east, and that he coordinated with 11 Platoon to do so.

As I approached the telegraph wires I moved back up to the top of the ridge. The first member of 12 Platoon I saw was Sergeant Meredith, and I approached him to ask where his platoon commander was. He wasn't particularly welcoming. 'Sod off, Sir. You're attracting bullets wherever you go.' Belatedly, I realized that this exposed part of the ridgeline was being peppered with small arms fire, not intense machine-gun fire, more harassing fire, but I couldn't work out where it was coming from – not from ahead, maybe from the lower slopes of Tumbledown, but that seemed extreme range. It was thoroughly confusing. I politely excused my discourtesy, crouched a little lower and followed Taff's pointing finger to Jacko.

I was impressed. Under the constant sniper fire their position was uncomfortable, but they had helped themselves to shell-holes, vacated Argentinian trenches and rock sangers. They looked ready for anything and amazingly relaxed. Jacko told me that he thought the enemy ahead had withdrawn as no more fire was coming from further along the ridge. Godfrey, still smelling somewhat from his encounter hours earlier with an Argentinian latrine, even asked if I wanted a brew. He probably needed warming up more than most. Nothing was going to budge 12 Platoon. As the tea would not be ready for several minutes, I declined their hospitality, explaining that I had to head back to the rest of the company.

I was just leaving when Jacko's signaller, Private Knight, passed me the handset of the platoon radio, a PRC 351 with sixteen times the power output of my 349. It was the CO, on the company net, loud and clear. '49, this is Niner. Why aren't you on the battalion net?' he demanded – 'a little peevishly' was how those around me listening in described it. 'I've been trying to get hold of you.'

'I've lost my signaller,' I replied – 'and his radio,' I added to clarify.

'Well, you should always be on the battalion net. He should be with you at all times. And where's your FOO?' he continued. 'We also tried to get you through the gunner net.'

It was probably as well that I still did not know that the CO had himself earlier lost touch with his battery commander in the turmoil of seizing *Apple Tart*, or my answer might have been rather more pithy. Instead, beginning to feel like a little boy who had dropped his gloves on a walk, I could only reply: 'I don't know. I've lost him too.'

'What about the Tango call signs?' he asked, referring to the light tanks. 'Who's controlling them?'

'We are.' This puzzled me. They were on my company net, as ordered, and anyway the CO had Roger Field with a radio on their own net acting as his liaison officer with the troop. It might have helped had he explained that he had despatched Roger to replace an injured crew member of one of the tanks, so no longer had communications with them. This was not the moment for a debrief, however.

I wondered also why, if he could not raise me, he had not instead spoken with Pete Adams on the battalion net, but then Pete might not have been in a position to shed much light on what had been going on or where I was. A lot was going on, visible from where the CO was, but the lack of information since we had finally launched our assault had clearly irked him. Unfortunately the reality of war had intervened, and keeping the CO happy had not been as simple in the preceding hour as on an exercise. I now tried to reassure him: we had secured *Dirty Dozen* but were attracting incoming artillery and sniper fire. 'Do you need any help up there?' he asked.

'No, it's hairy, but we're firm. More people up here will just offer more targets.' In my mind, also, was the fact that if Tumbledown did not fall by daylight, the fewer we had up here who might then have to withdraw, the better. The scolding over, I started back to 10 Platoon, heading quickly this time for the shelter of the northern slope.

As I got back to 10 Platoon, I was relieved to see that Ozzie was there, although he was a little the worse for wear. He had stumbled into an old shell-hole when we separated – another which seemed to have served as an Argentinian toilet, I reckoned from the gentle odour pervading the little rocky bowl in which he sat. Then, over the company net, Jacko Page's signaller, Knight, called: his platoon commander was down, he'd been shot. What was it about 12 Platoon commanders, I thought? Very soon after, however, came the news that he had survived the experience – 'just making a fuss' opined his platoon sergeant. Jacko later provided the detail:

> I had got up to check on the rest of the platoon and see whether we needed to adjust our position ... when I was struck by a round which hit my right ammo pouch and set off some of the rounds in the magazine I had in the pouch. Knight reported that I had been hit but seemed ok. I was but the impact caused my right hip and leg to seize up, reducing mobility somewhat. Like being hit by a sledgehammer and having an electric shock, both at once.

It was a very lucky escape. Jacko still has the mangled magazine. Sergeant Meredith questioned whether the fire had come from 10 Platoon. I assured him it hadn't, but the fact was that we were all still struggling to source this harassing sniper fire.

Meanwhile, in my absence Private Hanley had assumed the role of de facto company commander, sorting out arcs of fire between 10 and 11 Platoons, the odd 'Yes, Hanley' and 'No, Hanley' passing between him, Shaun Webster and Chris Waddington. I was chuffed to bits. From the training in Kenya, I had tried to get across that they should not depend on me but be prepared to act on their own initiative. They had taken me at my word, first during the initial night attack at Goose Green and now here.

I had just joked: 'Carry on, Captain Hanley, it's all yours,' when another call came from 12 Platoon. They could hear Argentinians to the east and south calling to each other. It seemed that they were rallying for a counterattack. With limited ammunition left, Jacko wanted indirect support to deal with the problem. Meredith later described how from where he was he could see scores of Argentinians on the southern slopes. Our mortar fire controller, with Ozzie, now stepped up. 12 Platoon were out of range of our 81mm mortars, which anyway had been struggling throughout the night with their baseplates sliding back in the soft peat. However, he passed the frequency of the gunner net to Knight. Knight retuned one of the platoon radios to the gunners and Jacko took it from there. During the trip south on *Norland*, everyone in the company down to section commander level had done some training in artillery and mortar fire control. For all his lack of experience and no Infantry courses behind him, Jacko was proving a very bright and capable young officer. It had been the first counterattack launched anywhere by the Argentinians throughout the entire campaign. The artillery, thanks to Jacko's initiative, quickly discouraged them. They withdrew.

Calm returned. A little later we were joined by Nobby Clark and the rest of Company HQ and our FOO. We were huddled out of harm's way in a defile of large rocks. Just ahead, 10 and 11 Platoons were spread out, also with some protection among the rocks along the top of the ridgeline. It looked like a matter of hunkering down until, hopefully, Tumbledown fell to the Scots Guards, and awaiting the arrival of daylight, still over half an hour away, when we would be able to make more sense of our situation.

Looking over towards 12 Platoon, I could just see the night sky on the horizon beginning to lighten when there were agitated shouts from Corporal 'Doc' Owen, one of Shaun's section commanders, and our volunteer company photographer: 'Stand-to! Stand-to! They're attacking!' Grenades began to explode around Owen's section. They began to respond in kind, throwing a mix of high explosive and white phosphorous grenades. Private Kenyon's legs were injured by shrapnel. The platoon's machine guns joined in and began to rake the hillside below with fire where they could see the flashes of the enemy's rifles. Within minutes the immediate assault was repulsed. I joined 10 Platoon on the edge of the ridge, which for a few yards dropped steeply and then more gently towards Moody Brook and Stanley Harbour 500 yards away. Further west, 11 Platoon fired a Schermuly flare, and in its light we saw below us scores of Argentinians, the closest only yards away. The source of 12 Platoon's grief had also become clear. 'Shit! Perhaps I should have said "yes" to the CO's offer of CVR(T)s.' But it was too late for regrets.

Both platoons were now engaging with their machine guns. Owen fired all eight of his M79 grenades. The attack began to falter. The FOO then called a fire mission from the guns into the Moody Brook valley below. That seemed to settle it, and in the slowly improving light we could see the enemy heading down the hillside and towards the old Marines barracks, leaving their dead and wounded behind them. The courage of these Argentinians could not be questioned, but once their initial assault had failed, they never stood a chance. It was all over in less than half an hour. Kenyon was quickly prepared for casevac, pleading with Soane, the platoon medic: 'I'm OK, I don't need that drip up my arse!' Clearly not seriously in shock, he was spared the indignity.

Recently I was contacted by one of the Argentinian platoon commanders in this attack, Victor Hugo Rodriguez, who retired as a lieutenant colonel. His company, A Company of 3 Regiment, which had been deployed on the northern slopes of Tumbledown overlooking Moody

Brook, were sent to reinforce 7 Regiment, the unit tasked to defend Wireless Ridge. By the time he got there 7 Regiment had withdrawn and his company had no communications with their superiors. In the circumstances their counterattack was a gallant effort. The company comprised mainly conscripts coming towards the end of their period of service so they had worked together for some time and clearly had some fortitude. Rodriguez talked of how one of his soldiers dropped his rifle and was allowed to walk over to care for his injured sergeant. Sadly I have been unable find out which of our soldiers showed such compassion, but it speaks to the way we conducted our business.

I checked with 12 Platoon. They were still getting inbound 155mm artillery fire, but the small arms fire had started to relent. Then Ozzie passed me the handset of the battalion net radio. He had been holding the CO at bay until I had a moment. I explained to an anxious CO that another counterattack had been repulsed. There was a lot of incoming enemy artillery, Tumbledown had still not fallen, but we were fine. Again, I suggested that, until we knew the outcome of the fighting for Tumbledown, bringing reinforcements here would just put more people at risk from the enemy artillery. Following the relative ease with which we had dispelled the last attack, I was more confident now that things were under control, but I felt that I hadn't convinced him.

'I'm coming up to join you,' he responded. That seemed a good call. The situation playing out was fast-changing and felt increasingly surreal. He needed to see it with his own eyes. My ability to paint the scene had probably reached its limits. For the first time in the 4 hours since the blue-on-blue incident, I began to relax. Time for a brew, and a cigarette. Hanley got busy. We'd lay on some hospitality for the CO. But in the 40 minutes before the CO arrived with his Tac HQ, the game changed completely.

All the platoons continued to engage with their GPMGs the mass of enemy around the near shore of Stanley Harbour and Moody Brook, now visible in the increasing daylight. At the extent of our range, it was patently having little effect. Suddenly realizing that I, personally, hadn't fired my SLR all night, I even indulged myself with taking a few pot-shots now things had calmed down. No reaction from the enemy. All it did was to confirm, to the Toms' amusement, that I should leave marksmanship to them. More significantly, wherever we fired from was immediately targeted by the Argentinian guns. Having been party to this, I sheepishly ordered the company to stop. We were just wasting ammunition and offering gratuitous targets.

Then we saw columns of Argentinians beginning to move southwards out of Stanley towards Sapper Hill, which dominated the capital. Probably, to judge from Rodriguez's account, this was the men of 7 Regiment who had earlier been withdrawn from Wireless Ridge. Minutes later, we saw others starting to march off Tumbledown towards Moody Brook and Stanley. At last Tumbledown appeared to be falling. The enemy, though, seemed to be preparing for their next battle: the defence of Stanley. I got the FOO to call for fire missions on both targets. 'Battery unavailable. Counter-battery fire' came the response. This had become like a long-playing record from the battery commander. 'Jesus Christ, we're still getting incoming. CB fire is doing nothing.' Here was a critical opportunity to disrupt the enemy's attempts to reorganize going to waste while the battery commander was still, as at Goose Green, playing BAOR Cold War doctrine. But this was far more significant – the chance of avoiding a fight through Stanley was being squandered.

The CO arrived and took in the scene. 'Why aren't you shooting at them?'

'Because the guns are unavailable. Counter-battery fire.'

'Well, what about your GPMGs?' I explained that we had tried, but that without SF tripods the range was too great to be effective, and all it had achieved was to attract incoming enemy artillery. He was not to be deterred, however, and ordered me to get my machine guns into action. Reluctantly I ordered 12 Platoon to open up with a gun from our furthest flank – not a particularly charitable gesture to them, but it was for the greater good, I told them.

The machine gun stuttered away, to zero effect. The enemy it was aiming at didn't even bother to run for cover. I waited, watching for the inevitable enemy shells to start harassing 12 Platoon. Nothing. I ordered 10 and 11 to start to engage. Still no response. It was as if, at the flick of a light switch, Argentinian resistance had been extinguished.

I felt rather foolish and started to explain to the CO. By now, however, his interest had shifted. The battery commander, on the other side of him, was now talking to the gunners. Lo and behold, he suddenly had the whole regiment – three batteries – available, although I did wonder at the speed with which the one that was reported out of ammunition had been re-supplied. The enemy continued to pour off Tumbledown in droves and along the road to Stanley. The CVR(T)s were also called forward to join the turkey shoot.

In the distance, now in full daylight, we could see the Argentinian guns on Stanley Racecourse. This was not what most people would think of as a

racecourse – really just a very large grass meadow, but that was also excep-
tional for the Falklands. There was no activity there but, to make sure, the
CO called up two Scout light helicopters equipped with SS11s – wire-
guided anti-tank missiles. We watched as they approached below us from
behind Mount Longdon, popped up just above the shallow col, fired and
guided in their missiles, and then dropped down below the skyline again.
All very slick, but of course no one was now firing back.

The penny slowly dropped. This battle, at least, was over. The CO
ordered check firing. The enemy were on the run, withdrawing from the
field; it was more important that we conserved our ammunition and set off
after them. We'd opened the gateway to Stanley, but we still needed to
deny them any chance to reorganize.

Chaundler immediately radioed Julian Thompson at Brigade HQ and
asked for permission to advance. Permission denied. The brigadier already
had other plans for the final advance on Stanley. The CO pushed back –
we were missing a huge opportunity. It was obvious that Thompson, like
Chaundler earlier, was unable to grasp the scale and abruptness of what
was happening. Indeed, even watching with my own eyes, I found it difficult to comprehend. Thompson, also, needed to see for himself. Some
15 minutes later he arrived in his helicopter. Seeing was believing. After
the briefest of discussions, he gave the CO the order for the battalion to
advance toward Stanley.

As 12 Platoon pulled back along the ridge, a number of Argentinians
began to emerge from nooks and crannies in the rocks that we had missed
in the dark during our headlong dash to secure it. Once these had been
disarmed and rounded up, they were handed over to the HQ team who
had arrived with a resupply of ammunition.

Now the plan was for B Company to move up to the col and on down to
clear Moody Brook and the old Marines barracks there. A Company was
then to pass through and lead the battalion into Stanley. D Company
would bring up the rear. I smiled – we were back to the alphabet. I didn't
care. We'd done our bit and I knew it was over. Job done.

As we prepared for the move off the ridge, I could see the Toms felt the
same, and they knew they'd done a good job. Red berets began to appear
from various pockets to replace the helmets on our heads. Here and there
sections got together to pose for their 'happy holiday' snaps, faces smiling
with pride, any exhaustion for the moment forgotten. Nobby called them
together. 'Okay. Endex. Make safe.' He reflected the atmosphere perfectly. At the end of every training exercise, this age-old command is given
for ejecting live rounds from the chamber of a weapon and returning them

to magazines, and when Toms relax and begin to think of a nice warm bed. I thought for a moment that he was about to order: 'For inspection, port arms,' when magazines are removed and weapons cocked to enable an NCO to look into every weapon and ensure the chamber was indeed empty and the weapon safe.

I discreetly intervened. 'Perhaps not just yet, Sergeant Major. Not quite sure the other side know it's Endex yet.' I was sure they did, but I wasn't quite ready to start counting my chickens. The Toms never miss much. A lively debate ensued. 'Of course they do, they're finished,' argued some. 'Better safe than sorry,' argued others, blithely unaware that that depended on which end of the telescope you were looking through. Nobby gracefully conceded, and rounds remained in the chamber. I notched it up as payback for his getting me to get my haircut six months previously.

In front of the company, with much laughter, Nobby and I shook hands. We set off for Stanley.

As we reached Moody Brook word came over the battalion net that the Argentinians had capitulated. The stash of maps that Corporal Owen had found back on the ridge showing all the Argentinian positions and had sent to brigade no longer seemed the gold dust that we had assumed. However, we were to remain ready for anything as formal surrender negotiations were still being set up. It really was Endex. Nobby's instincts had been spot-on, but we remained fully loaded.

Chapter 10

Into Stanley

As we entered Stanley, at some point we passed through A and B Companies. It was a dull, bleak day, the wind whipping up the sea in Stanley Harbour, but nothing could now dampen our spirits. The light was beginning to fade when I was ordered to set up a checkpoint just short of the war memorial to stop anyone going into the town until the surrender was formalized. Exhausted though I was, I could see it was a delicate situation. Anything precipitate or aggressive could set off renewed conflict with a still fully armed Argentinian garrison that heavily outnumbered the victors.

I tasked 10 Platoon with manning the checkpoint. Pete Adams and Nobby Clark went off in search of shelter for the company. The first person to approach the checkpoint was the *Evening Standard* correspondent, Max Hastings, who had spent the previous night as a guest of our battalion headquarters. The Toms tried to stop him just as I was approaching. 'I'm not under your orders,' he challenged dismissively. 'I'm Press.' The Toms were not impressed. This was at the end of a very long and testing day, and the tone of the exchange set the scene for a confrontation. I stepped in. 'Let him through,' I ordered, then, as an aside to calm the righteous indignation of the Toms, I added, 'If he runs into trouble, the bugger's on his own.'

What I didn't know was that Shaun Webster and Corporal Owen were already beyond the checkpoint and had decided to take a look at Government House, just around the corner. There they were invited in by an Argentinian major, who asked if they were the 'advance party.' Another officer entered the room. 'Gentlemen, may I present General Menendez.' The Argentinian commander then shook their hands. He asked Shaun how old he was, responding: 'Yes, I have a son, also 25, somewhere on West Falkland.' There followed a brief exchange about what unit Shaun was from. 'Ah, the 2nd Parachute Regiment. You fought our 7th on Wireless Ridge.' As he left, Menendez told them: 'We shall be surrendering at four this afternoon.' Shaun and Owen were then ushered out amongst much saluting and handshaking. Quite what Menendez made of this visit by a scruffy, dirty, young lieutenant and a corporal sadly is not recorded. Despite this unscheduled intervention, the surrender did indeed go ahead as planned, to Major General Jeremy Moore, the British land forces commander. Shaun himself did not disclose this encounter to me until after we got back home, doubtless fearing a serious dressing down. However, it was gratifying to think that while A Company was able to claim it was first into Stanley, and numerous others have claimed to be the first to raise the Union Jack above Government House, D Company was first into the seat of government.

That night the Toms were billeted in three houses that lined the road leading to the racecourse and overlooking Stanley Harbour. These houses had been occupied by Argentinians, and there was no sign of the owners. Three days later we did get a visit from a couple who owned the house my company headquarters and 11 Platoon were in. Sadly, I cannot recall their names, but we were able to assure them that their home was now in a much better state than how we had found it. They could not have been more welcoming: 'Stay as long as you need, we have somewhere else to stay.' Their relief at finding their home being spring-cleaned and their gratitude for their liberation had an evident impact on the company. We were no longer jobbing soldiers, but for a while at least, chivalrous knights of the Round Table.

Later that evening Pete Adams and Colour Sergeant Bob Powell returned from a logistics conference with the quartermaster. They bore with them two cases of Argentinian wine that they had 'stumbled' upon. This was shared out among the company. With a roof over our heads and a glass, or rather my brewing mug, of Argentinian Malbec to hand, I started to wind down, and to bask in our victory, and in the praise from the brigadier for a job well done.

Wireless Ridge was soon being promoted as a classic example of how an all-arms battle should be fought – optimal use of supporting firepower and concentration of effort at critical points, allied to good use of ground and manoeuvre to achieve surprise. Studying it became part of the syllabus at the Army Staff College, with David Chaundler, myself and other officers presenting to the students.

I'm not sure it would have happened without the arrival of Chaundler. He brought a fresh perspective both to preparing the battalion for further operations, and to the way in which we would undertake them. The withdrawal of the battalion to recover properly in Fitzroy, and his insistence that whatever our next battle would be, it would be adequately resourced with fire support had an undoubted material impact on our ability to deliver. However, it had at least as important an effect on our morale as well. The Toms had pulled the rabbit out of the hat at Goose Green, but without doubt they felt their necks, and nerves, had been stretched. They would have gone on, but tired bodies and ragged nerves can only achieve so much. Using Lord Moran's analogy in *The Anatomy of Courage*, our 'well of courage' needed topping up. I thus used to end my presentation at the Staff College with a quote from Mao Tse-Tung:

> Morale is an instinct that transcends the natural instinct for self-preservation and raises men above the pettiness of self-interest … The contest of force is not only a contest of military and economic power, but also one of the power and morale of the Man.

The other benefit that Chaundler brought was what today might be called a more collegiate style of command. With regard to the planning of Wireless Ridge, he got all his company commanders involved. We all looked at the ground together from Mount Longdon. It took Dair to notice the critical displacement of 3 PARA's C Company and the presence of an Argentinian company. Had they remained unspotted, we would have had another chaotic 'come-as-you-are' start to the battle with potentially disastrous consequences. With Chaundler by then back at Brigade HQ, the three of us, drawing on John Crosland's experience and with a bird's eye view of the ground, were able to suggest to him a pragmatic, indeed an advantageous, solution to this surprise. That enabled him, in an acutely tight timeframe, to adapt the plan and us to cross our start line on time.

Many have been tempted to compare the battle for Wireless Ridge – 'the perfect battle' – with Goose Green – the 'flawed battle'. To conclude, however, that 2 PARA had learnt from the mistakes made at Goose Green and applied them to Wireless Ridge is simplistic. The context of the two battles was completely different.

As the first major engagement of the war Goose Green was in a sense a step into the unknown, at least in terms of the calibre of the enemy. As such it was crucial not just for strategic reasons but to set the tone for the rest of the campaign. Nevertheless, it was a distraction to Julian Thompson's tactical priorities. His brigade, moreover, was struggling with huge logistical setbacks and challenges. Thus, the battalion figuratively, if not literally, limped to its start line under-resourced and with poorly considered and ambivalent intent. Of course, there are lessons here, but few were directly transferable to how the battalion chose to fight its next battle. In any event, no commander has ever had all the resources he would wish for, and waiting for that would render the opportunity lost, or worse, would hand the initiative to the enemy. True, there were mistakes at Goose Green, most critically the time and space appreciation, but so there were at Wireless Ridge. But then, as von Moltke said: 'No plan survives contact with the enemy.'

Wireless Ridge was an infinitely less testing affair. The enemy's will to fight had already been weakened by the battles two nights previously, and of course by Goose Green. There had been over two weeks of logistic preparation for the final battles. Identifying the aim and objectives was straightforward, uncomplicated by conflicting needs. The ground allowed scope for imaginative manoeuvre. Most significantly, we were the only combat or 'sabre' element of the brigade in action that night; thus we had their undivided attention and sole call on their resources. With the devastating amount of supporting firepower available, therefore, Wireless Ridge had been very much 'in the bag', whereas Goose Green had been touch-and-go from the start. Nevertheless, there were still unexpected challenges to be overcome on Wireless Ridge – not least the misreporting of the location of 3 PARA's C Company, and the tragic shortcomings of the artillery support prior to the attack on the final critical objective.

The styles of the two commanding officers were, of course, very different. The teasing question for me is how would Chaundler have tackled Goose Green, and how would Jones have approached Wireless Ridge? Both perhaps were the right men for their respective moments. Goose Green needed 'H's uncompromising aggression and self-belief in what was frankly a fairly desperate mission. Wireless Ridge benefited from Chaundler's more enlightened and considered approach which optimized all the available advantages and, despite the setbacks, delivered the coup-de-grace to the Argentinians in a way that made it seem easy.

By my second glass of wine, my 'Endex' elation had begun to give way to exhaustion and self-doubts. The previous night had been one of choices. Had I made the right ones?

The death of Private Parr at the hands of our own guns in the blue-on-blue fiasco was the bitterest moment. I already knew from Goose Green that my untrained FOO struggled with his map reading, as well as following the progress of and anticipating the needs of the battle. Perhaps therefore I should have more closely supervised what he was doing, although that would have been at the expense of the attention I could give to other aspects of the battle. The point is that a good FOO takes some of the burden off a company commander, rather than adding to it. However, there was perhaps more to it than that. Because he was untrained, I suspect that he did not get the respect and attention from the battery commander that some of his communications deserved, or indeed the support that his lack of training warranted.

Given that the other two companies were working in tandem that night, did they need a FOO each? I might have asked for one of them, or indeed the battery commander might have recommended it. However, when the final plan emerged with the increase in D Company's role, we were very short of time. No one likes to mess around with settled teams, especially at the last minute. The CO might have considered instead simply reallocating the companies' tasks, perhaps swapping D Company with A or B. That, for me, would have been the cure being worse than the illness. In all honesty, though, at the time I did not even consider these difficulties. I was focused totally on the job and on briefing my team. Sadly, issues side-stepped, even for the best of reasons, do have a habit of biting you in the backside. It still nags me that MOD penny-pinching and the slavish adherence to alphabetical order in the allocation of resources should have led to his death, but sadly it cannot bring Dave Parr back.

I had no regrets, however, in delaying my final attack until we had at least some measure of artillery support. To have done otherwise would most certainly have resulted in a much tougher battle for the final ridge and many more casualties. I was still rankled by the CO's impatience then, and later, about control of the light tanks, but remained unaware that, without his battery commander or CVR(T) liaison officer, he had his own frustrations to contend with. 'C'est la guerre,' I thought. 'Move on.'

Similarly frustrated by losing touch with Ozzie and my FOO during the initial assault on *Dirty Dozen*, I wondered whether I been too impetuous in pushing the attack headlong along the ridge without them? Had I perhaps, like 'H' on Darwin Hill, got too involved with that at the expense of my perspective and ability to marshal all the resources available to the company? Had it been an exercise, the directing staff answer would probably be 'Yes.' On exercises people only get shot by blanks, however; they are not actually wounded, nor killed. Nor are they in fear of their lives, faced with a 'fight or flight' choice. I could have paused to look for Ozzie, or alternatively Pete Adams with another signaller on the battalion net. But I felt our grasp on the ridge, still under heavy fire, was desperately tenuous. Quite probably, had I told the two platoons to push on without me, they would have done so successfully. At that moment, in the dark, I chose to push on with them to maintain the momentum – the fall-out I would deal with as it arose. Happily, 12 Platoon still got the artillery support they needed thanks to Jacko Page's initiative and quick learning.

I awoke refreshed. Allocating blame and ruminating over every choice that anyone had made now seemed unhelpful. Friction, I reasoned, was all part and parcel of the confusion of war. More important had been the resilience of the Toms not to lose faith and to bounce back when things went wrong because, no matter the care taken, in the stress and chaos of battle something invariably will. Indeed, the ability to bounce back faster and stronger than the enemy often decides who prevails.

At Goose Green and now at Wireless Ridge the company had met every test thrown at them – from friend and foe. Still they laughed. They had their regrets, comrades lost; maybe they were also worrying whether, had they done things differently, some of them might still be alive. I wondered whether they also were not so much mourning them as missing them, because these lost comrades would for ever be part of Penal Company '82.

Did they, like me, feel 'we're rather good at this. Bring on some more.' Or were they wise enough to recognize that this was perhaps because there was no more to bring on. After a testing climb in the mountains, sometimes I would think 'Thank God, we're down.' At other times: 'If we've survived that, we can do anything' – until the night before the next big route when the rat would return to gnaw at my insides once more.

Chapter 11

Back to the Mother Ship

Up and about on 15 June it was back to business. There were prisoners to be disarmed, escorted and guarded. The most immediate task for company commanders was to write up any of our people that we wished to put up for awards. There was a paranoia that the Navy, with their direct ship to UK communications, would steal all the glory. As a result, an unseemly race developed with Jeremy Moore, commander land forces, wanting recommendations that day but, in view of the telex bandwidth, in no more than twenty-five words each. I later learnt that these brief words were then turned into formal citations by a team of 'script-writers' in the Ministry of Defence. It was a shameful situation – impossible to do justice for some, or to fully research who did what and when and corroborate all that had happened. I gave it my best, but undoubtedly failed some individuals. Indeed, they were all heroes, so how to choose some over others was an invidious task. In the event I'm not sure it made any difference. When awards were announced months later, those for D Company bore only a passing resemblance to my recommendations. It was a sobering cold shower. Within 24 hours of having 'drunk delight of battle with our peers far on the ringing plains of windy Troy', we were already back to the venality and bureaucracy of peacetime soldiering.

As difficult, but more important, were the letters of condolence to the next of kin of those who had died. I had ten to write. From somewhere, Bob Powell, my CQMS, got me some unused 'blueys' – aerogrammes. Nobby, Pete Adams and I had each carried a copy of the company nominal roll with full next-of-kin details for just such purpose – in the pre-digital age such redundancy was seen as prudent. Thankfully, I was still around, so the others were absolved the task. I dug mine out of my bergen and set to.

After expressing my regrets, I briefly described the circumstances in which my ten men had been killed. If I knew their death had been quick and without suffering, I said so; otherwise I omitted such detail. In all the letters I affirmed that each man had died as a credit to themselves and to the regiment, making a crucial contribution to our mission for the freedom of others. I worried that it might seem trite, but I believed it then and I still do.

Some letters were more difficult than others. I had got to know and like Jim Barry well. Corporal Sullivan had caught my eye on the Kenya exercise as a particularly promising NCO, and I had met his wife. I knew that Lance Corporal Smith, who died with Barry and Sullivan at the white flag incident, had just got married, leaving behind his pregnant wife. I learnt, from the mass of letters that we received all at once in Stanley, that my wife had been in close touch with Gaz Bingley's widow.

The letter I had to think most about was to David Parr's mother. How could I square his death from our own guns with a crucial contribution to the mission? Did his parents need to know of his earlier injury, and that he had discharged himself from the field hospital to rejoin us for Wireless Ridge? I would have liked to vent my anger with the gunners in that letter, but that would not help his grieving parents. I chose, instead, to be 'economical with the truth'. I wrote that he had been killed by artillery fire in the course of the final phase of Wireless Ridge – omitting the detail of whose artillery it was. In the end it proved to be a misguided choice.

In the autumn of 1983 a book was published, based on a record of the campaign put together within the battalion. This book spelt out the incident and that Parr was killed as a result. RHQ received a pre-publication copy, so fortunately I was able to visit the family and warn them before it became public. It must have reopened terrible wounds for the family, but Parr's parents were incredibly stoical, and received my visit with amazing grace and courage. I should have perhaps realized that we had been part of history in the making and that at some point the facts were bound to emerge. At the time it never occurred to me, but it was probably better that the truth came out sooner rather than later. His fellow Toms were certainly pleased that it had. Dave's body had been repatriated and he had been buried at home in Lowestoft. A contingent from his platoon had attended the funeral and had found it harrowing not to be able then to share their grief fully and openly with his family.

The following days had a touch of deja vu. The Argentinian surrender in Stanley had lacked the controlled affair at Goose Green. An act of surrender had been signed, but with it went any command over the Argentinian forces. Many no longer remained as formed units, and officers deserted their troops, concerned for their own survival. They were armed still, although they offered no resistance, and looting was rife; to be fair our own troops were not above looting the Argentinian supply dumps. On 16 June the battalion found themselves back in a Northern Ireland internal security-type role, bringing law and order back to the capital. Over the following three days the enemy were slowly herded back to the airport where they were disarmed and searched. They were then embarked on the assortment of civilian STUFT vessels, including *Norland,* to be taken to Montevideo in Uruguay for eventual repatriation back to Argentina.

LSL *Sir Lancelot* had tied up alongside the harbour wall in Stanley, to be used as a prison ship. Thankfully, some bright staff officer had the better idea using it to provide each major unit with 24 hours of R&R. The battalion was invited aboard on 19 June, during a break from prisoner-handling chores, for a night in a bunk, a proper dinner on plates and a full English breakfast. Officers even had sheets for their bunks. I briefly dallied with the idea of using my sleeping bag out of solidarity with the Toms, but after a hot shower I could not face the prospect of then inserting my wonderfully clean body into my filthy green maggot. I used the sheets. My decision to decline a bath at Eric Goss's house in Goose Green to avoid having to acclimatize to the grime all over again was in another life. Sorry, chaps, I started with the best of intentions – rank has its privileges!

The next day, being Sunday and all of us clean and shiny, called for a battalion church service. This was held in Stanley's imposing cathedral under the tender loving care of Padre David Cooper. Even with the choir stalls turned over to the officers, it was a tight squeeze. A Padre Cooper sermon was never an event to be missed – always pertinent, but replete with pithy, sometimes outrageous, humour. The BBC filmed the event, and the prospect for the men of seeing themselves on telly appealed to the more vain. A few perhaps were there to thank God for being on our side, but for most, it was an eagerly seized moment to celebrate personal survival and, together, to mourn for our lost comrades. Until this point, apart, perhaps, from those up to their elbows in treating them, the pressure of events and the need to stay strong had inhibited any serious reflection of those lost. My main consideration had been the impact on our operational effectiveness. Now David Cooper led us robustly into the start of the grieving process. 'But what,' he enquired, 'did you really think about when you thought you were going to die? Was it your wife ... your girlfriend ... or even your dog? Or it may have been your own life itself?'

On 24 June *Norland* returned from dropping off prisoners at Montevideo, and we were told that we and 3 PARA were to be the first units of 3 Commando Brigade to leave. We would travel aboard *Norland* as far as Ascension Island, and in RAF aircraft from there. We started to embark on 25 June. One last task awaited, however. The residents of Darwin and Goose Green wanted us to attend a Thanksgiving service on 26 June at a memorial cross they had erected near where 'H' Jones had fallen on Darwin Hill. Bravo November, the only Chinook that survived the sinking of *Atlantic Conveyor*, was tasked to fly two loads, or sticks, comprising members of the battalion, but also many of the great and good of the Task Force to the service.

I was in the second stick. That morning I was waiting with seventy others at Stanley Racecourse, which had become the helicopter landing zone, for Bravo November to return from the first sortie. Minutes before it was due, I saw a Navy Wessex helicopter heading in. As it made its final approach, it snagged a telegraph wire with its little rear wheel – and crashed. No disaster, just a ruined helicopter. 'Must be Prince Andrew,' said some wag, as the crew crawled from the wreckage, although a loyal colleague was quick to point out that the prince flew Sea Kings. In the distance I saw Bravo November approaching. For once, my humour deserted me – I was a world away. 'Whose bright idea was this thanksgiving service?' I muttered to myself. 'We've got this far, still in one piece. Why take this totally unnecessary risk?'

The Chinook landed and we piled in. It was standing room only, cheek by jowl, seats and safety belts stowed out of the way. The engines groaned as they tried to get the Dunlops off the ground. I said a quiet prayer, preparing myself for the worst. Twenty minutes later we were on Darwin Hill, and the short service began. I remember little of it – I was there in body, but little more – the flight back was still to come.

Late that afternoon we were back on *Norland*. We were sharing the ship with 3 PARA so it was crowded, and for the officers it was now four to a four-berth cabin. Justice comes to all who wait. That evening we all gathered in the continental lounge for a farewell visit from Julian Thompson. In a brief address he spoke warmly of the honour and privilege of having the Parachute Regiment under his command. He finished with: 'As one soldier to another, I salute you all.' This gesture was treated to a heartfelt cheer from the assembled members of both battalions. We all respected him for the job he'd done in very difficult circumstances, but more we appreciated how graciously and even-handedly he had integrated us and our ethos into his brigade. There was not a jot of pomp or bravado about him, just a calm, quiet, modest professionalism which went a long way with us all. We felt very blessed to have had him as the key commander of the land war.

Shortly after that, we were under way. With no ceremony we eased seemingly unnoticed out of Stanley Harbour, the town soon lost to view in the evening gloom. I could not decide whether I was glad or sad that the great adventure was all over, but I do know I was enormously thankful that I had been part of it. I was glad to see the back of the Falklands and their grim winter. Back home it was summer, and a season in the Alps beckoned.

All too soon we were back to the real world. Post operations reports were required from each company, along with notes for the regimental magazine, *Pegasus*. Careers still had to be managed, postings sorted, specialist and career courses booked, and recommendations for NCO promotions made. I actually found the banality of it all surprisingly absorbing – perhaps it was the increased awareness that getting all this stuff right really mattered, or maybe I just needed something to deflate me from the frenetic activity of the previous weeks.

Two days out from the Islands we were told that we could all have a 3-minute call home, if we wanted one, on the ship's Inmarsat telephone. I immediately put my name down and the next morning my turn came up. I took my place in the queue. After 15 minutes I was next but three. I was getting increasingly anxious about what Rachel and I could say to each other in 3 minutes in such a public arena. There was no privacy, no booth, just a handset on a bulkhead. One of the battalion cooks, a catering corps sergeant, was on the phone. He looked stressed. Suddenly, he exploded. 'Bills! Bills! I've been risking life and limb for my country, and all you can do is bang on about bills!'

'Bloody Remfs!' I thought. 'Cooks were hardly in harm's way.' Probably an unfair sentiment: he would have spent much of his time with B Echelon on *Norland* in Bomb Alley. His phone call went from bad to worse, ending with a burst of swearing. The next person stepped up to the phone. I suddenly remembered there was something urgent I had to do. Making an exaggerated display of looking at my watch with concern, I stole away. My 'well of courage' had just run dry.

In fact, I did have something important to attend to. Airborne Forces Day was four days away. The annual celebration of the Regiment's formation in 1940 was normally held in Aldershot, then the Regiment's home, on the first Saturday in July. A parade, freefall displays, side-shows and other activities more typical of a village fete followed by parties in the officers' and NCOs' messes, while the Toms headed off to beat up the town were clearly not going to be possible on our car ferry in the middle of the south Atlantic. But with both Aldershot-based battalions on board, something was clearly going to have to be done.

I could see it coming a mile away. 'Phil Neame ran a very good sports day on the way down,' volunteered Chris Keeble. I smiled graciously and went to pull out my earlier plans. This time there would be the added dimension of an inter-battalion competition. I needed more events, but also had to cater for more spectators. I was sure that 2 PARA had the orienteering competition in the bag, as we knew the geography of *Norland* so much better. But to the previous events were added a Superstars competition consisting of timed trials for circuit training activities such as star-jumps, sprints, press-ups, etc. Tossing the sandbag also proved popular. To encourage spectator involvement, two free cans of beer for every man were authorized and provided by the ship – although maybe the NAAFI picked up the bill – plus two cans for each member of each winning team.

The finale was a chain of command race. Each battalion put forward a twelve-man team, comprising a member of each rank. Starting with a private and finishing with the commanding officer, each member in relay had to consume a boiled egg, a bag of crisps, a Mars Bar, a plate of custard (otherwise referred to as yellow phlegm) and a can of lemonade. This race, unsurprisingly, proved hugely popular and engaging with the audience – there's nothing the Toms like more than the sight of senior ranks suffering or making fools of themselves.

I like to think it was as good an Airborne Forces Day as any in Aldershot. The evening party, however, proved to be even more memorable and is still talked about today in the same breath as such legendary events as the Battle of Gun Hill, a landmark road in Aldershot that links the town's pubs and the barracks. With another two beers per man to move things along, the partying began. There had been a simmering resentment among our Toms at having to share their ship with 3 PARA. In respect to the crew's affections 3 PARA doubtlessly felt like second-class citizens. Starting in the continental lounge, but spreading to most parts of the ship, the Toms of the two battalions were soon beating the shit out of each other. Wisely, the two regimental sergeant majors left them to it until exhaustion brought an end to the fun.

In those days there was no such thing as planned decompression after a combat tour. We just called it letting off steam, but there's little new under the sun – Airborne Forces Day '82 served the same purpose.

Two days later we arrived at Ascension Island. The Chief of the General Staff, Sir Edwin Bramall, came aboard for a photo opportunity and to congratulate the battalions – the first of many ceremonies and events that were to follow. It was flattering to be so recognized, but he failed to make a lasting impression – I cannot recall a word he said. I was still finding the fuss for what I thought was just doing our job rather puzzling. In some ways I felt not a lot had changed and was beginning to feel rather flat.

It all felt rather alien. In my climbing world, understatement was the norm, and those inclined to strut their stuff were given short shrift. I learnt that one evening in North Wales returning to the hut of a Merseyside club that I had joined. It had been a drizzly day, but I and my mate had had a good one on the Anglesey sea-cliffs, ticking off two routes both with notable reputations. It was late and we were the last to return. 'What've you done then, lads?' someone asked. Trying to sound nonchalant and matter of fact, but patently too quick and eager to share our news, I replied: 'Oh, Wendigo and Red Wall.' From the far corner Marty piped up in his unmistakable Scouse accent: 'Yes, we had a bit of a poor day as well.' They're so much more refined from Liverpool.

Although it would have added ten days to our journey home, I suspect most of 2 PARA would also rather have gone all the way on *Norland*, but she still had several months more of ferrying Argentinian prisoners from Stanley to Montevideo. The next time I saw the ship was four years later. I was back as second-in-command of 2 PARA and attended a New Year's Eve party to which they invited members of the battalion every year until she was decommissioned in 2010. I only saw Don Ellerby once more when he visited the battalion to present the Norland Trophy for the first time to the 'Best Soldier'. By then he was retired. The bond between us and the ship was deep and long-lasting – an unexpected but hugely satisfying outcome from the pain of war. The crew's experience is touchingly and amusingly brought to life in Warren Fitzgerald's *All In The Same Boat*.

The next day we were ferried ashore and took off that evening from Wideawake Airfield, arriving at RAF Brize Norton early on 7 July. This time Prince Charles, our Colonel-in-Chief, was there to meet us. I confess to being rather underwhelmed. I was more interested in meeting someone else: it had been just over ten weeks since I had seen my wife. In that time a lot had happened. We had just sold our house, and I had left all the business of finding and moving into Army married quarters to her. I had a new home to return to.

We were just about to get into our car and drive home when an emotional-looking Nobby Clark appeared, running towards me. Nobby didn't do emotion. 'What cock-up's happened now?' I thought. 'Have we left someone behind? Has a member of D Company been disrespectful to the Colonel-in-Chief?'

Nobby grabbed my hand. 'Sir, I want to thank you. It's been a privilege serving with you. A great experience. We did OK!' I'd spent months trying to convince this cool and collected man that I was a good custodian of his precious D Company. Now, here he was, behaving in a way I had never seen or would have ever expected before. I hope I said something along the lines of: 'None of us could have done it without you.' I think we laughed together at our wives watching this uncharacteristic behaviour that, pre-Falklands, they would never have witnessed. I climbed into the car beside Rachel and set off for home. 'It seems I might have done some things right down there,' I said, still bemused but slowly realizing that the privilege had been all mine to have had this man of so many parts at my side. Sadly, Nobby has now died, and I shall never tell him that until we meet again on the other side.

Chapter 12

Homecoming: the Hard Part

Days before sailing we had sold our house in Hartley Wintney and had been looking for somewhere a little quieter than right beside the busy A30. With no chance to complete the search, I had left Rachel to try to get us Army quarters in Aldershot. This had been 'in at the deep-end' for her. She was younger than me and new to Service life, and we had been married for just one year. A quarter of that time had been our honeymoon on Mount Jiazi in China, our home a two-man tent in a high mountain valley which our expedition shared with a family of Tibetan yak-herders. Away to war, I had given little further thought to where we might live. It was a challenging start, perhaps, for any marriage.

All had gone well with her until the final day of moving out. Across the road was the local newsagent. Rachel popped over to get a paper as usual, and to say good-bye. This led the gentle old boy who ran the shop to ask why she had been sorting out the move on her own. That proved too much. 'Phil's on the way to the Falklands,' she explained and burst into tears. 'Don't you worry, he'll be OK,' said the little shopkeeper, and spent some time cheering her up. It appeared these little acts of kindness became normal while we were away. Indeed, I may have abandoned Rachel to go to war, but the battalion had not. John Holborn, the battalion's families officer and OC rear party, had been ever ready to help with advice and transport and even a team of hands to assist with the move. A battalion is very much a family.

After moving into married quarters in Aldershot, she at least then had the wives of several other officers of the battalion as neighbours and became more closely integrated into the wives club. This proved a mixed blessing. The 'patch' was naturally alive with rumour and speculation, not all of it positive, which had largely by-passed her until then. However, it seemed that the benefits of mutual support probably outweighed the downside. This was especially true after the sinking of HMS *Sheffield*, which, as on *Norland*, signalled loud and clear to those at home that we were now at war. It was only at this stage that Rachel learnt of the trip to

Portsmouth to wave us off, organized by the patch, that she had missed. It was something I should have known about, she often reminded me.

After five weeks the news of Goose Green changed everything. It is perhaps less so today, but in 1982 the wives of officers and warrant officers acted as unpaid assistants to their husbands, and few would have had it otherwise. The wives of my Toms living on the patch became an unwritten obligation for Rachel. The families of Corporal Sullivan and Lance Corporals Bingley and Cork, who had been killed, all lived in married quarters in Aldershot. Rachel now found herself helping John Holborn to provide comfort and support to their widows. Jane Bingley still speaks warmly of that time. All were also helped by the example of Sarah Jones, 'H's widow, who continued to give the leadership to the wives club that they desperately needed in such uncertain times, having at the same time to manage her own grief. It belatedly occurred to me that it hadn't just been tough at 'the front'. I did not have much to say on that drive home. I was still in my 'just another job' frame of mind. I was happy just to listen to my wife's story.

Anyway, there were holidays to plan. Before leaving *Norland*, we had been notified of two weeks' immediate leave, then a week at work to recover and refit the battalion for future operational preparedness, and then a full six weeks' leave to early September. The longest Alpine season I had ever managed was three weeks, and I had begun to dream of all the big routes I might knock off in six – maybe one of the Jorasses' north faces, even the Eiger Nordwand. I would need to discuss this with my great friend from Lamjung and Everest, John Scott. With our two wives looking after us at base camp in Chamonix, there would be no holding us.

On getting home, I was slightly surprised to find that Rachel did not share my enthusiasm for the Alps. I tried to tell her what a great opportunity it was. As I read up the routes, thought through how to minimize the risks on each, considered the bivouacs, checked my gear, I began to realize that I was going through the motions. After our expedition to Everest in the spring of 1976, John and I had gone to the Alps that same summer. It had been hopeless – Everest had, we realized, demanded so much that we just did not have the fuel for the big, neck-stretching routes. 'Everestitis' we called it. After the weeks of privation and perils in the Falklands winter I had just left behind, I was there again. By the end of that first fortnight of leave in 1982, I knew that I was just posturing. Rachel had been spot-on. We settled instead for a sailing holiday in the Ionian Sea – sun, retsina, friends, warm winds.

Returning from leave in early September was a shock. The battalion's time continued to be dominated by the war – thanksgiving services, memorial services, victory parades, visits from the great and the good, and to next of kin; later, repatriation of bodies and funerals. There was a need to regenerate our operational preparedness, but there was also grieving still to be done. A visit to Aldershot by Prince Charles, our Colonel-in-Chief at the beginning of October, for a Thanksgiving Service and to talk to the next of kin of both battalions was the start of that process. Ever the sceptic, I wondered how much it would actually help them, but he is very good at such moments and our families certainly drew strength from the day.

The next of kin were indeed our priority. Regimental HQ and our rear party and wives had done great work in trying to bring them succour and support, but it needed a more intimate touch. We made plans for those of the company's ten dead to be visited by an officer of the company, if for no other reason than that we were best placed to answer the questions that many would want to ask. They wanted first-hand information on what their loved ones were doing when they were killed, how they died, whether they suffered. Each platoon commander took responsibility for their own, and Pete Adams for Tam Mechan's parents. I arranged to meet Jim Barry's. For this, I was joined by Chris Waddington, who had become a close friend of Jim's.

My visit was easier than some. Jim's father was a former lieutenant colonel and had only recently retired from the security services. Both he and his wife knew the score. Facing them in their sitting room in St Albans, they were both putting on a brave face, but I could see they were devastated. They understood I was doing my duty, nevertheless appreciated it, and were determined to make it as easy as possible for me. Chris and I departed deeply impressed, but from what we had seen of Jim, not surprised. Over the years Rachel and I stayed in touch with them.

Human relationships can be messy, however. One had left behind a young pregnant bride, and his parents wanted as little involvement with her as possible. Another's wife, whom he had met during a tour in Northern Ireland, had gone back home, and solicitors were acting between her and his parents. Some wives had lost their entitlement to married quarters after the death of their husband and were at a loss as to where they would now live. On top of this, two families had received abusive letters from Ireland – no doubt a throwback to the battalion's two years in Northern Ireland that had preceded the war – saying their sons had got what they deserved. These visits therefore proved often to be much more than a matter of condolence. Supported though they were by Regimental HQ and the families officer, again I had to admire the way that that my young platoon commanders got on with it, just as they had down south.

One of the topics on these visits was to establish what the bereaved wanted done with their loved one. Since finishing its two-year tour in Northern Ireland in early 1981, the battalion's focus had been to train for overseas intervention operations in the Third World. 'H', perhaps impressed by the film of the day, *The Wild Geese*, had been fond of quoting the remark: 'We go in, and we bring everyone back.' We had all assumed that our dead would be repatriated, but the Falkland Islands was not the Third World. It was a British dependency – in a sense, it was 'home'. Moreover, there was a long tradition of the British Army burying its dead close to where they fell, surrounded by their comrades, in graves tended by the Commonwealth War Graves Commission. Anyone who has visited any of the graves at Arnhem, Normandy or the battlefields of the First World War will understand that these are anything but the abandonment of our dead in some foreign land. The Commission, with the Islands now back in British hands, was clearly able to replicate this in the Falklands.

Inflamed by the press, an emotional debate erupted, with everyone desperate to do the right thing. For the first time in history the government gave the choice to the next of kin. The choices were to have their loved one buried in a War Graves Commission cemetery at San Carlos, a monument to his sacrifice, together with his other fallen comrades; repatriate him to be buried alongside his comrades in the regimental plot in the military cemetery in Aldershot; or repatriate him for burial near his home where his family would be able to visit and care for his grave. What a choice for families to make. Had I been one of the fallen, I think I would have liked my family to leave me there with my comrades, but that could have been very different from what they wanted. I do not think they should have been obliged to make that choice. As it was, most of my dead were dispersed evenly between burial at home and in the regimental plot in Aldershot. Only one was buried in the San Carlos cemetery. Perhaps his parents' decision had been influenced by being one of the families to have received an abusive letter from Ireland. However, they called it well. He's lying there with his commanding officer, within sight of San Carlos Water where we went ashore, surrounded by a Falkland peat moor in a serene spot, beautifully tended and regularly visited. He'll never be forgotten.

The bodies of those being repatriated arrived in Portsmouth in early November. The month became a blur of four funerals in various parts of the country, and a final one in Aldershot Military Cemetery for those to be buried in the regimental plot. The Toms undertook the duties of pall-bearers and honour guards at the numerous funerals, providing comfort to bereaved families with grace, humour and sympathy. I found it a profoundly humbling time. Somehow we also squeezed in a two-day company exercise parachuting onto Salisbury Plain.

At the same time a swathe of postings began and people disappeared on specialist or career courses. It felt as if my 'band of brothers' was being torn apart. I could see a good argument for dispersing the experience gathered across the Regiment to training establishments, but the haste seemed indecent. After such an intense experience, there was also a strong argument for keeping us together until the post-war hullabaloo had died down. This happened at such a pace, however, that I even wondered whether it was deliberate policy. Was it feared that bonds seared in the heat of battle would make us ungovernable? If anything, it had the opposite effect to that intended. Among those posted was Nobby Clark. He was not selected for promotion to warrant officer grade 1 which he so richly deserved and would have put him in line for appointment as a regimental sergeant major, to which all senior NCOs aspire. He was sent instead to the regimental training depot just down the road as regimental quartermaster sergeant. The leaving party that the company held for Nobby was a heart-warming affair, but there was anger, even a whiff of insurrection, in the air. Nobby's posting had been announced at much the same time as the operational awards. There was also some bitterness over these. Nobby, as he stood to say goodbye, acknowledged the mood, and pointed out that I was still with the company, assuring the Toms that the company remained in good hands. I was touched by his generous words but, more important, the little moment of madness in the room passed on.

There were, nevertheless, still difficulties. Shevill had returned from hospital having apparently recovered from the extensive injuries he suffered at the white flag incident at Goose Green. Within days he was in trouble and in front of me several times on orders for insubordination, failing to carry out instructions or lateness. We arranged for him to see the padre, but that achieved nothing. He simply no longer seemed to care or wished to continue as a soldier and was becoming an increasing irritation to all around him. After three months I decided we had to let him go.

Looking back, I feel that we severely let him down. In those days we had heard of shellshock, but that was not his problem. Post-traumatic stress disorder, or PTSD, was quite simply not in our lexicon, nor did we have any means to look after soldiers so afflicted. I focused only on his impact on the company's operational effectiveness and the adverse effect he was having on morale. Shevill, though, was probably not beyond repair, and I for ever regret that we did not persevere with him or think more on what was happening to him.

My runner, Hanley, also presented some difficulties. We had all been warned not to keep Argentinian contraband, especially weapons. Wang had always ploughed his own furrow, which was why I so valued having him around me, and he chose to ignore this instruction. He would not have been the only one to do so, and would doubtless have got away with it had he not chosen to wave his Argentinian pistol around in a pub in Nottingham during his Christmas leave. He was arrested by the police who, given the circumstances, chose to pack him off to us to deal with. He was charged and marched into my office on orders. I had no choice but to remand him to the CO, knowing that he would get thirty days in the battalion jail. When he was sentenced, he pleaded with the CO to be released for his younger brother's wedding a fortnight later. Sadly, the CO was not to be moved. As Wang was marched off by the provost sergeant, he murmured to me that no CO and no jail was going to stop him going to Wing's wedding. I urged him not to be a cunt. He just smiled and assured me that he had no argument with me, but I knew his mind was made up. I just had to rely on the security of the guardroom and the alertness of the provost staff. Sadly, neither proved a match for Wang.

It was no surprise when I came in to work a week later to be told that Wang had escaped and was now absent without leave. He had managed surreptitiously to sneak a fire extinguisher into his cell after visiting the toilet. In the night he had smashed the reinforced glass of the window in his cell, climbed through and made off into the darkness. After the wedding he handed himself in and was returned to the jail. Once again, he was marched in on CO's orders. The punishment this time was another thirty days and then to be discharged the service. I pleaded with the CO that he was one of the best soldiers we could ever have on operations, and not to discharge him. It was to no avail. I got the feeling that the CO saw my recommending leniency as part of the problem. We were still Penal Company.

By March 1983 Hanley was lost to me and the company. Even my wife missed Wang, and his invariable advice to her at company piss-ups: 'You look after him, Rachel, or you'll have me to deal with!' In fact, he never was completely lost to the company, meeting up with us whenever possible at battalion reunions. Indeed, he still does, and every New Year I still get a call from him. Was PTSD part of Wang's problem? I think not, but

I do believe he never quite got over the end of his days in the Parachute Regiment. He was more than once involved in fights in Aldershot on Airborne Forces Days. On one occasion he took on a bunch of 'hats' and was severely beaten up, which left him with permanent damage. Thankfully he is now happily married to Molly and leads a calmer life. I still believe that he is another soldier who we should have looked after better after his service in the war, which I had recommended for formal recognition. I was gratified that at a battalion reunion a few years ago he was singled out for recognition by the then CO and his regimental sergeant major – something that clearly meant the world to him.

The truth is, we were all marked to some extent by our experiences in one way or another. Mostly for the good. Generally, discipline improved. There was no longer a need for the Toms to prove themselves by beating up Aldershot on a Saturday night. That now was regarded as pointless childish pranks; boys when they had left, they had returned as men, with nothing to prove. Nevertheless, many felt somewhat adrift. Interestingly, as I looked around, those one-step-removed from the close-quarter violence but who had had to cope with the aftermath seemed to be the most affected. Perhaps something like suffering by proxy. Steve Hughes, our wonderful young doctor, who will always be revered by every soul in 2 PARA for those four months in 1982, was the first to publicly 'come out' as suffering from PTSD. It took courage in the prevailing culture of the time, and it plagued him until he died. The signs were visible in others also, but we just didn't know what the signs meant.

At the time I thought I was doing fine, drawing the right balance for the company between giving due attention to the implications of the recent past and focusing on the future. Looking back, there were signs that I was possibly not. The first was one of pure farce. It was shortly after the decorations and awards had been announced and we had been rehearsing for a victory parade through the City of London on 12 October 1982. It was to conclude with a lunch in the Guildhall, with 'our Maggie' as the guest of honour. I had been appointed as deputy for the regimental contingent for the parade to Hew Pike, the CO of 3 PARA. A rehearsal had finished late morning near our quarters in Blenheim Park. I decided to go home for lunch, instead of going to the officers' mess. The trouble with these quarters was that the back door and the front door were both on the same side of the house, at the front. Ours was the second house in our close. My mind was miles away on a raft of pent-up frustrations. I counted to the second door, put my key in the lock, and tried to let myself in. It wouldn't turn. I rang the bell. Nothing. 'Damn and blast,' I muttered,

'Rachel's gone out and deadlocked the latch.' Without appreciating the impossibility of this, I stepped back and in a sudden fit of anger put my foot to the door. It gave way worryingly easily. The catch hanging off one screw, I entered the hall. I was immediately nonplussed: the carpet was mauve, not green – 'She's changed the carpet as well!'

The penny then dropped, quickly. I had entered the second door, not the second house. I quickly fixed the catch as best I could, pulled the door to, and stole a fearful glance across the road, thankfully seeing no prying eyes or fluttering net curtains. Like a thief, I crept two doors down, entered with no need of even a key, to see, with relief, familiar carpets in the hall – and my wife asking what the noise next door was about. She quickly saw the funny side and we laughed our way through lunch. Conversation turned to whether we should tell our neighbours, an army dentist and his wife, about what I had done. Reluctant to raise the spectre of them living next to a lunatic, I took the easy way out. I said nothing.

How life can catch us unawares. Three weeks later, after the victory parade was over and forgotten, there were church parades across the garrison for Remembrance Day. Rachel and I got back home at the same time as our neighbours, whom we did not often see. He wandered over to say: 'Just wanted to warn you that I think we had an attempted burglary a short while back. Might be worth us all being on our guard.' I tried to look surprised and concerned as I thanked him for letting us know. 'We did get the Military Police round, who found a boot print on our door,' he added. Should I tell him now that it was me and apologize? I decided that I had long since missed the moment, murmured 'Good thinking', and escaped indoors as nonchalantly as I could, to help myself to a quick whisky.

Better, perhaps, would have been talking more with Rachel about my experiences, but I didn't, or couldn't. In that respect we were like strangers. After all, she already knew what we had done – it had been on the news for weeks. Returning from big expeditions to the Himalayas, I always found the most pointless question was 'What was it like?' I would offer inanities like 'Great!' 'Hard!' 'Fantastic experience!' but always thinking: 'Where do I start? You've not been there, so you'll never get it.' Was that arrogance on my part, or laziness? I think neither. It was more that these intense experiences can be very public at one level, but very private at another. I needed years of processing before I was ready to share what it was like. In 1984 Max Arthur got in touch to interview me for his book, *Above All, Courage*. I clearly disappointed him. Eventually, he sent me a parcel containing a blank tape for a voice recorder and a bottle of brandy, with the instruction to take a drink and just blurt my thoughts out. Perhaps that was part of the process.

Speaking about what it was like, as opposed to what we had done, was important, but I could only do that with those who had had similar experiences. A year later, after a six-month tour with the battalion in Belize, I was posted to Regimental Headquarters based at the depot where Nobby was. I would regularly meet him for a beer and a sharing of thoughts in the sergeants' mess. On one occasion Rachel and I were due to have dinner with someone I had met in Belize and her husband, with whom we had become good friends. I had, however, got into a 'deep and meaningful' discussion putting the world to rights with Nobby in the sergeants' mess. Rachel turned up to drag me away. I was pissed off at the interruption and by the time we got to our friends I was beholden to no one. The worse for wear, I grabbed the car keys and drove off.

I was not traumatized, but I was disillusioned. It was not just Hanley's discharge that said that nothing had changed. There was an unfortunate incident in the sergeants' mess at an event to which the CO had been invited. At some point he was talking to my three platoon sergeants, O'Rawe, Light and Meredith, when he declared that he 'had given D Company the lion's share at Wireless Ridge because he knew we had not done much at Goose Green and was keen for the company to earn its spurs'. Leaving aside that the initial plan for Wireless Ridge did not have us playing a prominent role, and how he had got that impression, the three platoon sergeants had a very different view of what their men had done and sacrificed at Goose Green. With the losses we had suffered there still fresh in their minds, they were seething. The situation threatened to turn embarrassingly ugly until Glyn Grace, my new CSM, intervened. Glyn told me about it the next day. Much later he also told me that on being posted to D Company, he had been briefed to sort out the company and the mess left by Nobby – adding that he found nothing to sort and that it was among the best administered companies he had served with. Nobby himself never quite got over being so shamefully passed over for promotion. About the time I returned to 2 Para as 2ic, he came into an inheritance – the give-away being his turning up for work at the Depot in a new top-of-the range Ford Scorpio. A few months later he resigned and with his wife emigrated to Australia. Sadly, he became increasingly unsettled and died alone there six years ago.

The Belize tour from April to September the following year, in lieu of the tour we had managed to avoid by volunteering for the Falklands War, was confirmed in late 1982. The planned deployment of each company for the tour also spoke the same message. It was widely regarded that Airport Camp, defending the logistics rear but close to the fleshpots of Belize City, was the short straw. The task lacked excitement and the proximity of Belize City presented copious distractions of the flesh and the spirit. Neither was conducive to 'good order and military discipline'. Had we gone there in 1982, D Company was designated for Airport Camp, which then just seemed par for the course. We were last in the alphabet and I was the junior company commander – so be it. Dair and John had now left, so I was the senior company commander, and now I felt hints of a punishment posting for the company.

I started to worry that I was over-thinking these things. Then, early in 1983, we held a battalion level exercise in Norfolk. At some point I was confronted with a situation which required immediate action to pre-empt an unexpected threat. Unable to get the CO on the radio, I contacted Battalion HQ and briefed the 2iC, still Chris Keeble, who gave his go-ahead. Mid-way though our manoeuvre, I got a furious bollocking from the CO for moving without his authority. The look on my FOO's face (I had a qualified captain for this exercise) said everything. He had clearly never witnessed anything like it. I would normally have taken such a silly incident in my stride. Instead, I questioned whether I was the butt of the clear, but perhaps unsurprising, tension between Keeble and Chaundler, or of a continuing 'downer' on D Company.

Then, quite abruptly, everything changed. Discovering that, contrary to SOPs, no battalion log of our operations had been kept in the Falklands, David Chaundler instructed the battalion's signals officer, David Benest, widely regarded as the academic of the battalion, to compile an eye-witness record. This was then passed to Major General John Frost, the battalion's Honorary Colonel, who had led it through its defining moment at Arnhem in the Second World War. Frost had undertaken to publish a book of the battalion's exploits in 1982 based on Benest's notes but wanted to interview the main protagonists himself. Keeble returned from his interview with Frost and told me that the general also wanted to speak to me. I demurred; I had become heartily sick of the aftermath. Then David Chaundler returned from his meeting and gave me a direct order to see him.

I was a little over-awed at the prospect of my audience with one of the heroes of Arnhem. It was a friendly meeting, but nothing notable emerged. I just recited what D Company had done and in a sort of detached way he made some notes. From that moment, however, everything seemed to change, and D Company ceased to be the Cinderella of the battalion. Perhaps Frost shared with Chaundler and Keeble what he later wrote to

me, when we corresponded in November 1983 over the full disclosure of
how Parr was killed: 'Anyone following the campaign could not fail to be
impressed with the outstanding performance of D Coy ...'

By the time we deployed to Belize, D Company could do no wrong. The
CO graciously explained to the company that we had got Airport Camp
because he wanted the best company in the most challenging environment.
I played it as normal – I trusted my subordinates. I appealed to their
mutual loyalty, pointing out that no one any longer held their noses around
us, and I wanted it to stay that way. Motivation emerged when we un-
earthed a major drug smuggling operation among the Mennonite community in the north of the country. Our job was to protect the Belizean
border from the, by then, non-existent threat from Guatemala, with strict
orders not to get involved with internal Belizean affairs. Nevertheless, we
kept the Mennonite operation under continuous surveillance for the
whole tour with the tacit, but totally deniable, blessing of our brigadier.
I did not try to police what the company got up to in Belize City, but
simply decreed that anyone who failed to make the daily 6.00am company
run would be fined a week's pay, and senior NCOs, whom I didn't have
the authority to fine, would make a similar donation to the company's
R&R fund. It only had one such donation. In any event, it wasn't needed –
we managed to negotiate with the local mayor free hotel accommodation
on the offshore holiday spot of San Pedro in exchange for starting the
build of a new school on his island.

There were a few tricky moments. The Battle of Airport Camp became
for a while a battalion legend. During a major test exercise the company
had got very much the better of a visiting company of the Green Jackets
Regiment, who were providing the exercise enemy. This had caused them
some embarrassment and even more resentment. Exercise over, one night
they invaded our company's accommodation, Laundry Lines. They were
duly repulsed and, like the well-trained soldiers that they were, D Company set off in hot pursuit. I was summoned from the officers' mess and
told by the brigadier's staff that I would have to spend the night in the
lines to ensure no further trouble. I refused on the grounds that it would
undermine the authority of my junior NCOs who were in charge of the
lines. After giving them a quick pep talk, I retired. Trouble erupted again,
although this time it involved Hugh Jenner's Support Company, who
were in the camp as part of the exercise. The brigadier was not amused,
and the CO was summoned. All the blame fell on Support Company,
however. With the CO obliged to make a demonstrable example, they
were banished from the camp and despatched on a 40-mile route march

in full kit. D Company meanwhile basked in its successes against the Green Jackets both on and after the exercise. It was a close shave, enough for the battalion adjutant to mutter darkly as I left battalion headquarters: 'Bloody D Company. More like Teflon Company. Nothing sticks!'

When I handed over command in late 1983 on our return from Belize, I felt fulfilled. D Company was no longer Penal Company. Teflon Company would do nicely. Mission accomplished.

Epilogue

The passing years have provided time for reflection. The war itself was an anomaly that came out of nowhere. Some argue that it could have been avoided but, given the nature of the Argentinian dictatorship, which was desperate for short-term popularity, I do not subscribe to that. True, the UK prior to the war had no real interest in the Islands and was open to an accommodation with Argentina. Indeed, I speculate that had the invasion not taken place, the Islands might by now have been, at least nominally, Argentinian. That option is totally closed for the foreseeable future; the Islanders will never now accept any accommodation. For the same reason I cannot see how any British government at the time could have accepted any negotiated settlement to end the war against the will of the Islanders.

Invading the Islands therefore was a colossal and fundamental error by Argentina if they ever hoped to gain possession. I wonder whether doing so is in fact in its best interests. I once listened to a talk by a retired Argentinian officer. He opined that possession of the Malvinas was like a religion for the country, so the problem would never go away. He went on to add, however, that it is the one thing that unites the country. If they gained possession, what would then unite the country. Perhaps the Islands serve Argentina better by remaining, like the Holy Grail, a quest that can never be fulfilled. Maybe with mutual recognition of this, friendlier relations outside this insoluble problem would be possible. Argentina will, and must, continue to posture; if the UK accepts that, then both countries can quietly move on to where they can cooperate to mutual advantage. Certainly, from my experience, most members of our respective armed forces bear each other no hatred and have moved on.

The recovery of the Falklands was by no means a foregone conclusion, in the austral winter at the end of a problematic 8,000-mile supply chain. Our Navy was the more modern and powerful, but we were outnumbered in the air and on land by forces as well equipped as our own. The sinking of the *General Belgrano* was a fortuitous start, as thereafter the Argentinian navy appeared to give up, and returned to port. Their air forces were dedicated and highly skilled, although their focus on attacking the fighting ships of the Royal Navy was perhaps an error; had they concentrated their attacks on the STUFT logistics ships our land campaign might have ground to a halt. The loss of *Atlantic Conveyor* alone almost achieved that, and she was only attacked as the Argentinian pilots mistook her on their radar for an aircraft carrier. The loss was only overcome by the ability of Paras to tab and Marines to yomp across the desolate landscape and through the hostile weather of the Falklands. That was, perhaps, beyond the ken of our opponents.

Had either or both of our aircraft carriers *Hermes* and *Invincible* been lost then without the CAP air defence, operations ashore could also have been imperilled. Here was a fine compromise. Many of us ashore complained about the intermittent air support available. This was because the carriers were far to the east to put them beyond the reach of Argentinian aircraft flying from the mainland, but that in turn meant the Harriers had little operating time overhead. That price was worth paying to ensure that we still had some air support when it mattered most. Certainly, it was true of air support at Goose Green. That strategy would have paid off even more had the UK still possessed an AEW capability, enabling detection of approaching enemy aircraft early enough for the Harriers to be scrambled to intercept them before they reached their targets – the amphibious shipping. But AEW had been jettisoned in an earlier defence review, contributing to the loss of many from enemy air attack.

Had the Argentinians extended Stanley airport to enable it to take fast jets, then it might have been game up for the British from the start, in the same way that our fast jets flying out of Mount Pleasant airfield today is the single most important deterrent to any renewed adventurism by Argentina. On land, their major shortcoming was their army's inability to manoeuvre and their reluctance to counterattack. That made the selection of San Carlos, beyond the range of enemy artillery, an inspired choice for the amphibious landings – which were unopposed, even if it meant a lot of tabbing. At Goose Green a determined counterattack at certain points of the battle should have been possible and might well have turned the outcome. As it was, the only counterattacks experienced in the entire war were the two in the closing stages of Wireless Ridge – sporting affairs, but without a sporting chance – too little, too late.

All these factors left things finely balanced, which brings me back to the words of Mao Tse-Tung quoted earlier. What counts far more than manpower and materiel is 'the power and morale of the man'. We won because our individual soldiers were better trained, more determined and above all more resilient than the enemy's. Marines and Paras alike were better able to cope with the chaos, the uncertainty and the hardships. Above all, when mistakes were made – like the friendly fire on Wireless Ridge – and we were faced with setbacks – like the death of our commanding officer at Goose Green – we bounced back.

Lots of things go to enabling this resilience, but I think it starts with leadership. At every level, we were fortunate. Whatever their political leanings, I think that everyone of us felt that in Prime Minister Thatcher we had at the top an outstanding leader – 'H' spoke for us all in articulating 'We're doing this for Maggie.' In Julian Thompson, the unflappable commander of 3 Commando Brigade, we had a leader who conveyed utter competence and instilled quiet confidence. In 'H', by no means a paragon, we had nevertheless a leader of undoubted moral and physical courage with clear and inspiring values who could instil his faith and confidence in others like no one else I have met. His successors, Keeble and Chaundler, both brought their own and different brands of competence and distinctive contributions, but even after his death, it was 'H's ethos that continued to dominate the way 2 PARA went about its business.

Next, the cause. When we set sail from Portsmouth in the carnival atmosphere of 26 April 1982, most of us shared Wang's pithy scepticism about going to war 'for two thousand sheep-shaggers 8,000 miles away, at the arse-end of the world, in some place we've never heard of'. As events unfolded, our scepticism lifted. The freedom of two thousand British subjects became of growing concern, but we understood also that the cause was much bigger than that: we were defending a principle, resisting aggression, and restoring the honour, the reputation and the self-respect of the country. Unlike many asymmetric conflicts since, the cause was clear and just, and essential to our national interests. Moreover, it had unequivocal and readily identifiable aims and objectives. With these came a start, and a clear definitive end. As opposed to a war without end, it was all over in three months. It did not feel like it at the time, but it was limited and a relatively minor affair, but it was still of vital national interest.

Men don't risk their lives for a cause, however, unless they're zealots. I never saw my Toms as such. What I did see was young men with a passionate pride in their elite professionalism and an overwhelming loyalty to their mates. They needed a cause, but they would risk death rather than let themselves, their mates and their regiment down.

All these ingredients the Argentinians largely lacked. I suspect they also lacked one other, for me perhaps the most important: a sense of humour. The ability to laugh at the devil despite the most trying, sometimes tragic circumstances, I have no doubt prolongs the life of that 'well of courage' identified by Lord Moran. The constant ribbing, quips and the ability to laugh at themselves and their misfortunes that was ever present in D Company in 1982 certainly helped me to keep going.

Would I now have done anything different or did I learn anything fundamentally new? We all, I am sure, came back wiser and better soldiers in many ways. For the rest of my military career I remained heavily influenced by 'H's aggressive and inspirational approach to leadership, and his unwavering focus on succeeding, whatever. I don't know about faith moving mountains but it can certainly win battles. The overriding piece of advice I would give to myself forty years ago about to land at San Carlos, however, would be 'Keep thinking, keep questioning.' During the action, I think I did. In the battle preparation phase, I'm not so sure. In the pressure of the moment – the theatre of a formal 'O' Group and time against you – it's difficult. I am still aware that the deficiencies of the time and space appreciation for Goose Green should have been spotted and challenged. No one did. Another example at Wireless Ridge was when I might have requested the allocation of a fully trained FOO. On both occasions, in the moment, I was so focused on the process of disseminating the orders and allocating tasks to my company that I gave little thought to anything else. Then, I wonder, had I done so, would I have had the courage to speak up? Sometimes, at these highly charged moments, it's easier to 'Salute, do a half-turn to the right and get on with it.' I like to think that when 2iC on my second tour in Belize as CO Battle Group North, and when CO of 10 PARA, I encouraged an atmosphere where officers could so challenge. I probably flatter myself; such culture is very deep-seated.

Regarding Penal Company, I have often mused how it came to be thus. Maybe I was part of the problem. I confess to have never given much thought to 'managing upwards', and suspect that, from joining the RAF Regiment, I was perhaps a member of the 'awkward squad'. Soon after joining, for example, I was dissatisfied with my uniforms and refused to pay my tailors' bill. To apply pressure the tailors took the matter to my superiors. I responded by alleging that the tailors had libelled me. The station commander and my squadron commander amazingly quickly disengaged from the process, so the tailors issued a writ to take me to court. I took great satisfaction in being summoned to the station commander's office to be served this, and counter-serving my own writ on them for libel. The tailors and I soon reached what might be called an 'out-of-court' settlement. I failed to complete my law degree at university – climbing took over – but it was surely not time wasted.

D was known as Penal Company well before I arrived, however, so while I might have exploited and aggravated the situation, I cannot accept the credit for getting it its distinguished status. The alphabet doubtless had something to do with it, alongside perhaps the configuration of offices in Bruneval Barracks. But these are just reinforcing factors. Somewhere previously, involving a different OC of the company and perhaps a different CO, something seems to have gone wrong, maybe in the preceding Northern Ireland tour. Nor were relations between Nobby and the RSM particularly cordial, but I could never decide whether that was cause or effect. Nevertheless, a prejudice developed. We know well today that these can die hard and take some external intervention to break down. The efforts of myself and the gallant performance of my Toms in the Falklands was not enough; it took the intervention of General Frost, when writing his book on 2 PARA in the war, to trigger a change of mind-set.

So, was the reputation justified? A look at what many of the company have done since says 'No.' At the time I looked at my crew, individually, with short-sighted eyes. Could they do what was expected? Yes for 99.9 per cent. Were they promotable? Were they good for specialist work and training? Today, however, I never cease to be humbled at the talent over which I 'presided'. At least ten went on to join the SAS, one Tom (Wang's brother) making it to lieutenant colonel. Four others became lieutenant colonels within the Parachute Regiment and several others got commissions. Amongst my officers, two joined the SAS and one went on to become a lieutenant general (I foresaw the latter's potential at the time – although I had him pegged for CDS, so a slight disappointment).

Many left for successful civilian careers. I cannot recount all but I mention two. Private Colin 'Del' Delaney, our company medic, attended a 'Junior Brecon' course to qualify him for promotion to lance corporal, which he duly earned. However, he'd achieved what he most wanted in the Parachute Regiment, testing himself, and a fiancée and creating a family beckoned; like many that year, he resigned in late 1983. Colin trained as a surveyor and is now a co-partner of a multi-million-pound construction business. Private Tony Banks soon after, struggling with the aftermath, joined the Royal Army Medical Corps but could not fully move on. Having also decided to leave, he completed his accountancy studies and eventually got into the care home business. He now owns the largest chain of private care homes in Scotland. The memories of the war still dogged him, but it was not until he met another veteran in Liverpool, acting the part as television's 'Secret Millionaire', that he realized he was one of those also suffering PTSD. If ever there was a born survivor, it was Tony, but as with others who coped so well at the time, PTSD is an unpredictable predator.

As for me, I was promoted to lieutenant colonel in 1988 after completing a thoroughly satisfying posting back with 2 PARA as second-in-command, which included a further tour in Belize. The Falklands War still dominated conversation and the way we did things. I was then selected to take command of 10 PARA, the regiment's volunteer TA battalion based in and around London. That was a great tour, capped by leading a TA expedition to attempt a first British ascent of Everest in winter. I left the Army shortly after to go into business, and amongst other things set up my own software business – not a path I had ever planned, but I have always had a weakness for finding out what's on the other side of half-open doors.

The command of 10 PARA did not come up for a year, so I had to be found something useful to do, when most postings were for at least two years. By now, the Falklands had a garrison of 2,000 commanded by a 'two-star' officer, and a newly constructed military airfield at Mount Pleasant from which to operate fast jets and large transport aircraft. Most of the garrison were deployed for four to six months, but senior staff appointments in the headquarters were for a year to provide continuity. It was no great surprise to find myself at the top of the list to fill one of those. I could have demurred on the grounds of my previous 'extenuating' experiences. Although I was the butt of many jokes about who I had upset this time to get such a punishment posting, I accepted. Far from being disturbed by the prospect, I was curious to return, and anyway it would be better than possibly some blanket-stacking job in Catterick.

So, in 1989, with my wife and two young children, I returned to the Falklands. The Islands, particularly Port Stanley, were very different from what I had left nearly seven years before. Life in 'the camp', as anything outside Stanley was called, was perhaps little changed, but many 'camp' dwellers now owned their farms rather than working them as employees of the Falkland Island Company. In the capital there was a buzz and prosperity in the air. The wartime TEZ had become a Fisheries Conservation Zone. It was colossally rich in squid, and fishermen from across the world were paying large fees for licences to work the zone. Quite simply, the Islands were now wealthy and on the world map.

About ten days after I had taken over my post, which included responsibility for everything that was not day-to-day operations, the garrison was visited by the Army's quartermaster general, Sir David Ramsbottom, a very senior officer. My commander, Air Vice Marshal David Crwys-Williams, decided to fly him down to the Goose Green battlefield and invited me to join the trip. As we clambered out of the helicopter, I felt strangely detached, even confused, not knowing what I would make of it – like visiting a foreign country for the first time, or turning up at the wrong party, wondering why you didn't know anyone. Crwys-Williams, who had previously toured the battlefield, began to recount the story to the general. I was looking around, trying to work out where the hell we were. I had never been here before – or at least not in daylight.

Suddenly the surrealism of the situation dawned on AVM 'Chris', as we affectionately referred to him. 'Goodness,' he blurted, in his slightly plummy voice, 'what am I doing, telling the general about this. You were there, you tell him!' As I had done so many times before, in the middle of a series of hard moves on a rock climb to compose myself, I made an elaborate display of fishing in my pocket for my handkerchief and blowing my nose. Having bought some time, I launched forth. I doubt that I did our story justice, but the general seemed to enjoy it. We were in the area of our first night attack. A civilized man, I think he understood this was a little moment of catharsis.

To my surprise, I fell in love with the Falklands during that tour. The people, the wildlife, the sea trout fishing – and most of all the measured pace of life. Our family was welcomed by the Islanders, especially as I was a veteran of '82. Among the garrison, almost all of whom were on short-term tours unaccompanied by their families, our children were spoilt rotten. Senior though I was, our 3-year-old son was soon better known than me: 'Ah, now we know who you are, Sir. You're Freddie's dad.' We would happily have done more than a year. The MoD view that that was the most anyone could cope with seemed utterly misguided.

I have been back three times since – twice to help with films about the war. Despite having walked our two battlefields extensively during 1989, talking about events on the ground can still get to me. On the first occasion I was talking to camera about watching Dixon's life fading away after he was hit by enemy artillery shrapnel by the schoolhouse at Goose Green. I suddenly found myself cracking up. Fortunately, the producer cut the scene in his final edit. Then, on the next film, as I was rounding off with the 'Endex' moment at Wireless Ridge, I recited a prepared closing line: 'Now this fantastic little force I had helped build and worked with had done its bit and no longer had a purpose. It was a moment of sadness. We marched into Stanley knowing we would never do anything like that again. It was difficult to come to terms with.' As I reached the end, in a rush, I had to turn away.

I should finish on a lighter note. It was 1985 and I was looking forward to leaving RHQ and returning to 2 PARA as 2iC under a new CO, David Parker, whom I knew, liked and respected of old. The headquarters received a request to help a team of researchers at the department of mental health at the Maudsley Hospital. They had conducted a study comparing reactions to stress between decorated and non-decorated bomb-disposal operators in Northern Ireland. The decorated operators had shown a greater ability to cope with stress than the non-decorated. Now they wanted to repeat the exercise with veterans of the Falklands War. Not surprisingly, the request was passed to me, and I duly directed 2 PARA to provide the veterans, offering myself as one volunteer for the study. I found myself alongside thirty-three others – half decorated and half not – visiting the Maudsley as experimental guinea pigs. The level of stress was measured by heart rate when trying to perform certain tasks under threat of increasingly painful and randomly delivered electric shocks.

I felt like Peter O'Toole in the film *Lawrence of Arabia*, recalling the scene where Lawrence is seen slowly extinguishing a match from the bottom upwards with thumb and finger. When a companion tries to copy the trick, he cries out with pain: 'Cor, it hurts!' To which Lawrence replies: 'Of course it hurts, the point is not minding that it hurts.' Rather than stressful, I found the whole experience mildly entertaining, and amused myself by trying to 'game' the system. The results showed that, decorated or not, the Paras all showed similar low levels of cardiac response to laboratory stress, and in their ratings of fear. The report, published in the *British Journal of Psychology* in 1987, while pointing out that it is not the same as being courageous, concluded that paratroopers genuinely justified their reputation as 'fearless'. This provided a gratifying headline for the *Daily Express*, which got news of the study: 'PARAS ARE FEARLESS!'

Mine were also human. Ordinary lads, with loved ones at home, but together achieving extraordinary things. Like anyone else, we bled, we wept, we hurt, we knew right from wrong, we made mistakes – and through it all we laughed.

The Surrender Ultimatum to the Argentinian Garrison in Goose Green

To the Commander, Argentinian Armed Forces, Goose Green, from the Commander British Forces, Goose Green Area. Military Options. We have sent a POW to you under a white flag of truce to convey the following military options:

1. That you surrender your force to us by leaving the township, forming up in a military manner, removing your helmets and laying down your weapons. You will give prior notice of this intention by returning the POW under the white flag, with him briefed as to formalities, no later than 08.30 hours local time.
2. You refuse in the first case to surrender and take the inevitable consequences. You will give prior notice of this intention by returning the POW without his white flag, although his neutrality will be respected, no later than 08.30 hours local time.
3. In the event, and in accordance with the terms of the Geneva Conventions and the Laws of War, you shall be held responsible for the fate of any civilians in Goose Green and we, in accordance with those laws, do give you prior notice of our intention to bombard Goose Green.

Signed C. Keeble
Commander, British Forces Goose Green Area
29 May 1982

Enemy and Friendly Forces at Goose Green

Enemy Forces

12th Infantry Regiment (plus platoon of heavy machine guns)

4 × 105mm artillery

Elements of 601 AA Bn with 6 × 20mm and 35mm anti-aircraft guns

One coy of 25th Infantry Regiment (flown in as reinforcements late on 28 May)

750 FAA (air force) personnel (approx.)

Skyhawk and Pucara aircraft

Total Forces = 1,400 (650 Army; 750 FAA)

Casualties:
Killed	50 (approx.)
Wounded	120 (approx.)
Captured	1,200

Friendly Forces

2 PARA Group (less some support weapons)

3 × 105mm howitzers from 29 Cdo Regt

HMS *Arrow*: 1 × 4.5in gun (first hour of the battle only)

1 section 81mm mortars (2 tubes)

Blowpipe detachment

Harrier GR3s

Total Forces = 600 (approx.)

Casualties:
Killed	18
Wounded	37

Enemy and Friendly Forces at Wireless Ridge

Enemy Forces	Friendly Forces
7 Regiment (plus elements of Argentinian Parachute Regiment)	2 PARA Group
Company of 3 Regiment (counterattacks)	1 Troop of CVR(T) – 4 light tanks with either 75mm gun or 30mm cannon
4 × 155mm medium artillery	2 × batteries of 105mm howitzers (12 guns)
18 × 105mm light artillery	1 × 4.5in gun (HMS *Ambuscade*)
	3 PARA Mortars (6 tubes)

Casualties:

Killed	100	
Wounded	Not Known	
Captured	17	

Casualties:

Killed	3
Wounded	11

2 PARA's Fire Support

Weapon	Ordnance	Quantity
Naval Gunfire Support	4.5in HE	238
	Starshells	40
2 Artillery Field Batteries	105mm HE Proximity Fused	2,500
Mortars	81mm	1,800
Scorpion × 2	75mm	160
Scimitar × 2	30mm	660
Mounted GPMGs	7.62mm	24,000
GPMG (SF)	7.62mm	60,000

D Company Honours and Awards

Distinguished Conduct Medal
  Sergeant J.C. Meredith

Military Medal
  Lance Corporal G.D. Bingley (posthumous)
  Private G.S. Carter
  Private B.J. Grayling
  Corporal T.W. Harley

Mentioned in Despatches
  Private M.W. Fletcher (posthumous)
  Major P. Neame
  Lieutenant J.D. Page